Carl du Prel

**The Philosophy of Mysticism**

Carl du Prel

**The Philosophy of Mysticism**

ISBN/EAN: 9783742812933

Manufactured in Europe, USA, Canada, Australia, Japa

Cover: Foto ©ninafisch / pixelio.de

Manufactured and distributed by brebook publishing software (www.brebook.com)

Carl du Prel

**The Philosophy of Mysticism**

# THE
# PHILOSOPHY OF MYSTICISM

BY
CARL DU PREL.
*Dr. PHIL.*

Translated from the German
BY
C. C. MASSEY.

IN TWO VOLUMES.
VOL. I.

LONDON:
GEORGE REDWAY, YORK STREET, COVENT GARDEN.
1889.

#### This Translation is Dedicated

TO THE HONOURED MEMORY

OF

MRS. ANNA KINGSFORD, M.D.,

AT WHOSE INSTANCE IT WAS UNDERTAKEN.

# CONTENTS OF VOL. I.

| CHAPTER | PAGE |
|---|---|
| I. INTRODUCTION.—SCIENCE: ITS CAPABILITY OF DEVELOPMENT | 1 |
| II. ON THE SCIENTIFIC IMPORTANCE OF DREAM: | |
|     1. The Positive Side of the Sleep-life | 27 |
|     2. The Confused Dream | 38 |
|     3. The Relation of Sleep to Somnambulism | 44 |
|     4. The Metaphysical Application of Dream | 51 |
| III. DREAM A DRAMATIST: | |
|     1. The Transcendental Measure of Time | 87 |
|     2. The Dramatic Sundering of the Ego in Dream: | |
|         (a) The Body | 112 |
|         (b) The Mind | 122 |
|         (c) The Human Enigma | 133 |
| IV. SOMNAMBULISM: | |
|     1. Natural Somnambulism | 144 |
|     2. Artificial Somnambulism | 161 |
| V. DREAM A PHYSICIAN: | |
|     1. Dream-images as Symbolical Representation of Bodily States | 191 |
|     2. Diagnosis in the Somnambulic Sleep: | |
|         (a) Self-Inspection | 206 |
|         (b) The Diagnosis of the Diseases of others by Somnambulists | 232 |
|     3. The Curative Instinct in Dream | 252 |
|     4. The Health-Prescriptions of Somnambulists | 280 |

# TRANSLATORS' PREFACE.

THE work of which the following translation is now offered to the English public was published at Leipsic three or four years ago. In Germany it has been extensively noticed, and among other recognitions of its importance may be mentioned the fact that Edward von Hartmann has devoted a large part of one of his most recent treatises—'Moderne Probleme'—to an examination of it. The author, Baron Carl du Prel, Doctor of Philosophy, was already known by earlier works of a speculative character, especially marked by an attempt to appreciate the significance of the doctrine of Evolution, from a standpoint hitherto unrepresented in the prevailing treatment of the subject. Qualified by a philosophical training, not always found in combination with scientific studies, du Prel has ventured on the suggestion and discussion of problems for which that combination is eminently required. The list of his published works will be found on an outer page; 'Die Monistische Seelenlehre' and 'Die Mystik der alten Griechen' having appeared since the publication of the here translated 'Die Philosophie der Mystik.'

The influence of the philosophies of Kant, Schopenhauer, and E. von Hartmann is especially observable in the speculations of this author. It was necessary that the doctrine of soul (in the sense of a super-organic Subject) should pass through the solvent of those systems, that it might be freed from a dualism which neither science nor philosophy would permanently endure. If in this process—especially in its post-Kantian development—the doctrine itself seemed altogether lost, that was consequent on the assumption that no data existed for the empirical support of a reformed conception. *Behind* the phenomena of consciousness, both objective and subjective—thus, behind consciousness itself —must certainly be placed the ultimate reality or being of which consciousness offers only a reflection or representation. This inscrutable being is therefore termed 'the Unconscious.' But now the question arises whether this ' Unconscious ' lies *immediately* behind our physically conditioned consciousness, or may be pushed back indefinitely, so that there is room for a root of conscious individuality, only *relatively* unconscious for the organism of sense. Du Prel finds an answer to this question in the recognition and significance of what is now known as the psycho-physical 'threshold of sensibility,' and in its occasional mobility or displacement.

It is fortunately no longer necessary to contend against scepticism for the genuine character of the somnambulic (or Hypnotic) consciousness, spontaneous or induced. Even if the unanimous report, after full investigation, by the Committee of the Medical Academy of Paris in 1831, should still be ignored, recent scientific researches, especially in France, have placed the general fact beyond the possibility of dispute; at least, in any well-informed quarter.

But du Prel is the first, I believe, who has shown by systematic analysis and comparison, that somnambulism and cognate states are not essentially abnormal or morbid, but are in truth a mere exaltation of ordinary sleep, and that the faculties evinced in those states are incipiently manifested also in dream, and are even indicated, though still more indefinitely, in waking life. The importance of establishing the fact of this continuity in our psychical nature will be apparent to every attentive reader of the following work. For, far from reducing the advanced phenomena of somnambulism, as regards their psychological significance, to the level of the illusions which are the mere dramatic *form* of dream, the whole dream-life—emerging sometimes even in apparent waking—is reclaimed from its presumed worthlessness for scientific and philosophical purposes. But there is at the same time reclaimed from the crude or traditional *misinterpretation* in which 'superstition' really consists, a large field of *fact*, to which modern rationalism, for want of an explanation, has impatiently and rashly applied that term.

It may not be superfluous to direct the reader's attention, at the outset, to the essential difference between the dualism of consciousness as conceived by the author—the division of two 'persons' in one 'Subject'—and the traditional and popular idea of the dualism of soul and body. This is, in other words, the dualism of Matter and Spirit, of Nature and the Supernatural. It is here that Science, or rather scientific thought, has broken with Religion, or would, with Herbert Spencer, identify the province of the latter with the barren postulate of an ultimate Unknowable. This dualism reappears, in another form, as that of matter and force, receiving an idealistic solution in Schopenhauer's conception of all force as the Will behind consciousness and its 'Vorstellungen'—the phenomenal world. Physicists have already attained to a monistic conception of matter and force; or, at least, it is agreed that, though distinguishable as concepts, these factors are not therefore naturally separable. And it has become evident that force in its higher manifestation, as vitality, can no longer be supposed divorced from its material or medium, nor can consciousness be held potentially exempt from any sort of organic support or expression. This, indeed, is a conclusion long ago anticipated in ancient speculations* upon psychic bodies. That in modern times this conclusion has tended to materialism, or to those forms of pantheism which deny individual survival, is incontestable, though with the philosophical recognition by science of the converse proposition, that the world is objectively a phenomenon of consciousness,†

---

\* See Cudworth's 'Intellectual System,' for a collection of opinions on this subject.

† Huxley's 'Lay Sermons,' xiv. On Descartes' 'Discourse,' etc.

it is strange that the probability of other modes of phenomena, therefore of other sensible worlds than our own, which must be for us supersensible, though not supernatural, has been so little considered.*

The absence from Christian teaching of anything which can be called a psychology (such as occupies so prominent a place in some Eastern systems of religious philosophy) has left Western belief in immortality without any more definite conception of what survives in man, than that of a spiritual substance or principle, with which is identified the self supposed to be already known in consciousness. The Neo-platonic idea that the soul is only partially known in the physically conditioned consciousness—thus asserting a transcendental individuality—though not without some Patristic patronage, was not easily intelligible, and has long dropped out of view, as it is not to be confused with the doctrine of the trichotomy of man, which distinguishes soul from spirit. In the Christian belief, the soul is wholly introduced into a heterogeneous form, the body. That was a dualism which could not long survive scientific tendencies of thought; and as it is, in the West, the only traditional form of belief in individual immortality, that belief has long been decaying with the increase of intellectual activity among the people.

The dualism of consciousness, on the other hand—the discovery of an intelligence which emerges in clearness and power just in proportion to the cessation of the organic functions with which the consciousness of waking life is associated, carries with it no consequence inconsistent with the monistic conception of nature. But it would not of itself resolve the dualism of soul and body, without the evidence which this transcendental intelligence affords of another function connected therewith. The Subject, which includes the two halves of our consciousness divided by the movable 'threshold of sensibility,' is shown to be an

* Balfour Stewart's and Tait's 'The Unseen Universe' is the best-known English speculation in this direction.

*organising* as well as a thinking principle. The facts pointing to this conclusion which are adduced in the following work by no means exhaust the evidence for it. The history of inventions shows that the genius of discovery has unconsciously followed the organic constructions of nature, the principle of which is inferentially in ourselves. The numerous examples of this analogy, showing also the *antecedence* of the human invention to the knowledge of the natural construction—thus negativing the derivation of the former from such knowledge—are strikingly exhibited in a recent German work;[*] and another German author professes to prove that the very same law of proportion—that of the 'golden section'[†] — prevails alike in the organic and inorganic kingdoms of nature, and in the productions of human art, in architecture, music, poetry, and painting.[‡]

I will here translate some striking remarks of my author, from his 'Monistische Seelenlehre.' After referring to the first of the two just-mentioned works—that of Kapp—he says:

'At first sight it seems highly wonderful that technical products, invented and fabricated in the condition of clearest consciousness, should agree in fundamental character with products of Nature. And yet is this quite naturally intelligible. Our surprise springs from the supposition we make of a double source, a dualism of forces, which does not at all exist. The brain-processes on which those technical inventions depend are not evoked by consciousness, but only illuminated by it. As, according to Spinoza, the flung stone, if it had consciousness, would believe its flight to be voluntary, so we, when thought is lighted up by consciousness, suppose the process of thought to be an

---

[*] E. Kapp: 'Philosophie der Technik.'
[†] Euclid: Book II., Prop. 11.
[‡] Zeising: 'Neue Lehre von den Proportionen des menschlichen Körpers—Das Normalverhältniss der chemischen Proportionen.'

activity of consciousness. Instead of wondering that there is an unconscious thinking, we should rather understand that, in fact, there is none other: that is to say, there is indeed a thinking which is accompanied by consciousness, but none that is caused by consciousness. Organism and consciousness are not governed by heterogeneous forces, whose products, nevertheless, wonderfully harmonise, but in both provinces it is one and the same force differentiated, and therefore the products *must* agree. That surprise of ours arises from the presupposition of a dualism in man: in the monistic explanation of man it loses its justification.'

In art, following unwittingly the precedents of nature, there is the same activity, the same faculty of nature itself, only now raised to consciousness. The technical discoveries of inventive genius are secondary projections of the organising faculty of nature in man, and follow the type of the primary.

In the same work—' Die Monistische Seelenlehre '—other phenomena are brought into account for the further proof of an organising faculty in the human individual. These phenomena are chiefly of what is called in German *Doppelgängerei*, and are similar to some dealt with in the recent publication of the English Society for Psychical Research, entitled 'Phantasms of the Living.' Du Prel is, however, careful to discriminate the cases which may possibly come under the explanation (telepathic hallucination) most favoured by the acute authors of the above work, from those which seem to require his own hypothesis. As regards the evidential value of the testimony to such facts, as well as to those adduced in the following book, it is unnecessary to contend that the cases are all individually unassailable, if collectively and cumulatively they form a class with identical features pointing to the same theoretical explanation, when no other cause of such apparently significant coincidences can be shown. For it is just this recurrence, this community of features, which constitutes *experience*, and distinguishes that from the altogether exceptional and unrelated facts which must be proved, if at all, by particular evidence of such strength, that the improbability of its being forthcoming for what is untrue is greater than any improbability we can oppose to the facts for which it is found. The objection that the evidence in any special case does not come up to a certain standard, may be fatal when that case stands in isolation, but is much less formidable when the case in question is raised to probability by likeness to a class, *in respect of characteristics not includable in suppositions by which the class itself could be attacked.* The independent agreement of alleged facts, in particulars where agreement could not be anticipated on the supposition of a cause of fallacy common to the class (such as imposture, delusion, etc.), is a circumstance of evidence not less important for the establishment of the whole class, than is the independent agreement of witnesses for the establishment of a single fact; and a second-hand story, perhaps very loosely reported by an ancient author, may possibly in this way be corroborative of much better testimony to more recent facts.

But not only does an alleged fact gain in probability by a relation to other alleged facts, but also by a relation to our intelligence. It is the absence of this relation, even more than non-referability to common or admitted experience, which makes us unreceptive of evidence that would otherwise suffice to convince. When we see *how* a thing can have happened, we are much more ready to give a fair hearing to evidence that it *has* happened, than when the material offered is quite indigestible by our intelligence. And thus an explanatory hypothesis is hardly less necessary for the reception of facts of a certain character, than are facts for the support of a hypothesis.

If, moreover, the author has succeeded in showing, in what is perhaps one of the most impressive arguments of the book, that the faculties alleged to be displayed in the somnambulic state are antecedently to be expected upon the doctrine of evolution, and from the accepted physiological theory of cognition, the presumption is shifted, and the positive evidence must be more benevolently considered. The force of that evidence may be variously estimated; but it was at any rate strong enough, two generations ago, to convince such witnesses as the Committee of the French Medical Academy,* and later, as regards clairvoyance, (of the possibilities of simulating which he had made a special study), the celebrated expert, Robert Houdin;† and to elicit from such an understanding as Schopenhauer's the remark, that whoever doubted clairvoyance was no longer to be termed sceptical, but ignorant.

But, in truth, incredulity is a disposition that has very little regard for evidence. In his 'History of Rationalism,' Mr. Lecky has expressly pointed out that the tide of scepticism, as to phenomena hitherto accredited, which set in towards the close of the seventeenth century, was due entirely to general intellectual dispositions, and was not at all referable to more accurate conceptions of evidence. A few minds of a high order, exceptionally tenacious of facts, which they subjected to the severest scrutiny, attempted at that period to direct public attention to the evidential aspect of occurrences underlying what were, doubtless, very superstitious errors of interpretation. In vain. They were unanswered, unheeded. The Devil was going out of fashion; and as in popular belief the Devil was a principal party to most transactions exceeding ordinary powers of explanation, in the German phrase, 'the child was emptied out with the bath;' the facts were dismissed with the interpretation. And so it has been till recently; so, perhaps, it still is.

But to return to the philosophy of this book.

The hypothesis of transcendental individuality, coexistent with the earthly life, and constructive of the organism by which consciousness is (from the earthly standpoint) dualised, necessitates the doctrine of Pre-existence. That doctrine, though never popularly entertained in the West,

* *Post*, pp. 182, 183. † *Post*, p. 241.

has seldom been without distinguished representatives. The learned Dr. Henry More, towards the close of the seventeenth, or early in the eighteenth century, thus speaks of it in his treatise on the 'Immortality of the Soul' (Book II., c. 14): 'The consequence of our soul's pre-existence is more agreeable to reason than any other hypothesis whatever; has been received by the most learned philosophers of all ages, there being scarcely any of them that held the soul of man immortal upon the mere light of Nature and reason, but asserted also her pre-existence.' The same author also ascribes to the soul, not only consciousness, but an organising power and function. He defines the soul of man to be 'a created spirit endued with sense and reason, and *a power of organising terrestrial matter into human shape* by vital union therewith' (*Op. cit.*, Bk. I., c. 8). And further on he says: '... the frame of the body, of which I think it most reasonable to conclude the soul herself to be the more particular architect (for I will not wholly reject Plotinus his opinion), and that the plastick power resides in her, as also in the souls of brute animals, as very worthy and learned writers have determined' (Bk. II., c. 10). And, again: '... those two notorious powers, and so perfectly different, which philosophers acknowledge in the soul, to wit, perception and organisation.' Had Dr. Henry More gone a little further with Plotinus, to the doctrines of Pre-existence and the 'plastick power,' he would have added that of transcendental individuality, in distinction from the personal consciousness and functions, not conceiving the soul to be wholly plunged into the successive bodies it constructs. In any case, however, a restatement of the argument, as we have it in the following book, would now be necessary, to meet the advance of modern experience, thought, and science.

Many at the present day are independently of opinion (without having at all derived their view from the philosophers of whom More speaks) that individual survival of physical dissolution is only to be thought of in connection with the assumption of pre-natal existence. But the whole conception of immortality undergoes an important change, if we regard the personal consciousness, with its Ego, as a mere partial and temporary limitation of a larger self, the growth of many seasons, as it were, of earthly life. The substitution of this conception, with all that it involves in relation to ethical and social problems, for that of a mere continuity of the personal consciousness, whose interests arise entirely out of a brief experience and temporary conditions, is hardly less satisfactory than the provisional filling of the huge void between the personal life of average humanity, and the spiritual regeneration which is the only aspect in which religion can condescend to regard immortality. The scope of this speculation would, however, be quite misconceived, were it supposed to offer a substitute for religion, or to be inconsistent with higher and more spiritual truth, in whatever forms of religion that may be veiled. Rather might the contrary easily be shown to be the case. The transcendental does not drive out the Divine, but enlarges possibilities and opportunities in relation to it. The true theme of religion is not the future life, but the higher life. It does not offer to teach us a psychology, and any religious prejudice against an extension of our psychological conceptions would be only a repetition, in that province, of the still unforgiven error of opposition to the true astronomy; and with not so much excuse, since there is less that can be mistaken for psychology in the New Testament than that could be, and was, mistaken for cosmogony in the Old Testament.

If it should be asked, What, then, according to the theory of subjectivity propounded in this book, is the individual, or what is his state after death? the answer can only be given generally, in a similitude suggested by the author, of the smaller of two concentric circles expanding to the larger. The circumference of the inner circle is the organic threshold of sensibility, which death removes altogether, as it is already partially removed in states analogous to death, revealing then those phenomena the report of which excites incredulity, just because they exceed the faculties of the normal, or organic, consciousness. The psychological conception thus offered us of the more circumscribed personality, which we falsely suppose to exhaust our individuality, is somewhat that of a preoccupation of consciousness with its temporary circumstances; a limitation to which we can discover a resemblance in special preoccupations within the personal life itself. Often in childhood, or in crises of later life, our whole identity seems sunk in an absorbing interest, and only when the tension is relaxed do we again expand to our normal comprehensiveness of relations and interests, and recognise in the late contraction of consciousness a mere episode, which may soon be a forgotten one, of our life. But in those moments of concentration the attempt to reduce things to their true proportion, by reference to the total circle of the personality, would be scarcely more suggestive of the reality of that circle, than is now the philosophy of transcendental individuality recognisable as a true account of our identity. The submergence, the latency of general interests by preoccupation with particular ones, can even now contract the personality, the sense of identity, to a 'fixed idea,' and can amount to the insanity which blots even from memory our true relations to the world about us. The latency of the transcendental consciousness is only a stronger and more enduring case of preoccupation, just as the whole organic condition of our life on earth is more rigid and determinate than are the superinduced cerebral modifications which are the physical correlates of particular psychical states.

There is thus nothing unintelligible in the distinction between personality, understood of a certain fixed state, or preoccupation, of consciousness, the reactions of character on the special circumstances of a life-time, and the individuality of which those conditions are but a particular and transient determination. We often hear it said, in reply to metaphysical conceptions of identity, that continuity of consciousness is indispensable to the sense of identity, and that no doctrine which fails to take account of this can be regarded as a doctrine of individual survival. Thus, in Buddhism, the successive personalities, constituted and linked together by Karma, are quite inconceivable as a true case of Palingenesis, without the unitary bond of transcendental subjectivity. And it is probable that the unfamiliarity of this latter conception has caused European commentators on Buddhism to overlook indications of it which are certainly to be found in Buddhist books, and in recorded sayings of the Master. Other views of reincarnation, such as the French Spiritist doctrine of M. Rivail (Allan Kardec), identify the derivative and successive personalities, though without continuity of consciousness or memory. The nexus is here only a sort of heredity. But the personality is definable as the circle of consciousness, and is not identifiable with another and excentric circle, but only with the subject which has the same centre, though a larger circumference. Moreover, the consciousness of identity is indispensable, only we must not look for it in the wrong quarter, in the leaves of successive seasons rather than in the tree which puts them forth. Transcendental subjectivity makes provision for the continuity of consciousness; but, at the same time, it will be seen that the urgent demand for it of the personal Egoism greatly exaggerates its importance in relation to the total sphere of the subjectivity. The interest of the tree in last year's leaves is just the nutriment and growth it has derived through them. The experience and the whole activity of one of our objective life-times will be assimilated for results quite other, perhaps, than those the interest of the contracted Ego proposed, and probably bearing but a minute proportion to the gradually accumulated psychical content of the whole individual. The constant aim of philosophy, in its ethical aspect, is to bring the personal Ego to the point of view of the transcendental subject, to which the mere happiness of that Ego is indifferent. What to us, as 'persons,' are ideal motives, which only the noblest of the race can invest with actuating emotion, may, for the larger self, be of immediate moment, and alone of interest, except so far as it may also concern itself with maintaining the objective mode—the organic personality—which it has constructed for its own purposes. This, however, must be taken with the qualification mentioned in the text (Vol. II., p. 297). For, as the dispositions which manifest themselves in the personality are results of former life-habits, transferred to the subject (for which all is not gain alone), we can as little attribute moral perfection to the latter, as perfect health to the organism which always seeks to drive whatever may be morbid in it to the surface. Our earthly lives are just this surface, and the most rational conception of one aspect of Karma (of which this part of the text is evidently an independent exposition) is quite analogous to the process of Nature in the endeavour to expel disease.

With what admirable economy the doctrine of Palingenesis, associated with the truth revived in this book, that the soul 'does not sink wholly into generation,'* fits the progress of the individual into the progress of the race, avoiding all the waste of energy involved in the now favoured conception that the former is merely sacrificed to the latter; how the philosophy, or science, of biological evolution is shown to induce an expectation of the very phenomena which uninquiring rationalism would discredit; and how the materialist, who strangely claims a peculiar interest in that science, is found to be 'hoist with his own petard;' what probability there is, from the relative planetary ages and conditions, that exaltations of consciousness and faculty, which for us as a race belong only to the remote biological future, are already a realised attainment elsewhere in the Kosmos; how, as regards the value of life itself, Pessimism is reconciled with, or, rather, is subordinated to, Optimism, while its partial truth is admitted and its necessity is explained—all this, with much more than can be even

* Plotinus.

summarily alluded to here, seems to some students of the subjects dealt with to be expounded in these volumes with an ability and force which it is hoped may be appreciated by a larger circle of English readers.

The translation is as literal as I could make it. I have ventured occasionally to add foot-notes, intended to be explanatory or critical. I regret that the French word 'somnambule'—used throughout in the German text, and which I intended to retain only when a female of the class was denoted—occurs more indiscriminately in the first volume of this translation. Should the latter reach a second edition, the English form 'somnambulist' will be substituted in every case.

C. C. M.

# AUTHOR'S PREFACE.

It is not always the business of philosophy to split hairs, and to devise subtle problems. The weightiest problems are just those which are hidden by their every-day character, or behind unwarranted presuppositions, of which we are unconscious, only because we are continually making them.

Such a problem it is which I would suggest in the following work—the question whether our Ego is wholly embraced in self-consciousness. The affirmative answer to this question, the most proximate and constant of human problems, is evidently a mere presumption, and not less so because carried on through our whole life. Moreover, this presumption is not only logically unjustified, but is also—as will be shown—erroneous. Analysis of the dream-life leads to a negative answer to the question propounded; it shows that self-consciousness falls short of its object, that the Ego exceeds the self-consciousness.

If, however, we are more than that of which our self-consciousness informs us, and indeed not in the sense of a pantheistic dissolution, but with preservation of individuality, then it is evident that the question of the soul has been falsely stated. Instead of succession of the here and the beyond, we have their simultaneity, that is, the simultaneity of two Persons of our Subject.

Not always in the development of philosophy has this problem been concealed; it has already been suggested in Indian philosophy, later by Plotinus, and finally by Kant. But its importance and fertility can only be favourably conceived according to the degree in which our intelligible* being is held to be cognisable. Our problem must thus be recognised as the cardinal point of a philosophical system, as soon as it is provable that the intelligible being can be made accessible to experience. That is in fact the case.

The circuit of the knowledge and self-knowledge possible to an organised being is determined by the number of its senses, and by the strength of the stimuli on which its senses react; *i.e.*, by its psychophysical threshold of sensibility. In the biological process this threshold has been continually movable, and so in the succession of life-forms there has been not only a differentiation of the organs of sense, but also an exaltation of consciousness. But at the basis

---

* [The 'intelligible' being (or character) is a term of the Kantian philosophy, and is there used in opposition to the empirical. The noumenal, or intelligible, character corresponds, psychically, to the 'thing-in-itself' behind the phenomenal 'object.' The hypothesis in the text of the cognisability of the human noumenon supposes it to be potentially empirical—capable, that is, of presentation to consciousness under certain conditions. Such a presentation would reveal new determinations of the internal sense (in Kantian phraseology); in other words, would manifest another character, or personality, within the limits of subjective unity. The consciousness of the transcendental 'self' is of course only to be understood in the sense of ordinary 'self'-consciousness: *i.e.*, as objectification of the subject in its determinations, or inner content.—Tr.]

of this biological mobility of the threshold of sensibility, there must be the same mobility of it in the individual. This also is susceptible of proof from the analysis of our dream-life; but it is most strikingly apparent in somnambulism. The displacement of the threshold of sensibility is thus common to the biological process and to somnambulism; and hence results the weighty inference, that in somnambulism not only is the mode of existence of our intelligible being indicated, but also there is an anticipation of that future biological form which will have as its normal possession those faculties, of which we have now only an intimation in this exceptional condition.

Thus the negative reply to our question, whether the self is wholly contained in self-consciousness, throws light in its consequences as well on the direction of the biological process, as on the intelligible side of our being. Accordingly—and this is the most important result of our problem—the province of mysticism is revealed to the understanding. If man is a being dualised by a threshold of sensibility, then is mysticism possible; and if, furthermore, this threshold of sensibility is a movable one, then is mysticism even necessary.

This is in brief the purport of the following work. The latter will not deal with the historical, objective forms of mysticism, but the subjective foundation of all mysticism shall be investigated, in order then to turn to account the results obtained for a philosophical doctrine of man. Now, it is the rule, that only in the suppression of the activity of the senses can the inner working of our mystical, intelligible Subject occur, as the stars are first visible with the going down of the sun. We are therefore directed to the study of the sleep-state, especially in that deepening of it which we designate somnambulism. Modern science has lost intelligence for mysticism, only because it has almost entirely neglected the study of somnambulism, which is subjectively presupposed in the phenomena of mysticism. And yet there is no province which offers to psychologists and philosophers so rich a harvest as this; no other admits of so deep a penetration into the enigma of man and of his place in the universe.

Mysticism is not to be considered in isolation, but must be conceived in its organic connection with the totality of things. Every philosophy, in which mysticism is not a necessary part, must be from the outset defective in its principles; but conversely, mysticism can no more be arbitrarily extracted from the true view of the Kosmos, than can the focus from an ellipse.

Mysticism does not stand beside the other phenomena of Nature unconnected with them, but forms the last communication between all phenomena. So far from it being an obsolete view, much rather obsolete are those, though modern, conceptions in which it has no place. So far is mysticism from belonging only to a surmounted past, that much rather will it first attain its full significance in the future. As well the Kantian 'Critique of Reason,' as the physiological theory of sense-perception, and Darwinism, point convergently to a view of the world into which mysticism will be organically fitted.

The natural sciences have already reached their central depth, because in the conceptions, Force and

Atom, phenomena are reduced to the supersensuous. This must happen also in the science of man, and indeed—as shall be shown in this work—in a manner deviating as well from pantheism as from the dualistic doctrine of the soul. The phenomena of dream and somnambulism prove the existence of our intelligible Subject, and so we arrive at a closer definition and description of the Unconscious, which is to be conceived individually, and not pantheistically, and is not unconscious in itself, but is so only for the being of the senses.

The attempt to erect a philosophical fabric of doctrine on the empirical basis of the sleep-life can accordingly occasion no surprise ; for as soon as it is shown that this sleep-life possesses positive characteristics, peculiar to itself, it will become the duty of philosophy to apply to this third of our existence, not yet turned to metaphysical account, a like study, though it may be a more arduous one, as to the waking life. An essential part of experience has thus hitherto not been worked out, and it is just that which contains the reconciliation of the harsh antagonisms in modern intellectual development. Now since it is from these theoretical antagonisms that the harshness of our social antagonisms has grown, the reconciliation of the former must compose also the latter. And in this I see a proof of the correctness of my views ; for the conformity of theoretical truth with practical good is among my firm convictions.

Now if I, standing quite apart from the traffic of life, have not steered for this practical goal, but have been carried to it by inner necessity of thought, I shall still welcome an unprejudiced critical appreciation of my work, if only for the reason that in our social conditions the spread of reconciling and composing views would be very desirable.

Thus every criticism will be welcome which is adapted to advance the subject and myself. But I cannot hope for such from that sort of critics who are only able to explain every departure from their opinions by the insanity of the author; and who, while they attribute wild error to an author who has devoted years of study to a subject, think they understand the subject much better without such study. I have undoubtedly the right to demand from a critic, not only philosophical preparation, but also a knowledge of the most important of the works I have cited; but to emphasise this demand is unfortunately necessary at a time when journalistic reviewers, who have made no regular study in any direction, are thought capable of criticism in every direction, and who, without thoughts of their own, have leisure to disfigure and maltreat the thoughts of others. But apart from this limitation, I know very well that conflict, which Heraklitus called the father of all things, is also the father of truth.

DU PREL.

*June*, 1884.

# PHILOSOPHY OF MYSTICISM.

## CHAPTER I.

INTRODUCTION.—SCIENCE : ITS CAPABILITY OF DEVELOPMENT.

The endeavour of the human intellect is to explain the significance of the world and of ourselves. Religious and philosophical systems succeed one another, and each offers a different solution of the problems. Nevertheless, in this exchange of views there is progress. Truth is not a thing which can be accidentally and once for all discovered by genius as a complete structure, but is a growth, a slowly ripening product, and the process of scientific development is the evolution of truth itself, which thus first appears at the close of the process as its result.

Epochs of time follow one upon another, each with its characteristic representations of the meaning of the world and man's position therein. These representations impart to every period of culture its particular colour, even in relation to the practical conduct of mankind. The conduct of man always results from his idea of the world; the construction of his earthly life reflects metaphysical conceptions. The political and social quietism of the Buddhist peoples is thus a consequence of their aspiration for Nirvana, just as the precipitate material development of our time, with its worship of the golden calf, results from our recognising Sansara* alone as real. Whenever in history we come upon a generation sunk in materialism, we can at once infer that even in theory ideals have for it no value, and that it is no longer influenced by metaphysical conception, a fact which is most strikingly apparent in the irreligion of the masses. Disbelief in the metaphysical logically results in misplacing the emphasis on the earthly. Our century, indeed, lives in the delusion that it is thereby preparing the golden age upon earth; but whither we are in fact tending we may learn, for instance, from the statistics of suicide. From these it appears that in civilized Europe hourly three persons destroy themselves, and that for a succession of years the number of suicides has been frightfully on the increase.

Since a logical instinct leads to a correspondence between the conduct of men and their conception of the world-problem, it follows that whoever will improve men must first conceive that problem otherwise than they do; thus, that the moral progress of humanity is thoroughly dependent on the evolutionary capacity of science. If science has in itself this capacity, then there is at least the possibility of an impulse towards better conditions, and of again reaching a form of culture coloured by ideals; otherwise not. The question of the power of science to develop is therefore of the highest importance, even in practical regard.

* The vortex of life.—Tr.

The historical consciousness of humanity answers this question in the affirmative, so much so that many might consider a particular examination of it to be superfluous, since the self-evolution of science is not doubted by even the dominant opinion. But though such is the belief in intellectual progress, that one can no longer sit down on an ale-house bench without reproach, yet it is associated with completely false conceptions, and these can only disappear with the yet higher elevation of the belief, on the one side, and on the other with the renunciation of certain hopes which we now attach to it.

The first condition is that we should conceive progress otherwise than as mere breadth. True progress is always in the depth,* whereas every generation imagines that it leaves to its successors only the task of extension on the same level. The other misconception to be discarded is that, with the development of the sciences, the world-problem will become more comprehensible. The contrary is the case, at least up to the present, and apparently will be so for a long time, whatever the possibility of this hope being ultimately fulfilled.

Our inquiry is thus concerned with the two questions: how far intellectual progress takes a deepening direction, and what it contributes to the explanation of the world-problem. How intimately these two questions are connected will appear at the close; but

* As Bacon says: 'No perfect discovery can be made upon a flat or a level; neither is it possible to discover the more remote and deeper parts of any science if you stand but upon the level of the same science and ascend not to a higher science.'—'Advancement of Learning,' i. 5.—Tr.

they must receive separate treatment, in accordance with the axiom, *Qui bene distinguit, bene docet.*

The tendency of the self-evolutionary power of science to vertical progress may be illustrated by the following instances. Trusting the illusion of the senses, by which sun, planets, and fixed stars seem to rise in the east and set in the west, the old Greeks set astronomy the task of explaining these apparent movements on the supposition that they were the true ones. This task proved continually more difficult; more and more cycles and epicycles seemed requisite to account for the observations; but it was always believed that the method was the right one, and that future generations had only to labour further on the same level. But when the thought of Copernicus—anticipated in the secret teaching of Pythagoras and the Kabala—exposed the sense-illusion in which human understanding lay imprisoned, then it became also clear that success was not to be expected from further labour 'on the flat.' A new, vertical path of progress was laid down.

Similar examples might be drawn from other branches of empirical science; but it is more instructive to turn to philosophy. That would explain the world. But what world? The world which is manifested to us by our senses. And philosophy, like astronomy, took the appearance for the reality. It was an unquestioned assumption that our perceptions accommodated themselves to things.

It was believed that the whole world, as it lay outside of us, by means of our sense-apparatus, projected itself into the brain, and there produced a reflected image of itself. Thus truth was to be captured by investigation of the object. But now, again, when Kant (who himself compares his discovery with that of Copernicus) exposed the fallacy of the assumption actuating this endeavour, and urged the prior examination of the subject and its cognitional forms, the signal was again given to discontinue the level working, and to sink the foundations of research.

And it is only in Kant's sense that the modern evolution theory will work, however little this may be yet understood. The biological process begins with the simplest organisms, and it is in the complicated human organism that it has reached its present height. A tree stands in very few and simple relations to external nature; it reacts upon sunshine and rain, wind and weather, and unfolds itself accordingly. In the animal kingdom these relations to the environment have continually widened and multiplied, and hand in hand with the organic proceeds the intellectual development.

Organization and consciousness rise parallel to each other from the oyster to the man. And even if with contemporary man organic formation represented the most multitudinous relations possible with nature, yet would the circle of these relations be continually widened in the historical process, through the technical arts and theoretical sciences. The elevation of consciousness would thus still proceed, even were the evolution of organic forces concluded.

From the standpoint of every animal organism we can thus divide external nature into two parts, which are the more unequal as the organic grade is lower.

The one includes that part of nature with which the sense-apparatus establishes relations; the other is for the organism in question transcendental; that is, the organism lives in no relation to it. In the biological process the boundary-line between these two world-halves has been pushed continually forward in the same direction. The number of senses has increased, and their functional ability has risen. While, that is, the senses differentiated, and became sensitive to continually weaker degrees of physical influence, that which Fechner named the psycho-physical threshold was continually pushed forward. Influences behind that threshold do not come into consciousness. The biological rise and the rise of consciousness thus signify a constant removal of the boundary between representation and reality at the cost of the transcendental part of the world, and in favour of the perceived part.

Darwin thus has proved that from the standpoint of organism, a transcendental world is continually given; and Kant has proved the same for man by his distinction between the 'thing in itself' and the phenomenon.\*

The most extreme opposition to this conception is materialism, so that to regard the doctrine of evolution as supporting materialism belongs to confused thinking. The materialist is wholly imprisoned in

\* The 'thing in itself' is not identifiable with the transcendental, if the latter is conceived, as in the text, as potentially empirical. For what *can* be sensibly known is knowable only under percipient forms, whether these are a development of our present ones, or specifically different; the resulting 'object' being still phenomenon, behind which a reality, independent of perception, will be just as much in demand as for the world of our present senses.—Tr.

appearance. He holds the eye to be the mere mirror of phenomena, and the world to be just what it is for sense (im Kopfe); and so in the investigation of the object is to be found the solution of the world-enigma. Of Kant's problem he has no apprehension; he is like a man wearing blue spectacles, and explaining the blueness of objects from themselves. A part of the world having no relation to our senses has no existence for him. Materialism is the offspring of an assumption by which it stands or falls, namely, that all the real is sensuously perceptible. Feuerbach says that 'the object of sense, or the sensuous, alone is really true, and therefore truth, reality, and the sensible are one.' But this assumption, that to every force in nature there is a corresponding sense, that there are as many senses as forces, stands in contradiction with the demonstrable fact that consciousness is an unfinished product of evolution. The magnetic and electrical forces escape our direct perception, and could not be proved were they not convertible into equivalent amounts of other forces which address our senses. Only for this reason, that perceptibility and reality are not coincident, is the world an unsolved problem. Were they identical, a few centuries must suffice for the discovery of all truth.

The whole biological process is a protest against the presupposition of materialism. For every grade of organization there is a different circuit of the transcendental — the unrelated part of the world. Materialism also regards man as a product of evolution; yet is so illogical as to assert that the disproportion between perceptibility and reality, which exists in the whole biological process, exists for man no more. For materialism, the senses relate us to all external forces of nature, and with the failure of the relation fails also the force. That, however, is a *petitio principii*, implying the vicious circle: the sensuous alone is actual; there can be no supersensuous, since this would be sensuously perceptible. Contrary to this assertion of materialism, we must, therefore, rather say, as there are parts of nature which remain invisible to us, being out of relation to our sense of sight—for instance, the microscopic world—so are there parts of nature not existing for us, owing to entire absence of relation to our organism. 'The subtlety of nature,' as Bacon says, 'far exceeds the subtlety of sense and understanding.'\*

The proposition that every true advance of knowledge has a vertical direction was strikingly exemplified in the last century by materialism itself, when, constrained by natural phenomena, it had to give up its own assumption. In the physiological theory of sense-perception it became experimentally evident that perception and reality do not coincide. There are rays of the sun which we do not see, vibrations of air which we do not hear, etc. And in physics it became necessary to set up the atomic theory, so that now even materialism, making use of non-sensual concepts, has broken into the region of metaphysic, whose existence it denied, since it declared the identity of the perceivable with the real. Thus, while supposing science so near its conclusion as to be only capable of peripheral extension, mate-

\* 'Novum Organum,' i. 10.

rialism found itself compelled to carry on the work by a deepening of its central concepts.

In the history of science it has often appeared as if the objective horizon of knowledge was at least in sight, and as if nothing remained but to press forward upon existing lines for this horizon to be reached. Especially was this illusion excited by the development of the natural sciences, since it was believed that the only right method of research, the experimental (which certainly has led to undreamed-of advances in every department), had been found. Yet is Natural Science still very far from its goal, and already it is seen that after completion of her task new prospects will be opened in the vertical direction. Science has now herself acknowledged that when she has explained the world as it lays before our eyes, it is only a *represented* world that will have been explained—a secondary phenomenon, a mere product of our sense and understanding. Great, therefore, as her task undoubtedly is, it is but a preliminary labour of the human intellect; and she must disembogue into the stream of philosophy, that they may together solve the problem of knowledge. It will appear that the division of intellectual labour was only temporary, and that the opposition, amounting to hostility, between Philosophy and Natural Science, only confirms the words of Bacon\*—'Tum enim homines vires suas nosse incipient, cum non eadem infiniti, sed alia alii præstabunt.'

When each has performed its special task, the re-union of the divided tendencies will result in unexpected gains, which will also lie in the *deepening*

\* 'Novum Organum,' i. 113.

of conceptions. The question will then be further dealt with of the relation between the represented world and the real world, between things and our cognitional faculties. The inclination towards Kant, who raised this question, is already manifest in natural science, which no longer, as formerly, puts it aside as the offspring of an intellectual self-torture, but has practically justified it. Science herself is on the point of perceiving that the explanation of the empirical world is fundamentally nothing else than an explanation of the speciality of the human mind. And soon she will have nothing to object, if one says to her, with Schopenhauer: 'The being-in-itself of force, and the conditioning of the objective world by the intellect (wherewith is also connected the *à priori* certain truth that neither the causal series nor matter has had a temporal beginning) deprives physics of all independence, or they are the stalk by which the lotus of physics is rooted in the soil of metaphysic.'\*

The most distinguished representatives of science have already attained to this point, and it is with Kant they take counsel. Thus, philosophy and science are urged from different sides towards one point, where their union will establish a sure basis for further investigation of the world-problem. We know already, as a general truth, that we cannot grasp the whole reality with our present number of senses. Our external consciousness in relation to reality is quantitatively defective; it is similar to a sun, but its rays do not reach the boundaries of the all. The modern doctrine of evolution shows us

\* 'Parerga,' ii. § 87.

why it is so. But we have also to consider the quality of our consciousness in its relation to the world. The latter undergoes qualitative changes in the generation of consciousness; objects are transformed in sensibility. That which in nature is vibration of ether is in consciousness light; and atmospheric vibration, sound. We thus find ourselves, as it were, at a masquerade, since we are not truly cognizant of things, but only the modes in which our senses react upon them. So that not only are there more things than senses, but the things are also different, in fact, from what they seem in representation. Whence it follows that otherwise constituted beings would also have had another world.

The result of human thought on the world-problem may thus be expressed by saying: Consciousness does not exhaust its object, the world.

We pass to the second great problem for intellect to explain: man. As the world is the object of consciousness, so is the Ego the object of self-consciousness. As consciousness seeks logically to penetrate its object, the world, and to determine its content, so also self-consciousness the Ego. In the latter undertaking, almost everything has still to be done. As regards the world and consciousness, at least the conception of materialism has been eliminated; but it is still partially maintained in regard to self-consciousness and the Ego; materialism still flatters itself with the hope of being able to reduce all psychology to physiology. But even granting that it succeeded in this, it would then stand again at the point where further progress must be vertical. The problem of mind, even were it solved in the materialistic sense, presents immediately a new problem. The philosophy of the next century will undoubtedly include in its programme, as a pendant to the Kantian problem, the as yet scarcely propounded question, *whether self-consciousness exhausts its object.*

Such a question is just as warrantable in regard to subjective as to objective consciousness, and we have every reason to expect that in both cases the answer must be negative; thus, that the like relation exists between consciousness and the world, and between self-consciousness and the Ego. Self-consciousness may be as inadequate to the Ego, as consciousness to the world; or the Ego may as much exceed self-consciousness as the world exceeds consciousness. This is not only logically thinkable, but has also in its favour analogy and the doctrine of evolution. If nature has laboured for millions of years, by means of the struggle for existence on our planet, to raise the consciousness of the world so far that it perceives the enigmatical character of the world, and the obscurity of the metaphysical problems, it is a highly hazardous supposition that, on the contrary, the self-consciousness of nature, first kindled in man, has succeeded at the first cast, not as capability of development, but as an already completed product, comprehending, that is to say, its whole object, the Ego. Thus, if the existence of a transcendental world follows from the theory of knowledge accepted in this century, the theory of self-knowledge which will belong to the next century will bring with it the recognition of a transcendental Ego. It is also evident that the question concerning the relation of self-consciousness to its object, the Ego, has the same importance for the explanation of the human problem, that the question of the relation of consciousness to its object, the world, has already had for the explanation of the world-problem. The question of the soul, which has been stationary for centuries, would be advanced to a wholly new stage if it could be shown that self-consciousness only partially comprehends its object, whereby, indeed, the stumbling-block, Dualism, would be removed, and the question solved in the sense of Monism.

Meanwhile, it may suffice to call attention to this problem, in order to show that here also, when the present superficial work of psychology is accomplished, further advance will tend again in the vertical direction.

We can turn now to the second of our questions, namely, What contribution is afforded by the progress of the sciences to the explicability of the totality of things? The extent to which science is capable of development depends on the answer to this question.

Our century is characterized by the scientific contemplation of things, and so far from this period being near its close, it rather appears that the most important discoveries have still to be made in the vein which it is at present working, before a new period is ushered in by another deepening of the mine. Were the work of the human intellect always on one plane, the problem of the world must necessarily become continually clearer to us. But as every advance leads ultimately, as has been shown, to a deeper level, it follows, on the contrary, that the world-problem must rather become always more difficult.

It is remarkable in the process of intellectual development, that every discovery of a new partial truth does not diminish, but multiplies the number of given problems. The more we know of the world, the more extraordinary it is. To him who knows least of it, it appears far simpler than to genius. Thus culture makes us modest, if not in our human relations, yet certainly in regard to the riddle of the world. The opposite of this is what we see in the sufficiency of the average mind, which is also especially distinctive of our generation. Goethe describes it as the finest happiness of man to have investigated whatever can be ascertained, and silently to revere what is inscrutable. But now irreverence in presence of the world-problem, metaphysical conceit, is greater than at any former time, and the irreligion of the masses shows that this irreverence and this conceit have infected the whole popular consciousness.

It was this sense of the inscrutability of the world-problem that Socrates expressed in the well-known, but little understood, saying, 'I know only that I know nothing.' Certainly he did not mean thereby merely that there was knowledge to which he had not attained. There would have been nothing admirable for Plato in such a commonplace. Were the sphere of the problematical uniform, *i.e.*, if intellect had only to force its way upon the surface, then all knowledge would be attainable, given only a long enough life. Socrates rather meant that his ignorance had become greater with every addition to his knowledge, as indeed must be the case, if all progress leads into the profound. He felt that human consciousness does not exhaust its object; that thus, from the standpoint of intellect, truth generally is not knowable. In this sense Faust says, 'I see that nothing *can* be known' (Ich sehe, dass wir nichts wissen *können*)—a sigh which may be scientifically expressed : There are not only boundaries of knowledge which are historically surmountable, but also limitations of consciousness and knowing which are only biologically surmountable.

If every solved problem produces new ones—if thus the problems are continually on the increase—then will the most learned be the most modest, and to such will their ignorance appear greatest. Still more is it the case when we perceive that *every* phenomenon of nature, profoundly analyzed, draws us into the impenetrable darkness of metaphysic : that at bottom the tendency of a stone towards the centre of the earth is just as inexplicable as the thought of man.

Metaphysically, there is thus no distinction of intelligibility in things : all are alike incomprehensible. It is only an illusion of the materialists, that in the scientific treatment of things all obscurity is resolved into light. Force and matter they suppose to be intelligible—spirit is for them unintelligible ; therefore do they strive to resolve it into force and matter. Yet is the very opposite true. If anything is generally intelligible, it is spirit, consciousness, of which alone we know immediately, while all nature is only mediately cognizable, so far, that is, as it can affect our consciousness. All matter is thus resolved into states of consciousness. Of being, other than representation, we know nothing. To be and to be known

($esse = percipi$) are the same thing. Spirit is thus the primary and real; matter is merely a secondary phenomenon, whose reality stands temporarily therein; and the whole material world of representation would be otherwise, were the perceptive faculty of spirit changed. It may sound plausible to deny spirit, because it cannot be grasped with the hands, and to regard matter as real, because one can knock one's head against it; yet the reverse is true. Even Huxley, near as he stands to materialism, finds himself compelled to protest against it. ' But when the materialists stray beyond the borders of their path, and begin to talk about there being nothing else in the universe but matter and force and necessary laws, [and all the rest of *their* " grenadiers "]* I decline to follow them. . . . Matter and force are, so far as we can know, mere names for certain forms of consciousness. . . . Thus it is an indisputable truth that what we call the material world is only known to us under the forms of the ideal world, and, as Descartes tells us, " Our knowledge of the soul is more intimate and certain than our knowledge of the body." '†

It is, therefore, clear that we cannot discover truth in a one-sided investigation of the objective world; for this investigation leads us only again into the profound, and confronts us with the problem of spirit.

* The sentence in brackets, omitted in the German translation, refers to the following passage earlier in the same ' Lay Sermon': ' The method or path which leads to truth, indicated by Descartes, . . . refuses to listen to the jargon of more recent days, about the " Absolute," and all the other hypostatized adjectives, the initial letters of which are generally printed in capital letters, just as you give a grenadier a bearskin cap to make him look more formidable than he is by nature.'—Tr.

† Huxley, ' Lay Sermons,' xiv., on Descartes' ' Discourses.'

It is alike true of mankind and of the individual, that it is when we are only beginning to learn that we believe ourselves to know most. The world comes no nearer to our understanding, but the more we learn, the more wonderful and enigmatical it appears. 'The well of nature,' says Fechner, 'deepens the more, the more we seek to draw from it, our own organization itself lying in the deepest depth of it.'* Not in spite, but just on account of, the mountain of learning which we have already reared, but whose accumulation has only magnified our ignorance, does the world appear less simple to us than to a South Sea Islander.

The history of the sciences is therefore rather a rising consciousness of the world-problem, than its solution. Astonishment — as Professor Johannes Volkheit once wrote to me—is thus not only the beginning, but also the end of philosophy.

In the development of philosophy and the sciences the process of accommodating our representations and ideas to reality is accomplished. Truth is agreement of representation with actuality. Truth is anticipated before proof—it begins with hypothesis. As a rule, the capacity of a hypothesis—its explanatory range—is over-estimated; but in this tendency there lies a right logical instinct, which conscious logic expresses by saying that the number of explanatory principles must not be increased without necessity. Thus every hypothesis should aspire to extend its range of explanation as widely as possible. But the investigator should never forget that when the truth of a hypothesis is known, every further confirmation

* 'Zend-Avesta,' i. 426.

belongs to mere surface-working; and further, that every hypothesis has only a limited capacity. When its limit is reached further progress is on a deeper plane; and the first sign of this new period consists always in the discovery of phenomena which stand in *contradiction* to our hypotheses.

It is the characteristic of our modern science not to leave the discovery of new facts to accident, but to seek them with conscious purpose. But this should not be done only for ever to find new proofs of our theories, but rather in the quest of empirical contradictions to these theories, for thereon depends the true, the vertically directed, progress.

In regard to our understanding of the world all phenomena divide themselves into two categories, those which agree with our theories and those which contradict them. Were phenomena of the first kind only, no further progress would be possible; the process of accommodating representation to reality would be completed. Whoever believes progress to be as certain in the future, as is its continuity in the past, must admit *à priori* the existence of phenomena which conflict with our theories. To seek these, and to bore down with these, should be the task of every inquirer who is penetrated with the conviction of the intellectual progress of mankind. This is very finely expressed by John Herschell : ' The perfect observer will have his eyes, as it were, opened that they may be struck at once with any occurrence which according to received theories ought not to happen, for these are the facts which serve as clues to new discoveries.'*

* 'Preliminary Discourse on the Study of Natural Philosophy,' § 127.

It cannot be denied that our generation, intoxicated with its scientific successes, has almost wholly lost sight of this rule. Each of its imposing results in the horizontal direction strengthens the illusion that now at last has been discovered the single way to knowledge of truth. In place of the *à priori* conviction that experience must contain phenomena in contradiction to our theories, as certainly as future progress itself is certain, arises the *à priori* prejudice that such phenomena are not possible. This prejudice adopted into the programme of research would announce the arrest of science.

If we hold firm by the conviction that the human consciousness does not exhaust its object, but by ascending must gradually rank itself therewith, if we always keep before us the words of the Apostle, that human knowledge is only piece-work, then are we in the right intellectual disposition to open up continually new paths of progress. But if we revel in the enjoyment of the heretofore attained piece-work, if we begin to be enthusiastic about it, then however well we may have succeeded hitherto, the words of Bacon will apply to us : ' Imagined wealth is a chief cause of poverty, and reliance on the present leaves neglected the true resources for the future.'*

Doubtless, we should also endeavour to subject the phenomena of the world to our theories ; but never, therefore, to forget that this is only a part of our task, and that it is not upon those phenomena which appeal most to our understanding, and in

---

\* 'Instauratio Magna,' Preface.

whose agreement with our theories we are conscious of a victory of intelligence, that we can found true progress. More valuable are such facts as place our understanding in great embarrassment, for these necessitate reformation of our theories, and exalt the adaptation of our ideas to reality, which in the organic as in the intellectual region is only possible through alteration.

A negative case in opposition to dominant theories is thus the most valuable that an investigator can find. For so we can never apply the scale of acquired knowledge to that which has yet to be won, nor determine the range of the possible from past experience. A new phenomenon may easily contradict all our known laws, and yet be conformable to a law unknown to us, which suppresses the former. So, for instance, magnetism is in contradiction to the law of gravitation. That there are natural forces unknown to us, with expressions conformable to law, follows, however, immediately from the fact that the world never loses its problematical character. We must, therefore, not only admit *à priori* that experience will present contradictions to our theories, but we cannot even assign a limit to these contradictions; since it would be evidently illogical to assert that forces *unknown* to us can contribute only phenomena within a determined limit. The progress of the sciences continually widens the circuit of the possible. Instead, therefore, of always opposing impossibility to new phenomena, we should rather bethink ourselves that it is for Nature to determine the range of possibility, while we can know nothing of any impossibility, except logical and mathematical contradictions, the wooden iron and the crooked straight line.

Modern science does not possess this candour of judgment in regard to Nature in the degree to be desired. This is especially the case with the materialists. In their darkness they imagine that the materialistic consciousness exhausts its object; the future can only bring advance along the surface; and the intellectual labour of countless future generations is to consist only in a repetition of the eternal refrain: The materialists of the nineteenth century were right. In a minor degree, this is the fault also of the learned generally. Kant has said, the words 'I know not' are not easily heard in academies. Professional scholars are always disposed to regard every new discovery as a breach of patent.

It must be admitted, however, that this limitation of prospect has its use. It is a beneficent illusion, this belief of mankind that the goal of its research is in sight. They would falter in their pursuit of truth, could they imagine it only at an illimitable distance. Truth entices her followers ever further and further towards the far-off consummation, by suggesting that her favours are immediately obtainable. Thus it is that Kepler describes his search after Truth. Now vanishing from his sight, now reappearing and beckoning him on, she seemed to him like the coquettish Galatea in Virgil's 'Eclogue':

'Malo me Galatea petit, lasciva puella,
Et fugit ad salices, et se cupit ante videri.'

Now it is this illusion which interposes itself between human intellect and the perception that further progress is always in the direction of greater depth, and thus arises a disposition unfavourable to new discoveries. And as the best intellectual disposition for the inquirer is the most complete freedom from prejudice, that is often expressed in the paradoxical saying that ignorance makes us fitter for discovery than learning. Even the celebrated physiologist, Bernard, notwithstanding his materialistic bias, delivers himself in this sense: 'It has often been said that to make discoveries one must be ignorant. False in itself, this opinion hides a truth. It means that it is better to know nothing than to have in the mind fixed ideas, resting on theories of which one is always seeking confirmation, neglecting everything which does not harmonize with them. This disposition is one of the most mischievous, and is eminently opposed to discovery. In fact, a discovery is in general an unforeseen relation, not comprised in a theory, for otherwise it would be foreseen. An ignorant man, not knowing the theory, would in fact, in this respect, be in a more favourable mental condition ; the theory would not embarrass him, nor prevent his seeing new facts not apparent to him who is preoccupied with an exclusive theory. But we hasten to add that here is no question of elevating ignorance into a principle. The more instructed one is, the more anterior knowledge one has, the better will the mind be disposed to make great and fruitful discoveries. Only it is necessary to maintain mental liberty, and to believe that what is absurd, according to our theories, is not always impossible in nature.'*

But intellectual prejudice arising from theoretical

* Conf. Netter: 'De l'Intuition dans les Découvertes,' 53. Strasburg, 1879.

presuppositions not only suspends progress, but produces also positive ill-effects. For in our theories we have woven about the abundance of natural phenomena an ideal net, and have distributed them according to categories. Now if for the firm conviction that this system of categories has only a provisional value, we substitute the prejudice that it is complete—as the learned are much disposed to do—then must all newly-discovered phenomena adapt themselves to these categories, however alien in their nature, and though they should in fact necessitate an alteration of the system. If it is forgotten that the traditional distribution corresponds only to the material of our contemporaneous knowledge, new observations will be subjected to the old categories, and violence will often be done to them. Or should this not succeed, then are the unacceptable phenomena thrust aside with the well-known saying about 'isolated facts' proving nothing. As if in the domain of the actual there were degrees and scales of value, and only the facts of daily experience could rank as such! 'What is new,' says Bacon,* 'is usually conceived after the old fashion.' But it is to deny all future progress if we assume that all phenomena to be hereafter observed must necessarily fit into our old pigeon-holes. Suppose that Leverrier, the discoverer of Neptune, had conceived the remarkable eccentricities in the motion of Uranus, not as a new fact in itself, but in the old way, *i.e.*, as deducible from the then known factors. Reasoning under that prejudice he would not have found Neptune, but would have ascribed other masses or distances to the already known planets, to the

* 'Nov. Org.,' i. § 34.

deplorable confusion of astronomy. Such a confusion always arises whenever new phenomena are forced into an old pigeon-hole, a proceeding which, in modern science, is unfortunately very frequent, and which always reminds me of a certain chambermaid, in whose case the same sort of prejudice found a very comical expression. Wishing to pick up as much as possible of the conversation she overheard, and hearing of the just visible star, Aldebaran, she conceived 'in itself new' information 'in the old way,' and always spoke of the star as 'the old baron' (Alten Baron). And afterwards, when the same maiden, who had always lived in the plains, was taken by her mistress to the Tyrol, and saw mountains for the first time, she fell into the like mistake, and again conceiving this new experience in the old way, asked with much surprise for what purpose they had been heaped up. Still better may those scholars, of whom Kant says that they 'never see anything but what is conformable with what they have seen before,'\* be compared with the negro mentioned by Livingstone. The latter had presented him with a spoon, and taught him the use of it by drawing with it from a milk-pail. The negro, however, interpreting the new fact in the old way, took the milk out of the pail with the spoon, but then poured the contents into the hollow of his hand and drank from that.

That man in his attempt to make things intelligible should try to conceive new phenomena in the methods familiar to him is quite justifiable. But this endeavour should be hypothetical only, and should not proceed to a violent accommodation of

\* Kant (Rosenkranz, iii. 5).

phenomena, as is often the case, especially in modern psychology. So it is equally right for modern science to lay stress upon the inductive method, and to demand that all philosophical speculations should start from a basis of actuality. But these catchwords are often greatly abused. We must, indeed, turn to experience for enlightenment in the first instance; but we need not prescribe to experience what it shall offer us, and what not. We are not to expect that Nature, like the idol in a pagoda, will always incline her head to our theories, but must rather recognise, *à priori*, the certainty that there are phenomena for which we as yet possess no intellectual receptacles. While thus turning to Nature for enlightenment, we must not forget what Kant said: 'It is something very absurd to expect enlightenment from reason, and yet to dictate to her in advance upon which side she must necessarily determine.'* This is still more true of Nature, whose mysteriousness has been only increased since human intellect has applied itself to her. We have our reason for the investigation of the phenomena presented to us; but we misuse it when in our questions to Nature we already introduce half the answer : that is, when we presuppose that experience is only to be found within our theoretical limits. We thereby announce that human reason is incapable of development. In presence of high Nature, we should be naïve, and apply to the kingdom of truth what Christ said of the kingdom of God; that we cannot enter unless we are as children.

Briefly to resume the foregoing. We have seen that consciousness does not exhaust its object, but is

* Kant (Rosenkranz, ii. 577).

in a continual process of accommodation to it. The rise of consciousness, however, multiplies and complicates the problems. *Qui accroit la science, accroit le travail.* By the rise of consciousness in the biological process, the boundary between the sensuous and the transcendental world has been continually displaced, and it will be thrust back yet further, were it even by the addition of a sixth sense. The biological development is continued by the historical development of consciousness in the like direction, if only through modification of the organ of knowledge. We stand, moreover, in the presence of an inexorable alternative: either there is a progress for the future, in which case we must always and *à priori* grant the existence of facts which contradict our theories; or there are no such facts; and then we must also deny future progress, to which, at the highest, only a labour on the level could be ascribed. The choice cannot be difficult. If we cannot discover in the materials of our knowledge such contradictory phenomena, we have in that fact the clearest proof that we have fallen into the error censured by Bacon, of having conceived what is new in itself in an old method; that is, we have forced the contradictory phenomena into the old receptacles.

Owing to the capacity for development, not only of science, but of the human cognitional organism itself, it is therefore to be expected that progress leads always again in the profound, and intellect receives perpetually further accessions of problems. And if that enigmatical form of life, man himself, still at present toddling in child's shoes, shall retain maturity, yet will it even then be able to say with Solon: 'Learning without intermission, I advance in age.'

# CHAPTER II.

#### ON THE SCIENTIFIC IMPORTANCE OF DREAM.

1. *The Positive Side of the Sleep-life.*

In the ensuing inquiry, it will be especially and distinctly apparent that the empirical method of research, which applies itself exclusively to facts of experience, cannot lead to a successful issue unless accompanied by the purely logical penetration of the problem. It will also be shown that in the question here to be considered, mere experience must lead to false conclusions, and the right answer can only be obtained from the logical processes of thought.

The 'enlightened' sceptic regards simply the fact that on each morning he awakes from a more or less confused dream, and thence infers that 'all dreams are illusions' (alle Träume sind Schäume). To convert him from this opinion by an appeal to experience would be a quite hopeless undertaking; for it is characteristic of scepticism to allow validity only to such facts as compel attention through their frequency, the rare ones being suspected on account of their rarity. 'The sceptic,' said Jean Paul, 'disbelieves in meteorites because of the multitude of flints,' and all reports of remarkable dreams he would only meet with the usual evasions, with doubt and suspicion, with suggestions of deception or accidental coincidence. There is nothing to be done with him in this way. But if not destitute of all logic, he may be easily convinced that logical investigation is requisite to the discovery of truth. Placing one's self at the standpoint of the sceptic, and interrogating his thought by the Socratic method of intellectual midwifery, it is not difficult to bring him to the confession that dreams have a greater importance than is commonly believed; nay, that with great probability we may be visited every night by significant dreams, though in the memory of the morning only confused images thereof are preserved.

First of all, it is clear that for a scientific proof that dreams can be no more than illusions, it would be necessary to show that the organic conditions of dreaming admit of no higher significance. The causes of our dreams must be exposed; and it must be shown that from these causes nothing can result but phantasms without deeper sense, and that the course of our dreams can never be influenced by other causes. It is therefore necessary to investigate the nature of the dream-organ, and the source whence this draws the material of its representations.

Physiologists indicate the brain as the seat of consciousness in sleep as in waking, an opinion certainly supported by the experience that the impressions of the daily life pass over into dream, and mingle indiscriminately with the dream-images. But already the fact that much that was forgotten emerges again from the unconscious in dream, proves that in dreaming there is activity in folds of the brain, which in waking are either functionless, or whose functions remain below the psycho-physical threshold of sensibility, that is, do not result in consciousness. Sleep is induced by the quiescence of the nerves of sense, and of the outer folds of the brain in which they disembogue. The content of the waking consciousness is submerged; this must therefore be dependent on the activity of these outer folds. On the other hand, in sleep there is an inner waking—dream; the representations of dream, therefore, if they are to have their seat in the brain, must, at all events, lie in its deeper folds. But what the faculties are which accede to these, for the daily life unconscious, folds, can certainly not be antecedently determined.

But now, if the deepening of sleep implies the successive insensibility of the folds, that might easily extend to the cessation of function in the whole cerebral nerve-system, and the inner waking nevertheless continuing, and appearing to be even exalted, we should be obliged to transfer the dream-consciousness to another organ. But consciousness,[*] so far as we know, presupposing nerves, there would be nothing left but to suppose that in deep sleep the organ of dream is that nerve-system of ganglia, with the solar plexus for centre, which is still so little understood by our physiology. We know even less of the potentialities of this mysterious structure than of those of the brain. In short, physiology cannot demonstrate that the dream-organ is, from its nature, incapable of significant dreaming.

To inquire, now, into the sources of the dream-consciousness. We are capable of ideas in sleep,

[*] I have thus at this place and in the context translated the author's word 'Vorstellungen,' it not being essential to his meaning here to preserve the more definite rendering 'representations,' or 'ideas.'—Tr.

otherwise we could not dream at all ; but the dream-images are so heterogeneous, and so distinguishable from the content of our daily consciousness, that they must come from a region from which we are excluded in our waking life. The nerve agitations underlying these images must therefore in waking remain below the threshold of sensibility, and in sleep this threshold must be displaced. It is thus from the region of the unconscious that the dream-images emerge ; in sleep the unconscious becomes partly conscious, as conversely the conscious disappears.

Further, this unconscious region, thus illuminated in sleep, may lie either within our own organism or in the world external to it. In the first case, the exalted bodily sensibility, on which the dream-images depend, would be of interest only to the physician ; in the latter case sleep would produce a rapport with the external world distinct from that of waking sensibility, and thence, certainly, dreams of very real import would result.

Such a rapport is easily conceivable, for we are wholly ignorant *how far* the threshold of sensibility is displaced in sleep. Nor can we assert beforehand that our perceptive faculty in sleep extends only to the inner organism ; and it would be illogical to infer a determinate limit to the effect from an indeterminate cause, namely, from the unknown degree to which the threshold is displaced.

The external waking condition is partly subjective, partly objective ; that is, it includes bodily feelings and also extends to the outer world. The question thus suggests itself, whether the internal waking of dream has likewise both these characters; in other words, whether the displacement of the threshold can afford a relation to the outer world, by which we thus obtain information not accessible to us in the waking state.

This question must be answered in the affirmative. Physiology has long proved that consciousness is not co-extensive with the material arriving to the external senses. There is thus more relation between us and Nature than consciousness testifies. There are tones not perceptible for our ear, beams which produce no light for our eye, and substances which are indifferent for our taste and smell. Now, though our sensuous consciousness disappears in sleep, we nevertheless remain immersed in the general life of Nature, of which we are a part; sleep can only suspend the *sensuous* relation to Nature, but not that which is unconsciously present in waking existence. Rather can sleep alone, in displacing the threshold of sensibility, make this unconscious conscious. But it depends on the degree of this displacement how far the limits of our sense-consciousness are removed in sleep.

If sleep simply suspends the relation to the outer world mediated by the senses, but leaves that more general relation by which we are interwoven with Nature not only unimpaired, but even free to arrive at consciousness in the inner awakening: if thus, in order to produce significant dreams, it need produce no new relation, but only realize that which is already present, then not only is there no objection to the possibility of such dreams, but they are even necessitated by the mere displacement of the threshold of sensibility.

Sleep has, therefore, not only the negative side, that it suspends the sense-consciousness, but also a very positive one, if by it a relation to Nature which does not attain to consciousness in waking life becomes available. Dream is by no means a mere remnant of the daily consciousness, but a new consciousness qualitatively different from that. It being the task of philosophy to explain what man and Nature are, and what is the relation between them, if in sleep another relation obtains than in waking, then is our modern psychology, which treats sleep and dream as mere dependent phenomena, on a false path. Sleep and waking are of equally real importance for the solution of the human enigma; they are mutually complementary, and man cannot be understood unless we take into consideration both sides of his relation to Nature. And these two sides can the less be divided that they do not really alternate, but are always simultaneously present; the rapport with Nature given in sleep is not suppressed in waking, but only retires behind the threshold of sensibility: with the occurrence of sleep it is not newly produced, but is merely raised above this threshold.

Of the positive side of the sleep-life we can only speak in so far as through it there is a change from waking knowledge. This can happen as regards the content of the knowledge, and its form. It is therefore to be inquired how far these two factors are changed in sleep.

A new content of knowledge is delivered through every displacement of the threshold of sensibility giving occasion to new perceptions. The question thus arises: Are there forces of Nature of which we become aware in sleep, but which escape the consciousness of sense? We must reply in the affirmative.

According to physiological laws, weaker stimulations are suppressed for consciousness by stronger ones. The content of a consciousness is therefore furnished by the stronger stimulations, the weaker only acting below the threshold. The former being suppressed in sleep, it follows that the latter resume their sensibility. Wienholt made experiments with his perfectly healthy children in their sleep, which prove the existence of natural forces, whose stimulations are never felt in waking life. He made passes with an iron key at the distance of half an inch from the side of the face and neck of his son, fifteen years old, without touching him. After some passes the boy began to rub the place and make uneasy movements. On the other, still younger children, he made similar trials with lead, zinc, gold, and other metals, on which, in the great majority of cases, the children averted the parts so treated, rubbed them, or drew the clothes over them. The most remarkable impression resulted from the mere approach of the metal to the ear.*

Sleep, therefore, is accompanied by a perception at a distance, and announces the presence of substances which do not excite feeling in the waking man. But if these feelings contribute the material of our dreams, then, certainly, in the case of Wienholt's children, dreams must have been set up, somehow corresponding to his manipulations, and such dreams we may already with good reason designate as true. The far-feeling, by the dream-images it excited, was thus, in a certain sense, a far-sight, if only a symbolical one. Suppose, further, that Wienholt had approached

* Dr. Arnold Wienholt: 'Heilkraft des thierischen Magnetismus,' III., i. 234. 1805.

his substances from any distance towards a sensitive part of the body, the actual contact would have been temporally anticipated by feeling, supposing only that no deviation from the straight line of approximation were possible; that is to say, that this did not depend on Wienholt's will, but on a law of Nature. With the beginning of the far-feeling the children would have been also clairvoyant in the relation of time (previsionally).

Thus sleep not only brings a new material of knowledge, but even alteration of the forms of all knowledge, time and space, is also introduced with the new content.

But to the contemner of dreams the following consideration may lastly be commended, having reference to the as yet undetermined limit of our capacity for perception in sleep.

Ordinarily, we remember our dreams only in part; as a rule, only those which immediately precede our waking, those of deep sleep being lost to recollection. It is just in the latter, however, that the capacity for significant dreaming must especially develop itself, since the displacement of the threshold of sensibility progresses with the deepening of sleep. Remembered dreams can usually contain only unsignificant phantasms, since they are either those which immediately follow the falling asleep, or immediately precede the wakening, and are thus connected with the slightest displacement of the threshold. If we are ever to have an experimental psychology, and succeed in providing deep dreams with a mark for recollection on awakening, then shall we perhaps find that these dreams are unexpectedly noteworthy, while at present we are reduced to the exceptional cases, which are relatively so rare that the sceptic thinks himself entitled to disregard them.

Nor, assuredly, is the sceptic in any way bound to accept this expectation in place of present facts. According to the logical rule, that the burden of proof lies upon the assertor — *affirmanti incumbit probatio*—he has a right to insist on my proof for the assertion of even the exceptional significance of dream. The proofs from experience, which my treatment of the subject so far has not included, must therefore at length be adduced. But since in this debatable region each particular case is open to endless possible objections to which no determinate weight can be assigned, it will be well to strengthen the foregoing arguments, which had regard to the mere probability of significant dreams, by further ones from which even their *à priori* certainty may be inferred.

We have got thus far, that sleep has its positive sides, and that therefore we cannot estimate its faculties by those of the waking state. It is logically conceivable that we might be 'clairvoyant' while asleep, though not so while awake. Further, the circumstance that most dreams are unremembered, whereas the perceptions of the senses in the waking state could never pass out of recollection beyond recovery in a couple of hours, cannot otherwise be explained physiologically than by a difference of the organs with which the waking and dream states are respectively connected. Deep dream must, at the least, depend on the activity of other folds of the brain than those in function while we are awake: possibly even of another nervous centre altogether. For if we infer the similarity of the organ from that of the consciousness, the dissimilarity of the consciousness would imply the dissimilarity of the organ. And as the failure of memory in the case of deep dream can only be ascribed to the want of a common organ with the waking consciousness, the survival of memory between the light dream and waking must result from an at least partial community of organ. The withdrawal of the bridge of memory proves physiologically the change of organ; the preservation of the bridge, the community of organ. But inasmuch as it is only with the change to an organ of whose nature we know nothing that the significant dream can occur, the logical possibility of the latter must again on this ground be admitted.

But to add to this mere conceivability the *à priori* certainty, a double inquiry is necessary.

(*a*) Our remembered dreams—which are those of light sleep—we find to be without special sense and significance. Senselessness and possibility of recollection are thus given *together*, without the *connection* between them being as yet apparent. It is, however, quite possible that they are effects of a common cause, and for this cause we have to seek.

If the dreams of light sleep are remembered because the organ is partly the same as in waking consciousness, they being thus partly excited by the latter as it revives from its torpor and gradually resumes its functions, then in such dreams we have not the simple activity of one organ, but the mixed activity of two. The senselessness of these dreams is therefore to be explained by this mixture. They are implicated with too many ingredients of the waking consciousness. The same is applicable to the dreams immediately ensuing upon sleep, the waking organ not being yet completely at rest. To this organ, and to its insufficient suppression, the senselessness is to be ascribed, not to the true dream-organ. The confused dream thus belongs to an intermediate condition between sleep and waking, whereas the dream-organ can only exhibit its unmixed activity in deep sleep. Only then can the inner waking be present as a pure condition; the disturbing causes, the fragmentary sensations and ingredients of the waking memory, which are made over to the dream-organ to be worked up with its own products, having then disappeared. During their continuance an orderly activity is not to be expected. If, then, the confusion results from the community of the organ, it follows that this confusion will disappear with the change of organ, supposing—what is yet to be proved—there is then to be any dreaming at all.

The confused dream, therefore, claims our first attention. The causes of confusion being exposed, we shall know whether the dream-organ is responsible for it or not.

(b) From that inquiry it will appear that the dream-organ in itself, free from disturbing causes, is adapted to higher productions, the occurrence of dreams in deep sleep being presupposed. It is only in exceptional conditions that the dream of deep sleep can be ascertained, yet in these much better than the dream of light sleep. For the latter can only be recalled by the defective recollection of the dreamer; whereas the former in almost its whole course is

displayed to the external observer, so much so, that
the orderly activity of the dream-organ is found to
increase with the deepening of the sleep. It is in
somnambulism that the deep sleep exhibits itself in
connection with ideas, and in sleep-walking with acts
founded on ideas. It needs, then, only to be proved
that sleep, somnambulism, and sleep-walking are
intimately related conditions, to dispel the last objection against the possibility of orderly and significant
dreams.

This relation must therefore be the object of a
second inquiry. In this chapter, however, I may
properly confine myself to somnambulism, since we
are only concerned with the proof that deep sleep
has representations (dreams). I will only remark that
a false use of speech has established itself, which an
individual writer can no longer avoid. According to
literal meaning, *somnambulism* (*somnus*, sleep, and
*ambulare*, to walk) and night-walking are not distinguished, whereas the conditions indicated by these
words are in fact as different as idea and act, or, to be
more precise, as a dream associated with mere speech,
from one translated into acts.

## 2. *The Confused Dream.*

Falling asleep and waking up happen gradually.
It is in the transition state that those dreams occur
which we remember, so far as the community of the
organ extends, and which are confused owing to
failure in the unity of the organ. These dreams are
a mixture of fragments of the daily consciousness, of
functions of the dream-organ, and of images having

their origin in vegetative excitations within the organism. Excitations from three different sources thus cross each other in light sleep, and confuse the course of the dream.

For it is the peculiarity of dream, that in it all stimuli are forthwith translated into perceptual images, and hence a kaleidoscopic sequence of unordered representations is necessarily introduced. Abstract thoughts and memories immediately become imaginary percepts; the local direction of thought becomes a spacial transportation.

In waking, our thought is regulated; it receives direction from the conscious aim of the will and attention. But this order would be wholly lost if, as happens in dream, all the abstract were converted into images with apparent reality, if attention and aim failed, if every nerve excitation set up a representation of sense, every association of ideas becoming a combination of images, and every feeling connected with them asserting itself without restraint. There is in waking also a slight tendency to this continued perturbation, and as this has to be kept down, intellectual labour is attended with a strain which gradually tires the brain. But a dream, though ever so long, does not tire, no aim being kept in view, no order being attempted, and the inner consciousness being merely passive.

All these disturbing elements crowd in upon dreams with undiminished force. Every mental suggestion receives plastic interpretation as from sense. Since every nerve excitation is referred to a percept, all judgment must rest upon false premisses, and turn out distorted, as in madness. A very productive source of confusion are the associations, according to which thoughts enter consciousness in waking as in sleep, but which in dream become pictures, running off with more vivacity, and in a purely mechanical and unrestrained way. Every idea evokes, from the immense stores of memory, others connected with itself, and the consciousness of the sleeper is assailed by whatever can be dragged in by the laws of association. As these laws include mere temporal connection, without any intrinsic relations, so that even contradictions may be thus reciprocally elicited, such merely automatic play of association must result in great confusion.

Every emotion connected with a dream-idea has free play; every gentle movement of the will is translated into action. Finally, even the outer nerves of sense are in light sleep to some extent impressionable, and their stimulations turn into dream-images. The apparatus called the 'Volumeter' makes it possible to read off the degree of psychical agitation in the dreamer by the column of water in a glass tube, the depression of the column showing that the sleeper often still perceives remote sounds with mathematical certainty, and is not dead to external stimulations.*

By externally stimulating sight, smell, and hearing, the course of a dream may even to some extent be voluntarily determined. A person on whose mouth a few drops of water had fallen, had such a lively dream of swimming that he even made the usual

* Conf. 'Ausland,' Nos. 6 and 7.

motions with his hands.* Another, having some scent held before his nose, dreamed himself in a perfumer's shop, where he became faint and unwell.† Beattie relates the case of a sleeping officer, who, by words whispered in his ear, was made to dream all the circumstances of a duel, from the first interchange of words to the discharge of a pistol placed in his hand.‡ I myself, at a time when I regularly awoke from my first sleep, used always to remember dreams filled with noises and voices, till I observed them to be occasioned merely by the circulation of the blood, which became audible by laying the ear on the pillow, like the sound of a shell placed to the ear.

Even internal agitations of the brain prolong their influence into dream. If we read deep into the night till we fall asleep, we have dreams in which we are deluged with an uninterrupted throng of words. This, the after-effect of the reading, appears thus to be no mere abstract thinking, but tends always to sensible representation, and often, on gentle stimulation of the vocal muscles, produces movements of the lips, or, by transplantation of the brain stimulus to the peripheral extremities of the ear, seems associated with a soft hearing of the read words, only first perceptible, however, when sleep has deadened the stronger auditory excitations from without.

The dream of light sleep is often determined in its course by the last representation of the waking

* Nudow: 'Theorie des Schlafes,' 132.
† Spitta: 'Schlaf- und Traumzustande der menschlichen Seele,' 278.
‡ Beattie: 'Dissertations, Moral and Critical, on Memory and Imagination, Dreaming, etc.' London, 1783, 4to.

consciousness, a phenomenon which is also often met with among the insane.\*

As continual disturbers of the course of the dream are also to be mentioned those inner excitations connected with the nutritive processes, which influence the consciousness in dream, though not in waking. On this account authors who admit the possibility of significant dreams have always prescribed a light diet before sleep. Plato recommends moderation at that time, and the Pythagoreans especially interdicted beans, which, being with difficulty digestible, cause unquiet dreams. Artemidorus advises the interpreters of dreams to ask before explaining them whether the dreamer had retired to rest after a moderate or an excessive meal.† According to Philostratus, dream-interpreters would not condescend to expound dreams following on the enjoyment of wine, because it was only to the temperate that the gods had imparted the gift of seeing the future.‡ Similarly speak Pliny§ and many others.

Considering all these disturbing causes together, and remembering that every excitation is translated into a dream-image, the confusion of the dream of light sleep is very explicable ; and since it can only contain a succession of fragments without coherence, it is equally explicable that in the recollection of it, as a rule, only fragments are apprehended, not the whole course of the dream. As in waking one can only retain in memory an intelligible sentence, but

---

\* Griesinger: 'Pathologie und Therapie der psychischen Krankheiten,' 74.
† Artemidorus : 'Symbolik der Träume,' i., § 7, Vienna, 1881.
‡ Philostratus : 'Vita Apoll. Thyan.,' ii., § 37.
§ Plinius : ' Hist. Nat.,' x., § 211.

scarcely a senseless succession of words, so the succession of representations in dream, when without intelligible connection, is hardly recoverable by memory.

Thus we cannot hope to meet the characteristic functions of the pure dream-organ in the intermediate state between waking and deep sleep. Since, however, with the removal of the disturbing causes, the course of the dream is forthwith regulated, and even, as we shall see, with an aim, it can be accurately said that all the irrational part derives from the participation of the organ which is active in waking life, while all the rational is due to the freedom of the dream-organ from disturbance. Until the organ of daily consciousness is completely at rest, the dreams connected therewith — and these are just such as we remember—are worth no more than the delirium of a fever patient or the phantasms of a lunatic. Madness and dream exhibit, in fact, many common phenomena; whence it is said in the Talmud: 'No dream without folly.'

If, therefore, our dreams are confused as long as we are in some measure awake, the dream-organ being in no degree responsible for this, it of course follows that the effect must cease with the cause; thus, that in deep sleep the significant dream must be introduced, if there is any dreaming at all in that condition. But, as the bridge of memory fails between deep sleep and waking, the existence of the orderly and significant dreaming can only be proved when either the dreamer translates his dream into acts; or accompanies it with words; or lastly, when, contrary to the rule, it is recollected. The first case happens in sleep-walking, the second in the somnambulic state, while in regard to the third we are dependent on the reports of trustworthy vouchers.

### 3. *The Relation of Sleep to Somnambulism.*

With the deepening of sleep must diminish the confusion of the dream. As the cerebral nerve-system, sense, and brain become less sensitive, those disturbing contributions from the external, and from the remnants of the waking consciousness, disappear. The activity of the brain-organ must then be more orderly, and finally the confusion of the dream be completely removed. But perhaps the dream itself then ceases; perhaps these disturbing impressions are the sole material of dream; and deep sleep is not only without representations for the memory, but is altogether dreamless. This has often been asserted, and the question deserves investigation.*

Now, here it is somnambulism that helps us out of the difficulty. Induced by the treatment called 'magnetic,' but also spontaneously, it is a condition of

---

\* 'Hazlitt, in his "Round Table," has made an assertion which, if true, would go far to prove that the mind is perpetually active in sleep. He states that if a person is suddenly awakened at any given time, and asked what he has been dreaming about, he will be at once recalled to a train of associations with which his mind had been busied previously. This experiment has been tried upon myself, and I have tried it upon others, and I am satisfied from the result, as well as from reasoning, that the statement is not correct. In some few instances the persons would recollect ideas passing through their minds, but in a great majority of cases they had no recollection whatever of any such circumstances.'—Macnish: 'Philosophy of Sleep' (Glasgow, 1830), p. 81. On the supposition of another organic basis of the true dream-consciousness, the above experiment could not be expected to succeed, and its failure is no argument against a consciousness in deep sleep.

sleep which is also connected with an inner waking. In this state, however, a regulated series of representations are introduced. The consciousness of the somnambulist has no longer rapport with the external world through the external senses; the suppression of sensibility through them is at the greatest attainable point; instead of which a new, and at the same time orderly, rapport is established. From the self-consciousness of the somnambulist the 'I' of daily life has disappeared. It embraces, indeed, the material of this daily life, and that wholly, and thus coherently, not only in fragments, as in ordinary dreaming. But this total material is not referred to the 'I' of inner waking, but to another and foreign 'I.' The identical subject splits itself, therefore, into two persons. Somnambulism thus shows us that our daily consciousness does not exhaust its object, because to it that remarkable and radical prolongation of the Ego, which emerges in somnambulism, remains hidden, and belongs to the so-called 'unconscious.'

This somnambulism proves that the dramatic sundering of the Ego, which in ordinary dream only occurs phantasmically, has its truth in the real nature of man; that the daily consciousness includes one person only of our Subject, while to the other person emerging in somnambulism, the first appears as non-Ego. Mention of this relation is only made here in order to point out that the unity of the Subject of these two persons makes their severance by an insurmountable barrier highly improbable. Light sleep is an approximation to the state of somnambulism; the faculties of the latter will thus undoubtedly, if but exceptionally, be manifested in the former, and the belief in significant dreams, which has never been wholly extirpated, follows naturally from the fact that somnambulism differs only in degree from sleep. Hence these two conditions evince their relationship in a whole set of consonant phenomena, pointing also to the relationship of the psychical functions which are active in them.

The external condition of sleep-life is similar in the ordinary dream and in that of somnambulism. In the latter, the ball of the eye is directed inwards and upwards, and this appearance, as Aristotle noticed, is incident also, though less markedly, to common sleep. Ammianus Marcellinus cites it as an opinion of Aristotle, that as dream-images begin to occur, the eyes again look out straight in front;* but later observation has not confirmed this. Also that somnambulists accompany their visions with words, is only an extension of the experience that movements of the lips, if not articulate speech, often occur in sleep; and even in waking, when we are in a state of abstraction, the muscles of speech are frequently excited.

The phantasms of the dreamer, if different in regard to their content from the dream-figures of the somnambulist, are nevertheless so greatly related thereto, that if in the transition state both become mixed, they cannot be distinguished from one another; and hence the constant danger of confounding ordinary phantasms with [true] visions in the utterances of somnambulists. In the exceptional cases where somnambulists remember their visions after awaking, they themselves relate them as dreams, proving that the inner consciousness is similarly affected by the representations of both conditions.

* Ammianus Marcellinus: Histor. xxi. 1.

It has, moreover, been observed that as well the natural as the artificially induced somnambulism happens more easily by night than by day;* and according to Dupotet and others, actual sleep is the best condition in which to excite somnambulism.† Sleep is thus a mild sort of somnambulism; it lies midway between that and waking life. It is only by regarding somnambulism as a deepened or exalted sleep that we attain to a right comprehension of its phenomena; whereas a wholly false conception of it arises if we consider it, with Wirth,‡ as a mediate condition between sleep and waking. If somnambulists can undergo the most painful operations without feeling them, if in general they can be awakened by no pinching, cutting, burning, or the loudest noise, what is thus evinced is the highest extension of the insensibility of ordinary sleep, which, according to Wirth's views, ought more to resemble death.

This opinion of Wirth requires no special refutation, inasmuch as all the phenomena of somnambulism present themselves as an exaltation of analogous phenomena of sleep.

Thus in both conditions we find certain modifications of the faculty of memory, differing only in degree. Dream drops the material of daily consciousness, retaining only fragments; while, on the other hand, there is an exaltation of memory in the frequent recollection of long-forgotten scenes of our life. The somnambulist preserves the material of the daily consciousness in its entirety, and often shows

* Schindler: 'Magisches Geistesleben,' 26.
† Dupotet: 'Traité Complet de Magnétisme Animal,' 179. Deleuze: 'Histoire Critique du Magnétisme Animal,' ii. 236.
‡ Wirth: 'Theorie des Somnambulismus.' Stuttgart, 1836.

an incomprehensible memory of the past. Conversely, from dream we awake with defective recollection, from somnambulism with none at all. Exceptions are rare in relation to waking ; on the other hand, dream in this also shows itself an approximation to somnambulism, that it often supplies the bridge of connection for the material of the somnambulic consciousness.

In both states the visions are often only allegorical and symbolical representations of bodily or psychical condition ; in both, also, we find the phenomenon of the dramatic severance ; and it is another indication that sleep is a mediate condition between waking and somnambulism, when somnambulists, after the cessation of the magnetic condition, are still in sleep able to see their 'guardians' and 'guides,' the products of the dramatic severance.* The boy Richard said that though he was to come no more into the somnambulic state, yet he would see his guardian spirit in ordinary dreams, when necessary for the direction of his health ;† and Strombeck's Julia, one of the purest examples of natural somnambulism, said that for some time after the cessation of this condition she would still be able voluntarily to put herself into a slumber in order to learn what would be beneficial to her.‡

But even isolated somnambulic conditions are introduced, and again are terminated, by the natural sleep ; and when the aptitude for somnambulism has

* Gorwitz : 'Richard's Natürlich-magnetischer Schlaf,' 133, 139.
† Gorwitz : 'Idiosomnambulismus,' 192.
‡ Strombeck : 'Geschichte eines allein durch die Natur hervorgebrachten animalischen Magnetismus,' 115. Braunschweig.

altogether ceased, sleepiness and yawning often occur at the usual hours of its former occurrence.*

The analogies are thus very numerous, and since somnambulism always appears as a deeper sleep with exaltation of the phenomena of the latter, it is self-evident that the curative power which physicians value in sleep belongs in a still higher degree to somnambulism. It is incomparably more refreshing than ordinary sleep, as it is incomparably more intense; somnambules praise it with enthusiasm, and on awaking from it feel themselves wonderfully strengthened. Julie described her natural magnetic condition as a precious sleep, an hour and a half of which was worth six of common sleep.† Thus only is to be explained the successful prescription of a somnambule, to place her in a nine days' trance for the cure of her lungs.‡

If, now, sleep and somnambulism differ only in degree; if, further, the somnambule is not living merely in a world of phantasms, but stands in a veritable *rapport* with the external world, the dreams being true—even the apparently dead in this condition are notoriously aware of all preparations for their funerals, without any feeling of sense—it is not to be doubted that our everyday sleep likewise, if very deep, can be accompanied by true dreaming; and since the organ of external sense fails, it would be wonderful if just the limits of sense-perception were maintained. Horace's 'Post mediam noctem, cum somnia vera' has thus more truth than our school

* Kieser's 'Archiv. für tier. Magnetismus,' iv. 3, 132.
† Strombeck: 'Geschichte,' sc. 30.
‡ Schopenhauer: 'Parerga,' i. 275.

wisdom will admit, and we cannot doubt that if we could remember our deep dreams, we should meet in them all the so-called wonders of somnambulism.

But sleep is not only the negation of waking, but has its positive sides, as appeared in the foregoing by different characteristics which somnambulism contains on an augmented scale. Sleep and somnambulism, which are not diverse in nature, can therefore not be treated as different by the inquirer, as usually happens with very poor results. The phenomena of common sleep are magnified, and therefore more distinct, in somnambulism. On the other hand, the phenomena of somnambulism are relatively rare and are much contested. For one physician who has observed and studied somnambulism, there are twenty others who have seen nothing, and studied nothing of it, and who roundly deny everything, because it does not fit into their materialistic systems, and degrades the whole physiological psychology, with its vivisections, to a science of a much lower rank, one in which not causes but merely concomitant appearances are discovered. Thus it is that it has still required—and that a hundred years after Mesmer—the public representations of magnetizers to bring official science again to this point. But if now it is shown that the disputed phenomena of somnambulism are exhibited in elementary form in everyday dreaming, we thereby obtain a very certain measure of their actuality, and enlightened scepticism will be obliged to take in its sails still more than it has up to the present.

But sleep-walking also, as a third form of the sleep-life, in which visions are translated into acts, sensible excitations being transferred to the motor nerve system, cannot be arbitrarily separated from ordinary dream, but must be included in the comparative study.

Briefly to recapitulate our results up to the present, it appears that the common dream, so far as it is remembered, contains almost without exception only unsignificant phantasms. But this is due merely to the activity of external disturbing causes; in deep sleep these causes cease, and hence the effect, the confusion of the dream, must fall away. This cannot be proved directly, because the memory fails; but is indirectly evident from the thorough-going relation between dream and somnambulism, which not only brings a succession of regulated ideas, but also an orderly *rapport* with the outer world, and is thus a veridic dream.

No one to whom all this is clear will make any further opposition in principle to the numerous reports of remarkable dreams, an opposition which is unworthy of the truth-loving inquirer. It is very easy to assume the deportment of an enlightened sceptic and 'esprit fort' by joining in the vulgar cry that dreams are nonsense; it is, however, quite unscientific to infer the character of all dreams from our fragmentary recollections of those which are constantly perturbed from without. This will become more completely evident if—as there is reason to hope —experimental psychology succeeds in making the dream of deep sleep accessible to memory.

4. *The Metaphysical Application of Dream.*

That dream has had few philosophical results is not really its own fault, but that of its interpreters.

The content of our dreams is difficult to catch, and more difficult still is it to understand this content, since dream is a cluster of intricate problems. This intricacy explains the two extreme modes of regarding dream—that of the old philosophers, and that of the modern dream-contemner. One who knows that in dreams highly important phenomena are to be discovered, if only in a fragmentary form, is disposed to the superlative view by the very difficulty of understanding them. Thus the ancient Greeks. Others, again, will take the disorder of the presentations for mere presentation of disorder, and will deny to dream any scientific significance whatever. Thus the moderns. Extreme opinions are never true. We have here to hit the mean between the ancients and the moderns, between over-estimation and under-estimation.

As in the Bible, so among the old philosophers, many dreams were ascribed to a divine origin. Zenophon and Plato often speak in this sense. Aristotle thought, indeed, that only to the wise are illumative dreams sent by the gods;[*] but he does not deny them. These opinions are easily explained by their connection with the oracle-cult and temple-sleep among the Greeks. The ancients understood, with fine intelligence, that there is no essential distinction between the ordinary and the somnambulic sleep, the phenomena of the latter being only an exaltation of those of the former. It is, therefore, not strange that these philosophers scorned to contribute experimental proofs of clairvoyance in dream from private life. The modern reader certainly misses this evidence;

[*] Aristotle : ' On Prophecy in Dream.'

but a Greek author could content himself with a mere reference to the oracles, from which, as Plato says, it was generally known that Greek State polity had derived the highest advantage.

The Epicureans were singular in their view that dreams were thoroughly unsignificant phenomena. Gradually for inspiration was substituted the faculty in the human soul itself to lift the veil of the future; and Cicero ('De Senectute') believed that chiefly in dream the soul reveals its divine origin (*Atqui dormientium animi maxime declarant divinitatem suam*). Mahomet made his disciples relate their dreams every day, and believed himself also to be inspired in dream; and we find both opinions prevalent in the Christian epoch among the fathers of the Church (Tertullian, Augustine, etc.) and the laity.

That in our time, not reckoning a brief reaction at the period of the Romanticists, the pendulum of opinion has swung round so much to the opposite side, is due to the predominance of physiological methods of research over metaphysical and speculative theories of cognition, whereby the psychologies of waking and of dream were alike much affected. The result, especially in the materialistic schools, has been the prejudice that all psychical phenomena are merely the operation of organic conditions—*cum hoc, ergo propter hoc;* whereas it is apparent from the least consideration that physiology can never succeed in showing more than the mere *parallelism* of psychical and organic conditions. This parallelism, however, is not in the least decisive of the question which condition is cause, and which effect, or whether possibly both conditions, *as between each other*, stand in no causal connection at all, but are both effects of a common cause ; just as the appearance of the stars is neither cause nor effect of night, but their parallelism is produced by the setting of the sun.

Dreams are nonsense (*Träume sind Schäume*)—that is still the current opinion. But even were dream in fact only conditioned by bodily states, it would still merit scientific investigation ; we could conclude from the effect to the cause ; and at least medical science, which in this respect might learn from old Hippocrates, should concern itself with our dreams.

But, in fact, the study of dream frees us much more thoroughly from that physiological prejudice than can the investigation of psychical functions in waking life. The neglect of this study, arising from the under-estimate of the dream-life, has left a deficiency in the preparations for definitive judgments ; the material of empirical facts is still much in need of being supplemented. We must therefore devote a long inquiry into the mere analysis of the phenomenon, that we may not be misled to premature explanations, and deserve Fontenelle's reproach : ' Avant d'expliquer les faits il est nécessaire de les constater ; on évite ainsi le ridicule d'avoir trouvé la cause de ce qui n'est point.'

If, however, in the following there is more than a mere aggregation of empirical facts, the purpose is not to deliver a definitive explanation, but only to indicate the direction in which empirical investigation of dream-life must be instituted, in order to obtain a scientific result. It will thereby appear that dream has not merely a scientific importance in general, but one *peculiar* to itself, and that it fills a vacuum, so that the analysis of waking consciousness cannot be substituted for it. It will further be shown that metaphysically, also, dream has a real value, and is a door through which we can penetrate into the obscurity of the human enigma. In dream are exhibited *other* forces of the human Psyche, and *other* relations of the Psyche to the whole of Nature, than in waking life ; and those inquirers stand in their own light who treat dream as a mere chapter of physiology. By missing the *peculiar* importance of dream, they renounce to their own disadvantage the data which it offers for the nearer determination of the human Psyche, whose definition is still in such confusion. As yet a whole third of our existence has scarcely been realized for metaphysics ; an omission the more improper in that the psychology of waking life is unadapted to this phenomenon of dream, which teems with specific characteristics. To judge dream-life merely by its analogies with waking life is an actual contradiction, for the foundation of the former is an entire negation of the consciousness and self-consciousness which are the basis of the latter. Just from this fact is derived the hope of attaining to a rational doctrine of the soul, for the question what the soul is, evidently demands a preliminary inquiry, whether soul and consciousness are identical. Now, this prior question is answered in the negative by dream, which shows that the concept of soul exceeds that of consciousness, as, perhaps, the attractive force of a star exceeds the sphere of its light.

The investigator of dream-life is distinguished, then, from the physiologist who identifies consciousness and soul ; and from the metaphysician who, while believing in a metaphysical substance behind consciousness—variously called thing-in-itself, or idea, or will, or the unconscious—yet seeks no metaphysical kernel of individuality beyond the sphere of the self-consciousness, but holds that the individual Psyche is rooted immediately in the thing-in-itself, the individual having therefore a merely phenomenal significance.*

The physiologists are very summarily disposed of, since, as already said, at most the parallelism of bodily and psychical conditions can be proved, from which a causal relation is far from following. But on the supposition of such a relation, dream could still be studied with advantage by physiologists, as from its special characteristics they might strengthen and multiply the evidence for their views. A detailed refutation of these physiological views can the more

---

\* In strict metaphysical propriety, any distinction of the soul, whether mediately or immediately, from real or noumenal being, leaves it only a phenomenal significance. A transcendental consciousness—such as the author infers from the evidence adduced in this work—would still be phenomenal, though in another order or degree. The metaphysician who limits individual consciousness to the mode at present known to us—who denies transcendentalism—can have no other warrant than a supposed absence of positive evidence of other states of consciousness; as a metaphysician he has no right to pronounce upon this question, as it does not concern the distinction between noumena and phenomena, but the possible range of the latter. On the other hand, he is clearly within his right in pronouncing, rightly or wrongly, on the question whether a noumenal definition of individuality is at all possible, and in maintaining that subjectivity must *ultimately* be sought in the Absolute Spirit, of which *all* consciousness can only be phenomenal, or *manifestation*. It is very necessary to keep clearly in view the distinction between the *noumenal* and the *transcendental*; a positive knowledge of the latter being always possible or conceivable; whereas the 'thing-in-itself' can never be *object* in or for consciousness, however we may exalt our conception of the latter.—Tr.

easily be dispensed with, as the most distinguished psychologists—Maudsley, Fechner, and many others—hold them to be completely fallacious.

Those phenomena only of dream-life are scientifically applicable which can be recovered on waking. But of what we dream our memory includes only a slight fragment, and thus there is a great *quantitative* disproportion between remembered and forgotten dreams. Moreover, the dreams preceding and following deep sleep are penetrated by the materials of the waking consciousness, becoming filled with images foreign to this, as sleep deepens. The signature of the memory diminishing with the depth of the sleep, while, on the other hand, the special peculiarity of dream accedes in the same proportion, there results also a great *qualitative* disproportion between remembered and forgotten dreams. This is certainly the chief reason for the contempt of dreams, which is almost justified as regards the generality of remembered dreams, but not as regards others, lost as a rule for memory, but of which sometimes fragments at least survive in waking consciousness. The majority of intrinsically remarkable dreams are unfortunately lost; even when we wake from them immediately, only obscure ideas and feelings can be traced, and the deepest degree of sleep, that induced by magnetism and hypnotism, is followed by complete oblivion.

But from the fact that the representations of deep sleep are obscure upon awaking, it does not follow that they were so also during the dream. 'I rather conjecture,' says Kant, ' that these may be clearer and more extensive than even the clearest in the waking state; for this is to be expected from a being so active as the soul, when in complete rest from the outer senses, although corporeal sensation being absent at the time, on awaking there is a failure of the association by which the continuity of personal consciousness is sustained. The acts of some sleep-walkers, who in such condition sometimes show more intelligence than at other times, though recollecting nothing thereof on awaking, confirm the possibility of what I surmise concerning sleep.'* It is thus only in the waking reproduction, not in the production during the dreaming, that those representations are obscure. And somnambulism is the evident confirmation of this.

But for the scientific significance of the dream-images it is necessary, not only that they should be clear, but that they should also be regulated in some way, not be a mere confused medley, as the contemners of dreams assert. Now, the fact is that long dreams often exhibit as logical a concatenation of incidents as could come before us in the waking state. It is also the fact that in other dreams the law of causality seems to be completely in abeyance, or at least that the causation is being constantly broken, the play taking a collateral, or a wholly new direction with interruption of all continuity. Therefore this continual disruption either belongs peculiarly to the nature of the dream-organ—in which case dream could have but slight scientific interest—or, referring the order in the representations especially to the dream-organ, we must regard the almost constant aberration as a constant disturbance of the course of

* Kant : 'Träume eines Geistersehers.'

the dream, and must show the cause of it. In light sleep such disturbances continually occur. The susceptibility of the senses is not completely suppressed; not only peripheral excitations, gleams of light notwithstanding closed eyelids, impressions of sound, of pressure, of skin-sensibility, are conveyed to the brain, but also internal irritations of the organism due to the greater activity of the vegetative functions in sleep. Such stimulations are referred by the dream-organ, often with strong exaggeration, to a more or less adequate cause, transposed into outer space, that is converted into a perceptive image. This is the same process from which, in waking also, the represented world takes its rise, peripheral stimulations being referred by the *à priori* causality function of the understanding to an object in external space.*

So long, therefore, as outer and inner stimulations can be conveyed to the brain, the course of dream cannot be regular; there is a continual metamorphosis of the dream-images, which pass over into one another, and all logical concatenation fails. This must be all the more the case, inasmuch as dream, as Volkelt† very well demonstrated, has the characteristic of not enduring abstract conceptions. All thoughts which

---

\* In a mere allusion to the idealistic theory of perception, the author is not to be reproached for the apparent inconsistency of postulating 'peripheral' stimulations of an already objective organism as the occasion for the construction of a world under the form of space. But it may be as well to remark that the inconsistency is apparent only. If in 'perception' the subject is active, and in fact constructs its objects, the result being a world thoroughly conformable to the law of causality, the very occasion of this process must have its external representation in the completed product, implying the objectification (representation) of the subject itself, as organism, or body, in a world of space.—Tr.

† Volkelt : ' Die Traumphantasie.'

introduce themselves immediately take on a sensuous form ; what is in waking an association of ideas, is in dream an association of images.

If in dream I find myself in an empty room, which I recognise as the dwelling of a friend, the latter forthwith steps in at the door ; if I find myself in the company of a friend, and some peculiarity of his dwelling occurs to me, instantly I am transported to it.

Attention and consciously directed reflection have no place in dream ; rather are we completely passive, the images being evoked according to the laws of association with as little regularity as in waking also, when perhaps we are lying on the edge of a wood, and turning over the leaves of half-forgotten memories in the book of our life without regard to date.

The peculiar nature of the dream-organ, and therewith the scientific importance of dream, can be first recognised when such outer and inner stimulations of the organism cease, and association no longer intrudes fragments of memory into the dream-world. The precondition is a very deep sleep, wholly excluding the outer senses from the outer world, and breaking down the bridge of memory.

The diversion or breaking off of the series of representations thus always results from disturbing causes. On the other hand, it cannot be proved from deep sleep itself that the self-determining dream-organ produces an orderly series, there being as a rule no recollection ; but quite apart from somnambulism, it can be proved from a certain species of very remarkable dreams, even of light sleep, in which a dream-play *of long duration* is wound off, while, nevertheless, the possibility of interruption is excluded *by want of time*. These dreams offer a very good opportunity for observing that the undisturbed dream-function produces coherent sequences of representations.

I select an instance from my own experience whereby the apparent contradiction in the above concise expressions will at once explain itself.

I dreamed that I entered a friend's room, and to my surprise found it divided by a curtain waving down from the ceiling to the floor. We conversed together for some time without my putting any indiscreet question; but he guessed my curiosity, and saying he would show me what the curtain hid, he stood up and raised it. This caused a noise like the unrolling of a starched material. At the same moment I awoke, just as my brother was crumpling together a stiff paper, occasioning the same sound that I had heard in my dream. In a single case such a coincidence might of course be regarded as accidental, but this sort of dream is so frequent that that explanation appears quite inadmissible.

This dream was thus elicited by a peripheral excitation of the hearing, while yet the dramatic preliminaries to the dream climax, corresponding to the excitation, apparently preceded the latter. Beginning and end of the dream are therefore contemporaneous, or are so closely compacted that we can regard as contemporaneous the lapse of time during which the dream-organ functions according to its own nature, a disturbing cause being excluded *for want of time*. Since, however, the course of the dream took up *a not inconsiderable time*, at least apparently, and was thoroughly coherent, the elicitation of co-ordinate, dramatically accentuated sequences may be regarded as of the nature of the dream-organ. The contemners of dream, therefore, direct their reproaches to a false address. Disturbing causes are always throwing impediments in the way of the natural orderly activity of the dream-organ, which takes them up with the result that it seems to be in the nature of the dream-organ itself to piece together heterogeneous, senseless fragments in a mosaic patchwork.

It is, moreover, to be observed that the high scientific importance of this species of dream appears also from the disproportion between the short, vanishing point of time, and the multitude of representations crowded into it. Such dreams afford almost a sufficient proof of Kant's doctrine of the ideality, *i.e.* of the merely subjective validity of the time-form ; but even for the transcendental realist, for whom time has both subjective and objective validity, they prove at least this much, that subjective time does not coincide with objective, that different beings may have different scales of time, and that even one and the same being has not always the same scale.

Kant has shown that all the content of perception clothes itself in the cognitional forms of time and space. But it now appears that these forms are only unchangeable for the sensuous daily consciousness, and that sleep provides a new measure of time and space. In this respect, also, has sleep a whole positive side of its own, and thus the psychology which takes for its object only the waking man, must necessarily miss the correct definition of man. Philosophy deals with nature as perceptible by sense, with man as he perceives by sense, and with the relation between the two ; on this basis its systems have been erected, yet the world and man are still problematical. But now that sleep is seen to have positive sides, a philosophical system has to be founded on the basis of the dream-life, since therein man and nature alike appear otherwise than in waking life. When this hitherto wholly neglected third of our existence has been likewise turned to philosophical account, we may perhaps hope that the nature of the world and man may be thoroughly explored.

The interruption of the orderly dream-function by outer or inner irritations suggests the comparison with insanity. As the dream-function is in itself quite orderly, and confusion is only introduced by disturbing fragments which the dream cannot reject, so it has long been recognised by physicians that the thinking of the insane appears quite logical as soon as one knows from what presuppositions it starts. The lunatic errs in his premisses, *e.g.* in his fixed idea, not in his consequences. He often refers mere inner feelings to outer causes, which to him, just as to the dreamer, acquire the actuality of sense, and dramatically influence him ; but his feeling is real, he reacts quite logically upon it, and his insanity lies only in his projection of it into the external world.

The psychical activity of the dreamer is thus not in itself absurd ; it first becomes so when disturbing matter is presented to it from the bodily sensibility ; and so also the infirmity of the insane is not really infirmity of intellect, the appearance of which is only produced by the intellect having to operate with the false material imposed upon it by nervous sensibility. Only from this necessary distinction between intellectual disease and brain disease is to be explained the frequent observation that insane persons in their last hours exhibit full clearness of consciousness, apparently then first recovered. Lemoine* knew an insane person who suffered under an hallucination, but attempted to explain, quite in a scientific manner, the images hovering before him. His senses erred, therefore, but not his intellect.† It is so also in our dreams; and we must all the more recognise the rational concatenation of ideas, when we see that the dreamer endeavours to weave into the sequence the most heterogeneous and disturbing feelings, as well can be done.

Confusion is thus the rule of dream from the standpoint of memory, but not from that of the dream-organ; it is only in appearance that the criterion of memory makes the confused dream the rule, and it is only in appearance that the absence of that criterion makes the orderly dream exceptional.

The vegetative functions of the organism, respiration, circulation of the blood, digestion, etc., still introduce disturbance into the course of the dream, even if peripheral excitations have ceased to be possible. The sensibility to internal stimulations is even heightened during sleep, such coming then to be perceived which could not penetrate the waking consciousness owing to the prevalence of peripheral excitations. Dream is therefore very unquiet after meals or after excesses in drinking. Therefore the Brahmins and the Greek

---

\* Alb. Lemoine: 'Du Somneil.' Paris, Baillière, 1855, § 211.
† Probably no physician would consider this a case of insanity. It is like the celebrated case of Nicolai. The accepted test of insanity with hallucination seems to be the acceptance of the latter as objectively real.—Tr.

philosophers always prescribed temperance, which alone makes us susceptible to significant and divinely-inspired dreams. Of this opinion were also the priests of the temple of Æsculapius.* And Cicero says,† 'It cannot be doubted that the number of true dreams would be greater were we to fall asleep in a better condition; but filling ourselves with wine and flesh, we have obscure and confused dreams.' So in the Middle Ages, Agrippa von Nettesheim and others recommended fasting with fumigations and anointings.‡ And to this day, Indian parents prepare their children by fasting for prophetic dreams. This is founded on a true insight that the dream which is characteristic of the dream-organ, and is determined by its pure activity, does not occur as long as the internal vegetative irritations of the organism exercise a disturbing influence.

It becomes a question, therefore, whether this pure dream ever occurs at all. Hitherto we have only got so far, that the dream-organ exercises a pure function in the measure that sleep gains depth and the disturbing excitations diminish. The peripheral nerve-extremities of the external senses are the first to obtain rest, the brain remaining still sensitive to internal irritants; and in so far as these may arise not only from the regular internal functions of the organism, but also from the same when irregular and diseased, dream has a great importance also for medical diagnosis, even if the diseased motions are only represented by symbolical images.

* Philostratus: 'Vita Apollonii,' i., c. 6.
† Cicero: 'De Divinatione,' i., § 29.
‡ Schindler: 'Der Aberglaube des Mittelalters,' 247.

The relaxation of the nervous system thus proceeds from without inwards, and if this process went on without arrest, insensibility must finally extend to the central nerve-system, the brain ; but this stage would only be reached in the deepest sleep. Now as physiologists certainly know little about the causes of sleep, neither can they determine the limits of its operation. But here, again, the magnetic sleep is instructive, as this has very often been utilized for the most painful operations, no feeling whatever being conveyed to the brain.

If, now, in the deepest sleep of which the organism is capable, we should still dream, though without subsequent recollection, and if the brain-life has no participation in this experience, the importunate question arises (as already remarked), with what organ then do we dream, if not with the brain ? As long as the brain is active, it is easy to speak of a dream phantasy ; but since this can only be thought of in connection with the brain, or at least as accompanied by phenomena in the brain, this phantasy, regarded as the cause of dream, is wholly excluded by the dream of deep sleep. In the remembered dream, the activity of the phantasy is easily to be traced ; it cannot, however, be regarded as the peculiar cause of dream, because, as Aristotle remarked, it is to be placed within the dream,* and because the significance of the dream-images rises with the depth of the sleep, whereas the contrary must be the case if we think of the phantasy as in connection with the brain-life.

* Aristotle : 'On Sleeping and Waking,' k. 2.

Upon these grounds, and further, because dreaming even in the deepest sleep is a fact which, though in natural sleep seldom, in magnetic sleep always, can be proved, it follows that Schopenhauer was completely justified in admitting a special organ of dream. The phenomena of magnetic sleep and the statements of somnambules suggest a connection of the dream-faculty with the ganglionic system, a connection easily explaining the fact that dream can be remembered only in the degree to which the brain-life is still participant; and that the absence of memory of deep and magnetic dreams results from the transfer of the faculty of conscious representation to another seat, of which the brain on awaking consequently knows nothing.

Schopenhauer says that in dream, somnambulism, and related conditions, we obtain the objectively represented intuition by a different organ than in waking, that is to say, not by the outer sense, and he speaks therefore of a special dream-organ.* Fechner also is of opinion that the psycho-physical scene of our dreams is different from that of the impressions of waking life, and that 'with the temporal oscillation of the psycho-physical activity of our organism from waking to sleep is connected a spatial [local] oscillation or circulation . . . such, that during waking the stage of dream remains wholly beneath the threshold, while that of waking impressions is somewhere and somehow above it; in sleep, on the other hand, the stage of waking life sinks quite beneath the threshold, while that of dream is elevated *relatively* to this completely submerged stage of

* Schopenhauer: 'Über Geisterseher.'

waking life, and with the occurrence of actual dreaming rises even above the threshold of consciousness. . . . Were the psycho-physical stage of dream and waking consciousness the same, dream would be a mere continuation of the latter (as happens when the eyes are closed [without sleep [during the stillness of the night), and material and form would be the same, whereas it is quite otherwise.' Finally, Fechner agrees with the view that in light sleep both stages can be animated, and he thence explains the confusion of our dreams, there being no partition wall between the stages, but interaction between the two.* These considerations, and the proof adduced by Reichenbach, that the seat of the odic brain-activity shifts according as we sleep or are awake, the odic intensity predominating in the large brain during waking, in the small brain during sleep,† favour the view that in sleep an organ is active, which in waking is either functionless, or whose functions remain below the threshold of sensibility. With this displacement of the stage of consciousness must evidently be connected the remarkable faculties of somnambules in the deep sleep, however premature further hypotheses may be. But even if every impression of consciousness could only be connected with the brain, it must yet be conceded that in deep sleep there must be quite other avenues of perception leading to the brain than in waking, so that we are connected with the world by other threads than the outer senses, as necessarily follows from the fact that our dreams are not produced by the activity of

* Fechner: 'Revision der Hauptpunkte der Psycho-physik,' 286-288.
† Reichenbach: 'Der Sensitive Mensch,' i. 409, ii. 627.

the brain, but that it passively receives them from the Unconscious. Experience alone, however, not *à priori* theories from this standpoint, can decide of what faculties we may be capable by means of these new avenues.

The material and formal difference of our dream-representations from those of waking thus only necessitates the hypothesis of new avenues of perception; but if we consider the fact of absence of memory on waking from deep sleep, that suggests an actual transposition of the stage of consciousness, and thus an interchange of functions between the brain and the ganglionic system.

Now, as this forgetfulness after waking resembles a change in the sense of personality, all the more as this alternation of consciousness contains a material and formal difference of representations, so in fact the change of sleeping and waking presents a temporally successive dualism of personalities, locally comprehended in the human subject.

But this problem belongs no longer merely to physiology, for these proceedings in the ganglionic system are to be regarded only as concomitant, not as causative phenomena, and so the scientific investigation of dream passes into the domain of metaphysic, so far as the latter has the nature of man for its object. The attempts heretofore to attain to a definition of man by analysis of the waking consciousness have led to no undisputed results. Now, however, it is shown that we have a second consciousness, and therewith is discovered, not only a second way to solve the problem of our interior life, but also the cause of the former miscarriage.

When the proper dream-world arises, when the brain-life is reduced to latency, or, at least, is restricted to vegetative functions, then we have a phenomenon to which none other approaches in importance, since it signifies nothing less than that man is a double being, though not in the dualistic sense of the old doctrine of the soul. It is thus dream, not waking, which is the door of metaphysic, so far as the latter deals with man.

If we have two consciousnesses, rising and sinking like the weights in a scale, then from the investigation of both can we first attain to the definition of man; and the opinion that the human psyche possesses other faculties in dream than in waking, that it, moreover, stands in other relations to the whole of Nature, appears at least logically admissible. If, further, the disappearance of the cerebral consciousness does not signify the disappearance of consciousness generally, then it becomes clear that we can alternately pass through two different states of consciousness, that is, in alternation of waking and sleep. But this is only possible if both states *contemporaneously* exist, though unconsciously to each other. Potentially, the dream-consciousness must be given even in waking, and the waking consciousness in dream, just as the light of the stars is present when the sun shines, but is first visible when that sets. One may then well say that scarcely any fact is of more remarkable import than that one subject can embrace two persons.

By attending only to the remembered content of dream, we do little more than supply a chapter to physiology; whereas the gravamen of dream lies in the problem before us, 'for which the weighty and primary fact is *that* we dream ; the content of dream being of secondary consideration. According to the logical rule, the actuality of a fact proves at the same time its possibility. *Ab esse ad posse valet consequentia.*

But in the case of facts which appear to us unintelligible, we are always prone to convert this into an impossibility for intelligence—an illogical proceeding—in order to prove their non-existence. Now, since the assertion of man's double nature may certainly be considered one of the strangest, and is, certainly, the most important inference from dream-life, further elucidation is indispensable. It will thereby appear that this assertion does not imply a return to the dualistic doctrine of the soul, but that in existing philosophy we have already the germs of a monistic doctrine.

There are two problems, with which all philosophizing is concerned, the World and Man. Into the one our consciousness seeks to penetrate ; into the other, our self-consciousness. Philosophizing upon the world has taken the following course : it started with an investigation of the object, and ended by perceiving that the subjective condition of cognition must be investigated first. At this point stands Kant. As result it was recognised that consciousness does not exhaust its object. This is the quintessence of the philosophical theory of cognition. Our thinking on the world ends with contradictions, whose solution lies in a region not illuminated by consciousness. Here, now, is the point where Science, Physics, Physiology, and the doctrine of Evolution flow into philosophy. Theoretical Physic shows that not only our practical powers, but even the number of senses, are inadequate to objects. All operations of Nature depend on minute processes, which escape our senses, in the interior of bodies, and for the understanding of which we have set up the atomic theory as a provisional hypothesis. Finally, the doctrine of evolution shows why the world exceeds our consciousness. Consciousness is a product of evolution, and, in the biological process, has emerged from constant and painful struggle for existence; it grows up, therefore, to its object, the world, only by degrees, as a creeping plant to its support. So also are we men, as the highest existing products of evolution, yet limited by our whole organization to relations with only a fragment of the whole of Nature; the transcendental world beyond our senses remains closed to us.

Thus, in brief, is the relation of consciousness to the world-problem characterized, as has gradually become historically clear.

We pass to the other problem, man, to consider the relation of self-consciousness to that. It is at once presumable that self-consciousness also does not exhaust its object; a presumption which rises to certainty when we consider that self-consciousness is only a special case of consciousness, not different in itself, but merely by its direction—that is, by its object. This object is ourselves. Thus what is true of consciousness generally must also be true of its special case. Self-consciousness must be capable of evolution, of exaltation, thus gradually illuminating the outline of its object. In the biological process, self-consciousness appears first with man. The biological evolutionary capacity is illustrated by the individual. The child still speaks of itself in the third person; it is by degrees that its consciousness reaches this inner object, and thus becomes self-consciousness, which cannot sooner arise; as the sunbeam in space first gives light when it is intercepted by an object. But were this light in us all not so weak, there would have been no need for the inscription on the temple at Delphi: 'Know thyself!' Nor would Plato have said that most men only dream, the philosopher alone strives to be awake.

Self-consciousness, this latest bloom of the biological process, has in man only its first foundation, and its content is therefore exceedingly poor. Analyzing this content we find, as Schopenhauer has shown, the primacy of will in self-consciousness. In all our sentiments, feelings, and desires, we recognise ourselves as a willing substance, and also the identity of this substance through the whole course of our lives. That this will is blind would imply the assertion that self-consciousness exhausts its object—a very disputable proposition. On the other hand, it is clear that in self-consciousness we can find only a blind will as object; for were we even cognizant in our metaphysical substance, yet could this knowing not in itself be known as object, just as the eye can see everything but itself. This could only then be the case if man had two consciousnesses, one of which had a greater sphere than the other. Only thus would a self-mirroring take place. If we, as metaphysical beings, comprehended ourselves as earthly beings—as a larger circle is concentric to a smaller one—we could then, to a certain degree, be even cognitionally an object to ourselves. The content of self-consciousness could become an object of consciousness, and, with Descartes, we could propound as a fundamental fact: 'I think, therefore I am.' But even then we could know ourselves only *wholly* on the side of will; the will would still have the primacy in self-consciousness; and cognition, as fact of our inner being, would be only a secondary phenomenon to the will, cognizable itself only as turned *outwards;* but would be no apprehension of our metaphysically knowing part. Our earthly consciousness can thus be object to our metaphysical eye, but the latter cannot see itself; and still less can our earthly consciousness, as the smaller circle, embrace the larger circle of the metaphysical consciousness, though the converse may well be. As will, on the other hand, we are in both circles identical, and the earthly consciousness can only apprehend this will by the direction which brings it to self-consciousness, and, at the same time, it cognizes this will as apparently blind.*

* Some attempt to explain the above rather difficult passages may not be unacceptable to the reader. The object in *self*-consciousness is the will-character or disposition as motive power in thought and action. This is the only *self* cognizable by the merely reflective consciousness. But the very cognition of the will-self proves that the whole self is not cognized, since therein is also this very act or faculty of cognition, which cannot be at the same time its own object. To the self-consciousness of the 'earthly' (*i.e.*, the physically organized) man, the 'will' thus necessarily seems 'blind' (without conscious intelligence), just because we have to divorce it, as object, from cognition. So that by the merely *reflective* self-consciousness, consciousness itself can never be discovered in that which is its only possible object. But it may be quite otherwise if this object, the self, is *more* than it can appear, as object, to the reflective consciousness. Its two moments, will and cognition, would then be reunited in a *direct* cognition of the external, derivative, 'earthly' self, which

It is evidently an error of omission that the question has not been investigated, whether self-consciousness exhausts its object, or is not rather capable of evolution, reaching the limits of its evolution only with the limits of its object, as also consciousness would be no longer capable of evolution were it to comprehend the whole world, peripherally and centrally. A presentiment of the true state of the case has certainly existed in religious and philosophical systems. The doctrine of the soul proves this. But the latter does not indicate the true relation, as well because it divides man dualistically into body and soul, as that it conceives the earthly self-consciousness as a function of this immaterial soul—in which process the eye would see itself, the knowing subject would be its own object—instead of simply saying that we ourselves are in part unknowable, transcendental, that we can only know ourselves in the will, whereas to a transcendental self-consciousness the knowing substance can be object only as directed outwards, as empirical consciousness.

In modern philosophy and science this doctrine of the soul has therefore been abandoned, but 'the child has been shaken out with the bath.' It is understood, indeed, that soul and consciousness are not identical

---

it would envisage as both volitional and cognitional. And yet the metaphysical self would be under the same disability of cognizing its own cognitional part; and thus the 'blindness' ascribed to Will, as thing-in-itself, by Schopenhauer, is shown to be a *necessary* illusion of self-consciousness; or, rather, it is thus shown that this *apparent* blindness is no proof of the fact. Behind self-consciousness is the incognizable consciousness itself; incognizable, however, to the *same* mode of consciousness, or personality, but a quite possible object to another, higher, more interior and comprehensive consciousness of the same subject.—Tr.

concepts, and the advance to the doctrine of the Unconscious is quite consequent. But science knows only the physiological unconscious, philosophy only the metaphysical unconscious, and that not in an individual, but in a pantheistic sense. Hegel calls it Idea, Schopenhauer, Will; with Hartmann it has two attributes, Representation and Will. Germs of a rational doctrine of soul in the sense above indicated are to be found in Kant and Schelling, but hitherto they have only been turned to advantage in Hellenbach's 'Individualism.'

That these germs have now to be developed is an anachronism, since this task should have been appointed for the reformation of the old doctrine of the soul, which it would thus have followed in historical succession; and its accomplishment would then have preceded the rise of the pantheistic systems, to the considerable advantage of the latter. That these should have been the immediate solvents of the old doctrine of the soul was thus a leap, the intermission of a stage, with the result that the new systems could not penetrate the popular understanding. The latter has appropriated only their negative side, and is gone over to the comfortable materialism which flatters its lower instincts, but which owes its apparent clearness only to its dryness, and must draw after it the destruction of our culture, unless belief in metaphysic can be revived.

The modern pantheistic systems are all rooted in transcendental idealism. They have in them tendencies, however, partly to transcendental realism (which with Hartmann has even a systematic foundation), and partly to metaphysical individualism. Pure idealism must logically leave out of account the question whether there is a metaphysical quintessence, even in the individual as such. That Schopenhauer should have even suggested the problem: how deeply the roots of the individual Will extend into the thing-in-itself? was in direct opposition to the idealistic foundations of his system. If time and space are the *principia individuationis*, having no validity for the thing-in-itself, then is the thing-in-itself One only, which in the world of phenomena is, as it were, optically divided into a multiplicity of individuals, by means of the representational forms, time and space. For idealists there can be no third interposed between phenomenon and thing-in-itself; man as individual is not of metaphysical nature. But at all events the question of the metaphysical root must have been as applicable to every atom as to man. That Schopenhauer raised this weighty problem at all can only well be explained as an inclination to individualism, of which his later works contain several indications, as already his earlier view of Nature shows him disposed to realism. Schopenhauer would doubtless in time have given up his pantheism in favour of Individualism, and his Idealism in favour of a Transcendental Realism; it being natural to every philosopher, his term of life corresponding, himself to bring to maturity the latest germs in his system, instead of leaving their further cultivation to the historical development of philosophy.

If self-consciousness does not exhaust its object, then corresponding to the transcendental world must be a transcendental Ego; and our sense of personality, by which we know ourselves as mere willing beings, does not coincide with our whole Ego. The sphere of our earthly personality would be only the smaller circle included in the larger concentric circle of our metaphysical subject, and the earthly self-consciousness would not cast its beams to the periphery of our being. Secondly, the question would arise whether the metaphysical subject is in itself unconscious, or only relatively so, as lying beyond the illuminated sphere of the earthly self-consciousness, so that this Unconscious would be only an Unconscious for us as earthly persons.

The thought that individuality extends its roots down into the thing-in-itself is thus at least logically admissible, and it is therefore a neglect of philosophy to put aside this possibility, and to proceed forthwith to the definition of the 'thing-in-itself.' The actual proof could certainly only be afforded by experience; but empirical proofs of supposed impossibilities are not sought for, and it may be that it is only for that reason that they have not been found.

But from the mere conception of metaphysical individualism may be obtained indications where and when such empirical proofs must be discovered, and of what character they must be. For the terminology to be adopted in this inquiry a few words will suffice. The whole circuit of the human being shall be designated Subject. As in regard to the world, we distinguish between the transcendental—beyond consciousness—and the empirical—within the reach of consciousness, so in regard to man, the empirical Ego, the person with self-consciousness, is to be distinguished from the transcendental Subject, which could only be named a transcendental Ego, if to this Subject not only willing, but also knowing and self-consciousness are to be ascribed.

If, now, the earthly self-consciousness, like the consciousness of the world, were capable of evolution, then would the boundary-line between the empirical Ego and the transcendental Subject be no impenetrable partition-wall, but from the standpoint of biology would be instable. But from the instability of this boundary-line would follow the *à priori* probability that the germinal dispositions to extension of self-consciousness beyond its temporary limits must now and then come into action, so that intermediate conditions of empirical and transcendental psychology could be observable.

The thread which holds together the personal self-consciousness consists in memory. Without this, personal identity in self-consciousness would be suspended; the feelings would be only experienced in isolation: there would be no survey of them in their succession. Were there no bridge of memory from feeling to feeling, self-consciousness must begin anew with every new feeling, and be again dispossessed with every following one. The feeling of personality would be atomically broken up, as pearls on a string roll asunder when the string is unknotted. Now from this it becomes *à priori* certain, that occasional functions of these germinal tendencies of transcendental psychology must be associated with modifications of memory of some sort. It is thus of the greatest importance to track the functions of memory in all our psychical conditions, especially in the very abnormal ones. It is of course implied that an occasional displacement of the boundary between transcendental and empirical Ego must be connected with corresponding changes in the state of empirical consciousness and self-consciousness.

Should man be a double being in the sense indicated—which duplicity would not be dualistic, but only, as it were, optically produced by the boundary-line between conscious and unconscious—these two halves must be related to each other like scales of a balance ; in proportion as the empirical Ego retreats, must the other advance, and conversely; as the stars optically disappear with the sun's rising, and appear with his setting. Corresponding to this relation will be the proportionate content of memory.

On the given presupposition of metaphysical individualism, we can next say, proceeding deductively, that it can only be proved from psychical conditions in which the retirement of empirical consciousness and self-consciousness would facilitate the emergence of the transcendental Subject. Such conditions we live through experimentally in dream, and they fill a whole third of our existence. Dream thus offers most chances of proving a metaphysical individuality. The dream-world is therefore the empirical basis for individualism ; as the external world should afford the explanation of the world-problem, so the dream-world that of the human problem.

It would be a mere misunderstanding to refuse to the world of dream the dignity of an empirical basis for the reason that its presentations are illusions and not reality. They have, at any rate, the reality of appearances, and, moreover, for the present purpose it is absolutely indifferent whether dreams are illusions, which as to their content they certainly in most cases are; but we are concerned solely with the mere facts *that* we dream, and that in our dreams, be their content what it may, definite functions are recurrent which have no analogy with waking life.

Individuality being presupposed, something can be affirmed *à priori*, even concerning the quality of these functions. If, that is, our Subject falls apart in two halves, the empirical and transcendental, only apparently, in consequence of the limits of the self-consciousness which does not exhaust its object, these halves cannot possibly be of wholly heterogeneous natures, therefore their modes of functioning cannot be thoroughly different, and both must be related, as well in knowing as in willing. Thus the functions to be expected from the transcendental Subject, which were above determined only with reference to the occasion of their appearance, may now in some measure be defined with reference to their quality, and indeed so, that now no objection can be made to our speaking of a transcendental, willing, and knowing *Ego*. From the conception of individuality, yet further *à priori* determinations may be deduced. For our cognition, for instance, all things act in time and space, and our whole conceptual understanding of Nature depends on expressing the modes of action of things in relations of time and space. Now had these cognitional forms of ours no validity whatever for the transcendental world and the transcendental Ego, the capacity of consciousness and self-consciousness, for evolution in the direction of the transcendental, could not be at all thought as possible, and as the two worlds would be separated by an insuperable chasm, we could never set foot in that region which exceeds our empirical consciousness. These representational forms of time and space, however, even though corresponding to transcendental reality, might have a signification for our transcendental Ego *other* than for the empirical; it is still, at least, not decided *à priori* that the same *measure* of time and *measure* of space must avail for the transcendental as for the empirical Ego. If, therefore, any psychical conditions whatever could be shown in which there is cognition with modifications of time- and space-relations, this again would warrant the inference of a transcendental-psychological function.

Our demands on the transcendental Ego thus constantly gain in definitude. Whether it exists remains, provisionally, still undecided. But if it exists we are logically safe in deductively pronouncing on what occasions, that is, in what psychical states of the empirical Ego, it can come to the front and exercise its functions, and, approximately, how it must exercise them. The result up to the present may be comprehended in a few words; if a transcendental Ego exists, it will be manifested in the following determinations as facts of experience:

1. A duplication of human consciousness.
2. An alternation of the two states of consciousness in inverse proportion to their intensity.
3. Modifications of memory in connection with the alternation of the two states.
4. Functions of knowing and willing in both states, and that probably under
5. Modifications of the measure of time and space.

We at once see that it is the dream-world which

presents the facts of experience thus theoretically resulting from the conception of metaphysical individuality. The dream-world, therefore, must contain the solution of the human enigma—if that is possible at all. Of course only an exact analysis of our dreams could afford the reliable inductive proof that metaphysical individuality is the true solution of this enigma. Provisionally, however, and deductively, has been shown the great probability that the enigma will in this way be solved. For if the logical consequences of a presupposed hypothesis are found to agree with facts of experience, the truth of the hypothesis is in the highest degree probable.

If there is a transcendental Ego, we stand with only one foot of our being in the phenomenal world. But then it is also clear why the relations of man to this phenomenal world, as known by self-consciousness, cannot offer the solution of the human enigma. Only by including in our regard the other side of our being, can we succeed in that. In waking, we know nothing of this other side; the empirical self-consciousness does not comprehend the transcendental, but is comprehended by it. In sleep is given at least the negative condition for filling the empirical self-consciousness with a transcendental content, which content would present itself as dream-image. It is true that even the empirical Ego must encounter influences from the transcendental world, inasmuch as the two Egos are indeed identical; but for the empirical consciousness such influences remain below the psycho-physical threshold of sensibility, the susceptibility being first exalted in the degree that the influences from the empirical world cease; the threshold is depressed, that is to say, new material of sensibility is afforded, and the deepest sleep brings with it even the greatest susceptibility for such influences, which otherwise remain unconscious.

But though in this we have evidence of the capacity of the empirical self-consciousness for evolution, we are not to suppose that even in deepest sleep the psycho-physical threshold is altogether removed. We have the germ only of this evolution in us, and even in trance, ecstasy, and similar conditions, it may not be susceptible of a development which would correspond to a biological process of millions of years. This consideration alone should suffice to restrain us from an over-estimation of dream. To which is to be added that transcendental influences, if they are to be perceived by us, must always clothe themselves in the cognitional forms of the empirical consciousness, and thus have only the value of allegories, symbols, perhaps only of emblems. That is the case also with supersensuous conceptions. If, for example, we cannot represent time otherwise than under the figure of a line which we draw, that is because supersensuous conceptions, to be represented to us, must clothe themselves in the forms of our consciousness. In like manner dream-images of true transcendental content can be only symbolical, that is, true only somewhat in the sense in which it is true that time is a line.

In the alternation of sleeping and waking we have thus identity of Subject and difference of persons. We are at the same time citizens of two worlds, and it is merely the alternate latency of each consciousness that presents this contemporaneity as mere succession. Still more distinctly than by the mere alternation of waking and dream, this duplication of our nature is revealed in that remarkable class of dreams in which our Ego is dramatically sundered. If in dream I sit at an examination, and do not find the answer to the question put by the examiner, which then my next neighbour, to my great vexation, excellently gives, this very clear example shows the psychological possibility of the identity of the Subject with the contemporaneous difference of persons. The example is even more remarkable than if it were our real double nature, for in this dream the two persons even know of one another, and that not in regard to their identity, but in regard to their difference. To object that a possibility in dream does not prove real possibility would be to misconceive the problem. The *psychological* actuality, thus possibility, is not in the least affected by the example being taken from the mere world of dreams, and the illusory nature of dream here disparages only the one circumstance that the two persons of the Subject stand opposed to one another perceptibly. Thus the existence of a transcendental Object is proved by the cognitional theory of consciousness; the existence of a transcendental Subject by the cognitional theory of self-consciousness. There the world of sense is the basis from which we must proceed, here, the dream-world. Only upon the basis of this dream-world can an empirical establishment of the doctrine of soul be undertaken, this endeavour being hopeless as long as we limit ourselves to the analysis of the waking half of our being, even were the strife between physiologists and psychologists at length decided in favour of the latter. Logical speculations alone will no more establish the doctrine of the soul than the mere emotional needs of believers, in which only the wish is father to the thought.

If philosophy, starting from the empirical facts of dream, shall have accomplished this task, then, and first then, will be the time for it to attack the further question, whether that which is proved in dream in relation to the Microcosm repeats itself in a larger sphere, in relation to the Macrocosm. The question then will be whether there is an all-embracing World-Subject, dramatically sundering itself in millions of suns and milliards of beings in space and time.

## CHAPTER III.

#### DREAM A DRAMATIST.

### I. *The Transcendental Measure of Time.*

THE more familiar we are with the history of philosophy, thus the slighter our hope that its study will yield us new data for the solution of the world-enigma, the more does that enigma oppress us. This suggests the review, within experience, of such phenomena as have not yet been duly explored, and from which the metaphysical information latent in them as not yet been sufficiently extracted. This undertaking is additionally justified in that modern philosophy has abandoned the construction of *à priori* systems, and knows that only in facts of the phenomenal world should its foundation be laid.

Such insufficiently utilized facts of experience are indeed numerous, but even the existence of most of them is contested, because they do not belong to every-day experience. Inferences from these can therefore for the present have no cogency.

But we are about to discuss a phenomenon which enjoys the advantage of being wholly undisputed, without having been as yet sufficiently turned to account. This phenomenon belongs to the world of dream. It has, in the first instance, a high interest for Æsthetic and Psychology; but on closer inspection it will be found also to contain, and at the same time to solve, a metaphysical problem.*

The poetical endowment of our fantasy in dream has found many admirers; but it has been supposed that this endowment is only of a lyrical nature. This is plainly said by one of the latest inquirers in an otherwise highly interesting work :† 'The æsthetic value of dream lies not in its dramatic, but in its lyrical element.' The following investigation will give chief prominence to the dramatic element of dream. Then, when we seek the force of this dramatic endowment, we shall attain to some important consequences in which physiological psychology will be reconciled with the spiritualistic doctrine of the soul with regard to the legitimate ingredients of both.

To evince the importance of the dream phenomenon under investigation, a short preliminary remark is necessary. It was, I believe, Helmholtz who first proved experimentally that the transmission of excitations in the nervous system requires a measurable interval of time. There is therefore a moment of suspense before consciousness comes into play. From an excitation in the peripheral nerve-extremities of our external senses, to the occurrence of a sensation in the central organ of the nerves, the brain, a time elapses, only indeed the fraction of a second, but with a duration proportionate to the intervening extent of the conducting nerves. Fechner, moreover, has shown in his 'Psychophysics' that the antecedent conversion of the excitation in the brain into a con-

---

\* Volkhelt: 'Die Traumphantasie,' 189.
† Müller's 'Archiv für Anthropologie,' 1850, 71-83.

scious act of sensibility claims a further particle of time, so that there is here also another moment of suspense.

The functions of the nervous system are therefore associated with a definite measure of time. Since consciousness is awakened by means of an organic basis, the nervous system, it is subject to the delays occasioned by the limited celerity of the nerve-excitations. Within a given time only a definite number of sensations is possible. Thus if with the change of object an uninterrupted succession of atomic processes is completed in a minimum of time, the translation of physiological changes into consciousness does not represent them individually, but the resulting sensation is the equivalent of their completed sum. We perceive nothing of the continual growth of a blade of grass, but first such amounts as we can compare; the transitory intervening stages being lost for our consciousness.

If, however, it could be proved from experience that in certain conditions consciousness takes place without any retardation, it would follow that such acts of consciousness are no longer associated with the material substration of the nerves to which the restrictive interval of time is due. And if, further, we can comprise in a *minimum* of time such a succession of representations as in the normal state would require hours, it is incontrovertible that this sort of consciousness is independent of the nerve-apparatus, whose functions are, as experimentally demonstrated, much more restricted in point of time.

If, now, there were beings whose measure of time in perception did not coincide with our own, but was longer or shorter, it would follow that the world would be wholly otherwise presented to them than it is to us. We could never come to an understanding with such beings concerning objects; we should not believe that we and they were living together in the same world; each class would probably impute illusion to the other. This question has been examined by a very circumspect writer, Ernst von Bär, the forerunner of Darwin, and he has shown that the phenomenal world would undergo a powerful transformation, were our measure of time in perception altered.* The same inquiry has been taken up more recently by Felix Ebertz;† so that I was able to found upon these works an attempt at a scientific solution of the question concerning the intellectual nature of the inhabitants of the planets.‡ As certainly as we are able to say with regard to the physical nature of such inhabitants, 'other worlds, other beings,' so certainly, with reference to their intellectual nature, can it be said, 'other beings, other worlds.'

We mark off a space of time according to the number of changes in Nature comprised in it. This number for us, however, depends upon our subjective celerity of apprehension, that is to say, upon our congenital scale of time. A definite sum of perceptions thus produces for us the appearance of a definite duration, the foundation of which is this our congenital scale. Were the whole process of Nature quickened or retarded, with a corresponding change in our measure of time, we should be quite unaware

---

* Ernst von Bär, 'Reden,' i. 257.
† 'Die Gestirne und die Weltgeschichte.'
‡ 'Die Planetenbewohner,' 114.

of the fact, and should not believe our life to be longer or shorter than in our present condition.

But though these arguments cannot be logically assailed, the reader will be prepared with the objection that the conceivability of a thing does not prove its reality, and would have to be satisfied that such hypothetical beings, with an altered scale of time, actually exist upon other stars. Now the question, whether there are such beings, admits of an answer, without the necessity of a journey to other worlds than our own.

We are ourselves such beings, and that not only exceptionally, but during a whole third of our existence, that is to say in dream, as also in certain other conditions.

Collecting facts of experience, we may in the first place refer to the observations of physicians who have stupefied their patients by narcotics. Usually this condition lasts only a few minutes; but on awaking the patient believes a much longer time to have elapsed. This can only result from the fact that in the narcotic condition he has experienced a much longer succession of representations than would be possible for the normal consciousness in the same duration. He has changed his scale of time, whereas in memory the represented series is judged according to the normal scale, and is thus believed to have occupied as long a time as would be required upon that scale. Now as such a process is impossible according to physiological laws, it necessarily follows that this process is not a physiological one, in other words, consciousness is here independent of the nervous system.

A like change of the temporal scale, with the disappearance of normal consciousness, is also incident to indulgence in opium and hashish. The faculty of representation is thereby enormously accelerated. One of the strongest opium-consumers, De Quincy, says that under its influence he had dreams of ten, twenty, thirty, even up to sixty years' duration, some even which seem to exceed all limits of human experience.* A hashish-eater described a dream to Hervey,† in which the representations ensued with fabulous rapidity. 'It seemed to me,' he said, 'as though something had been taken away from my brain, like a spring from a watch, and that the whole chain of my recollections ran off of themselves with unheard-of rapidity and incoherence.'

At the approach of death, also, the extraordinary exaltation of memory, connected with a change in the measure of time, has been frequently observed. Fechner‡ relates the case of a lady, who fell into the water and was nearly drowned. From the moment when all bodily movements ceased till she was drawn out of the water, about two minutes elapsed, during which, according to her own account, she lived again through her whole past, the most insignificant details of it being represented in imagination. Another instance of the same mental action, in which the events of whole years were crowded together, is described by Admiral Beaufort from his own experience. He had fallen into the water, and had lost (normal) con-

* Spitta: 'Schlaf. und Traumzustände der menschlichen Seele,' 203, Aumerkung.
† Hervey: 'Les Rêves et les Moyens de les Diriger,' 480.
‡ 'Zentralblatt für Anthropologie und Naturwissenschaft,' Jahrgang 1863, 774.

sciousness. In this condition 'thought rose after thought, with a rapidity of succession that is not only indescribable, but probably inconceivable by anyone who has not himself been in a similar situation.' At first the immediate consequences of his death for his family were presented to him ; then his regards turned to the past ; he repeated his last cruise, an earlier one in which he was shipwrecked; his schooldays, the progress he then made, and the time he had wasted, even all his small childish journeys and adventures. ' Thus travelling backwards, every incident of my past life seemed to me to glance across my recollection in retrograde succession, *not*, however, *in mere outline*, as here stated, but the picture *filled up* with every minute and collateral feature ; in short, the whole period of my existence seemed to be placed before me in a *kind of panoramic review*, and every act of it seemed to be accompanied by a consciousness of right and wrong, or by some reflection on its cause or its consequences. Indeed, many trifling events, which had long been forgotten, then crowded into my imagination, and with the character of recent familiarity.'* In this case also, but two minutes at the most had passed, before Beaufort was taken out of the water.

We thus possess a faculty, ordinarily latent, of looking into the inner world of our Ego, with a measure of time other than that of our waking life. In other words, the normal self-consciousness does not exhaust its object—the Ego. This normal self-consciousness with its physiological measure of time is only one form of our self-consciousness. Man has a double

* Haddock: 'Somnolism and Psychism,' p. 213.

consciousness, the empirical with its physiological measure of time, and a transcendental with another measure of time peculiar to itself. Now, that this transcendental consciousness forthwith emerges, as soon as the empirical is set to rest, is most strikingly evinced by our dreams. Since the transcendental measure of time is a characteristic incident of these, it is evident that the physiological scale is inapplicable to them.

Jean Paul, in his 'Musæus,' makes the short but striking observation, that the dreams of one night would require more than a day for their narration. In fact, we can always convince ourselves that the number of our dream-representations are temporally so crowded together as often to seem to fill enormous spaces of time; yet, notwithstanding the rapidity of their passage, without the loss of one of their moments. As in waking we estimate our subjective time-consciousness according to the number of representations experienced, on which, indeed, rests the conception of duration, so also in dream. Since, however, the dream-representations ensue according to the transcendental scale of time, we dream of long episodes of life, journeys, etc., a whole flood of representations precipitate themselves upon us; and in the briefest period we believe ourselves to have lived through months, and that not first in the ensuing recollection, but in the dream itself. Thus we carry over into dream the waking habit of estimating duration according to the number of perceptions upon the physiological scale of time, while our consciousness is, in fact, then subject to the transcendental scale. Thus one, intoxicated with hashish, believes himself to live through tens of years; confirming what has been already said, that the process of Nature might run off at any rate whatever, without our detecting the difference, supposing only a corresponding change in our measure of time.

These comparative scales of time are very finely illustrated by a Turkish fable, related by Addison :*

'A Sultan of Egypt, who was an infidel, used to laugh at a circumstance related of Mahomet in the Koran†, as what was altogether impossible and absurd. But conversing one day with a great doctor in the law, who had the gift of working miracles, the doctor told him he would quickly convince him of the truth of this passage in the history of Mahomet, if he would consent to do what he would desire of him. Upon this, the Sultan was directed to place himself by a large tub of water, which he did accordingly; and as he stood by the tub, amidst a circle of his great men, the holy man bid him plunge his head into the water, and draw it up again.

'The King accordingly thrust his head into the water, and, at the same time, found himself at the foot of a mountain on a sea-shore. The King immediately began to rage against his doctor for this piece of treachery and witchcraft; but, at length, knowing it to be vain to be angry, he set himself to think on proper methods for gaining a livelihood in this strange country. Accordingly he applied himself to some people whom he saw at work in a neighbouring wood. These people conducted him to

---

\* *Spectator*, No. 94.

† The story from the Koran is here given after Addison's narrative.—Tr.

a town that stood at a little distance from the wood, where, after some adventures, he married a woman of great beauty and fortune. He lived with this woman so long that he had by her seven sons and seven daughters. He was afterwards reduced to great want, and forced to think of plying in the streets as a porter for his livelihood. One day, as he was walking alone by the seaside, being seized with many melancholy reflections upon his former and his present state of life, which had raised a fit of devotion in him, he threw off his clothes with a design to wash himself, according to the custom of the Mahometans, before he said his prayers. After his first plunge into the sea, he no sooner raised his head above the water but he found himself standing by the side of the tub, with the great men of his court about him, and the holy man at his side. He immediately upbraided his teacher for having sent him on such a course of adventures, and betrayed him into so long a state of misery and servitute ; but was wonderfully surprised when he heard that the state he talked of was only a dream and delusion ; that he had not stirred from the place where he then stood ; and that he had only dipped his head into the water, and immediately taken it out again.'

There is a passage in the Koran in which Mohammed relates what might suggest the suspicion that he had substituted hashish for wine.

'It is there said\* that the Angel Gabriel took

---

\* I copy this account from the *Spectator*, where, however, the note is appended : ' No such passage is to be found in the Alcoran, though it possibly may be in some of the histories of Mahomet's life.'—Tr.

Mahomet out of his bed one morning to give him a sight of all things in the seven heavens, in paradise, and in hell, which the prophet took a distinct view of, and after having held ninety thousand conferences with God, was brought back again to his bed. All this, says the Alcoran, was transacted in so small a space of time, that Mahomet on his return found his bed still warm, and took up an earthen pitcher (which was thrown down at the very instant that the Angel Gabriel carried him away), before the water was all spilt.'

Turning now to the analogous phenomena of ordinary dream, it will be seen that this fable has, in fact, discovered with great insight a characteristic of the condensation of impressions by means of the transcendental scale of time : viz., the dramatically pointed succession of the representations. For we find the same distinctive mark in a certain sort of dreams, by no means rare, and which experience can always verify, since they can even be artificially induced. It had already been remarked by the elder Darwin, in his 'Zoonomy,' that external sensations affecting the consciousness of the dreamer, and thereby awakening him, can nevertheless be the occasion of a long, spun-out dream, interposed in the brief moment between the sensation and the awakening.* But the awakening thus externally caused is, at the same time, internally motived by the dramatic climax of the dream. Thus, for instance, Cartesius was once awakened by a flea-bite, and, at the same time, from a dream which concluded with a duel in

* J. H. Fichte: 'Anthropologie,' 470.

which he received a stab in the same part of his body.

Even during sleep our sensory nerves are exposed to various external irritants. When these impressions are transmitted to the brain, it reacts, as in waking. It is in the nature of the brain to refer these impressions to causes in external space. Thus arises the phenomenal world, in waking, as in dream; only that in the latter the cause is taken from the imaginary world, and in place of *one* cause, a whole chain of causes is made to bring about the sensation. In this chain it is that Dream appears as a dramatic artist, and as well in that, as in the process of condensation connected therewith, may be compared to the magician in Addison's Turkish fable.

Some characteristic examples will serve for illustration. Hennings\* relates the dream of one who had fastened his shirt-collar too tight, and had a painful dream of being hanged. Another† dreamed of a journey in an American prairie, and of an attack by Indians, who scalped him. He had drawn on his night-cap too tightly. Another dreamed that he was attacked by robbers, who laid him on his back on the ground, and staked him to it through his teeth.‡ On awaking he found a straw between two of the latter. Gregory relates that another took a hot bottle to bed with him, and then dreamed of an ascent of Etna, in which he found the heat of the ground almost unbearable.§

\* 'Von Träumen und Nachtwandlern,' 238.
† Lemoine: 'Du Sommeil,' 129.
‡ Scherner: 'Das Leben des Traumes,' 233.
§ Scherner: 'Das Leben des Traumes,' 234.

The distinctive peculiarities of these dreams—their dramatic character, and the condensation of representations—are still more significant when the exciting cause is some external accident suddenly occurring. To begin with a dream which has become historical. Garnier* relates that the first Napoleon was asleep in his carriage when the infernal machine exploded under it. The report roused him from a long dream, in which he was crossing the Tagliamento with his army, and was received by the cannon of the Austrians; so that he sprang up with the exclamation, 'We are undermined!' and awoke. Richers† mentions the dream of a man who was awakened by a shot fired off near him. He dreamed that he had become a soldier, had suffered unheard-of hardships, had deserted, was taken, tried, condemned, and finally shot. This whole dream was thus the work of a moment. Steffens‡ relates: 'I was asleep in a bed with my brother. In dream I saw myself in a lonely street, pursued by a strange sort of wild beast. As is often the case in dreams, I could not cry out, and ran along the street. The animal gained on me. At last I came to a flight of stairs, and being stiffened by terror, and exhausted by running, I could get no further. I was seized by the beast, and severely bitten on the thigh. The bite awoke me, and—my brother had pinched me on the thigh. Reflection,' says Steffens, 'somehow connects this external event with the dream. But it remains to be explained, how that which was the subjective *climax*

---

\* 'Traité des Facultés de l'Âme,' i. 4, 36.
† 'Geist und Natur,' 209.
‡ 'Karrikaturen des Heiligsten,' ii. 700.

of a whole succession of dreamed incidents could be at the same time the external occasion of them! Or shall we here adopt the invariable refuge of superficial minds, accidental coincidence? Such facts instruct us rather that those perceptual forms, which for the waking state have an unconditional reality, are proved by even ordinary dreams to belong to a condition which is only relative.'

Volkelt* says: 'A composer once dreamed that he kept a school, and wished to make something clear to his pupils. Having explained, he turned to one of the boys with the question, "Have you understood me?" The boy screamed out like one possessed, "Oh yes!" He angrily reproved him for so yelling. Then came a chorus from the whole class, "Oh yes!" followed by "Curjo!" and finally, "Feuerjo!" And then he was awoke by an actual cry of "Feuerjo!" in the street.'

Count Lavalette† relates: 'One night, asleep in prison, I was awakened by the Palace clock striking twelve o'clock. I heard a sound as of the grating being opened, and the guard relieved. I fell asleep again immediately, and had a dream '—then follows the account of a frightful dream, the particulars of which, according to the feeling of the dreamer, must have occupied at least five hours—'when suddenly the grating closed again with great violence, the noise of which awakened me. I made my watch strike; it was still twelve o'clock, so that this fearful fabric of imagination could have lasted only two to three minutes, the time necessary for the relief of the

---

\* 'Die Traumphantasie,' 108.
† 'Mémoires et Souvenirs du Comte Lavalette,' i. 28.

guard, and the opening and shutting of the grating. It was very cold, and, therefore, the relief was very quick; moreover, the gaoler next morning confirmed my reckoning. And yet I can recall no event in my life, the duration of which I could assert with greater certainty, of which the particulars were better impressed upon my memory, and of which I was more completely conscious.'

Maury[*] was ill in bed, and dreamed of the French Revolution. Bloody scenes passed before him. He spoke with Robespierre, Marat, and other monsters of that time, was dragged before the tribunal, was condemned to death, and carried through a great crowd of people, bound to a plank. The guillotine severed his head from his shoulders. He woke with terror, to find that a rail over the bed had got unfastened, and had fallen upon his neck like a guillotine, and, as his mother, who was sitting by him, declared, at that very moment.

Let us now analyse the problem which is to be solved. Accident explains nothing in these cases, since such dreams are very frequent—I have, myself, elsewhere[†] reported about a dozen from my own experience—and always the awakening cause agrees in character with the final catastrophe of the dream: flea-bite and dagger-stab, report of shot and being shot, falling rail and guillotine, etc. For the same reasons we must reject the supposition that the imagination only skilfully weaves into the course of the dream the material imported by external accident.

---

[*] 'Le Sommeil et les Rêves,' 161.
[†] Oneirokritikon: 'Deutsche Vierteljahrschrift,' 1869; and 'Psychologie der Lyrik,' 28-30.

Dream is rather a completely accentuated drama. Its apparent duration, however, cannot possibly be the actual one, since we often dream of whole days, whereas at the most hours, and often even only minutes, have elapsed. Did the two durations coincide, then, inasmuch as the final event of the dream is only the awakening cause disguised by imagination, the effect must have preceded the cause,* which is impossible. It is, therefore, absolutely certain that a process of compression takes place in the series of representations, and thus also that we dream with a scale of time other than the physiological one. But even so, the difficulty is not yet removed; since the awakening cause forms in these dreams always the *final* event, and, moreover, determines the whole purport and course of the dream. However compressed may be the whole series of representations comprised in the dream, still that would not alter their relative position as antecedent to the awakening cause. It thus appears that we still have the effect before the cause, since it is quite indifferent whether this effect has lasted only a second or whole hours.

For the solution of this problem a further point of attachment must be reached. The necessity of seeking for this solution is apparent from the fact that all our dreams seem to contain the same problem, those of the above-mentioned class having merely the advantage of

---

* According to what has been above pointed out, and is indeed sufficiently evident in the class of dreams described, viz., that they are a dramatically connected whole; the climax or catastrophe being not only the subjective aspect of the external awakening cause, but being also the strictly appropriate conclusion of the dream. Thus the awakening cause must have suggested the *whole* sequence of representations constituting the dream.—Tr.

presenting it more distinctly than others; owing to the circumstance that they are excited by the same cause which also awakens; thus making the process of compression in the sequence of representations clearly apparent. But the same would undoubtedly take place, were the exciting cause transmitted to the brain without interrupting the sleep and becoming an awakening cause. The transcendental measure of time cannot possibly be due to the awakening: it must thus be incident to all our dreams, if only the external irritant is strong enough to affect the consciousness of the dreamer. It is indifferent which of our peripheral senses is affected. The ear appears to be the most sensitive; but the above-cited examples show that dramatic dreams can be produced by external accidents conveyed through other senses also. The deeper the sleep, the more are the outer senses closed; but as dreams still occur, it follows that the greater number of them are to be ascribed to exciting causes within the organism, that is, to the vegetative functions which go on during sleep. These also produce dramatic dreams. Thus one of my friends dreamed of receiving a letter summoning him to Berlin to be present at an execution. He set off and came to the scene of punishment, but was made so unwell by the sight of the spurting blood that he was sick. And this actually happened, he awaking at the same moment. Macuish relates a case in which a man afflicted with chronic and acute gout dreamed every night that he was in the dungeons of the Inquisition, suffering the most ingenious tortures. This horrid dream did not leave him for a long time, so that the invalid every evening looked forward with dread to the coming night.

Here is an instance from my own experience. I had an apparently very long dream, towards the end of which I lost myself in a long gallery of an extensive building. There came towards me from the other end of the gallery a lady with a rustling train. I went close by her in order to discern her features in the dusk, and recognised a lady whom I seemed to have known long ago ; whereupon, with the imagination still available in dream, I went through the ceremony of my introduction to her. But in saluting her as I passed, I caught my foot in her train, and at the same moment awoke with a nervous spasm of this foot, by which it was turned a little outwards, so as quite to correspond with its situation in the dream. Now, this long dream was evidently elicited by the spasm, and took up so short a time that my cigar had not gone out.

It seems, then, that all our dreams in fact happen in the same way, whether the exciting cause is within or without us. The brain receives a stimulus, and applies to that its own inherent law of causality, that is, constructs by imagination a corresponding cause. This cause is objectified, and through the transcendental scale of time assumes the form of a concentrated series of representations, with dramatic reference to the conclusion. But this will not always suffice to explain the final event, the length of the sequence of representations varying exceedingly. As we cannot assume that the transcendental scale is different according to the individual, this difference of length must either lie in the peculiarity of the exciting causes, or depend upon the degree of imagination in the dreamer ; or perhaps the length of the dream is conditioned by both causes co-operating.

A comparative glance at artistic production will here be not without interest. In the mysterious laboratory of the poet, dramatic conceptions originate, for the most part, in some scene hovering before him, the dramatic motivation of which, intuitively epitomised, often presents itself to him suddenly. How far this brings him, evidently depends on the degree of imagination. The close and frequently observed affinity of dream to the poetic art is thus revealed in a further particular. The condensation of the ideal sequence seems to obtain in every kind of artistic creation, and to belong generally to the nature of intuition; so that even scientific or philosophical problems are often suddenly penetrated in a series of unconscious and condensed conclusions. A hypothesis is for the most part the child of imagination, and all great theories have come into the world as hypotheses.

Mozart has made the following interesting statement about his own productive faculty: 'When I am all right and in good spirits, either in a carriage or walking, and at night when I cannot sleep, thoughts come streaming in and at their best. Whence and how I know not—I cannot make out. The things which occur to me I keep in my head, and hum them also to myself—at least, so others have told me. If I stick to it, there soon come one after another useful crumbs for the pie, according to counterpoint, harmony of the different instruments, etc. This now inflames my soul, that is, if I am not disturbed. Then it keeps on growing, and I keep on expanding it and making it more distinct, and the thing, however long it be, becomes, indeed, almost finished in my head, so that I can afterwards survey it in spirit like a beautiful picture or a fine person, and also hear it in imagination —not indeed successively, as by-and-by it must come out, but as all together. That is a delight! All the invention and construction go on in me as in a fine, strong dream. But the overhearing it all at once is still the best.' Mozart did not foresee how interesting would be his involuntary comparison with dreaming. Giving to his words a rather more precise expression, they mean that the secret of musical compositions lies in the compression of auditory representations. One is involuntarily reminded of Luther's forcible saying : ' God sees time not lengthwise, but crosswise ; all is in a heap before Him.' Here Luther refers the omniscience of God, to whom he ascribes the transcendental measure of time in its highest degree, to the compression of representations, and compares it with the intuitive cognition of genius, wherein that, which to the man of ordinary reflection appears as a temporal succession, is changed into a juxtaposition to be surveyed at a glance.

If, now, we compare these results, to which we are led by regarding the mode in which dream and genius operate, with the theories of materialists, who see in all thinking only modifications of the brain, it is intelligible why we seek in vain in such theories for any fine conception or great discovery. There functions in them only the physiological measure of time, not the transcendental ; so that here, too, we may say : Thou resemblest the spirit thou conceivest (' Du gleichst dem Geist, den du begreifst '). Nor, on the other hand, can I wonder, especially having regard to the above-quoted saying of Luther, that

Splittgerber, in an otherwise excellent recent publication,* finds the problem of the dramatic dream so difficult that he is driven to the following hyperbolical explanation : 'There remains at last no other solution of the problem before us than that of the supermundane origin of the soul, according to which she is confined to the limits of space and time only through her connection with a material body in the present world ; and is relieved from these fetters, if only approximately, in the early stages of the dream-ecstasy, recovering her higher freedom and divinely-related nature.' Such explanations recall Plato rather than Aristotle ; but at least they prove that Splittgerber has recognised the whole importance of the problem, and has taken up his own position very clearly.

From a psychological-æsthetic, our problem has gradually assumed a metaphysical character. The chief question remains to be answered : how can a dream which is induced by an excitation of sense close with an event apparently contemporaneous with that excitation ? If this contemporaneity be real, then, however compressed may be the dream, it still antecedes that which excites it ; and we have the impossible supposition of an effect before its cause. The solution can, however, be extracted from the results already obtained.

It is experimentally certain, that in the waking state the process of representation in consciousness requires a measurable time. But it is also a fact of experience that in certain conditions of the mind this law no longer obtains. Consequently our physiological measure of time does not lie in the nature of the mind,

* Splittgerber : 'Schlaff und Tod,' i. 131.

whose cognition is retarded by the nervous system. In artistic production and in dream this hindrance is thrown off with the reflective consciousness, and the transcendental scale of time is set free. But the same consciousness, in which lies compressed the series of representations in the dramatic dream, must also somehow become aware of the exciting occasion before the latter, according to the physiological measure of time, can inform the brain, *i.e.*, the physiologically mediated consciousness. In this brief interval the condensed series of representations is inserted, and at the very moment at which the exciting cause enters the brain, consciousness closes with a corresponding event in the dream. For that mode of apprehension which takes place with the transcendental measure of time, the effect is thus ended when the cause first presents itself to the apprehension associated with the physiological measure of time. The enigmatical phenomenon, that in dramatic dreams the effect apparently precedes the cause, is explained therefore by the duality of our consciousness, that is, by the duality of persons of our Subject. But whoever will not accept this solution of the problem has necessarily to choose among the following hypotheses :

1. The effect in dramatic dreams antecedes the cause. This is logically excluded.

2. There is in the nature of dream a teleological arrangement, by which, at the moment that waking is caused by an external excitation of sense, the dream concludes with an event corresponding in character. This supposition is indeed logically admissible, but is purely arbitrary because unevidenced.

3. This teleological arrangement might also be brought about by the clairvoyance of the human Psyche, foreseeing in its transcendental consciousness the awakening cause, and teleologically disposing the course of the dream, either so that the future awakening cause determines the course of the dream as its *final cause,* or that the transcendental consciousness so contrives it that the sudden disturbance of sleep should be mitigated.\* This supposition can be dispensed with by those who recognise the process of condensation in the series of representations in dramatic dreams.

4. The temporal and qualitative agreement between awakening cause and dream-climax is only apparent and accidental. To this opinion rationalists will incline, in order to escape the hypothesis of a transcendental consciousness, and thus of a second person of our Subject. But that the rationalistic view is untenable we learn by experiment, since the dramatic dream can be artificially excited, in which case the simultaneity and agreement between an actual event and one dreamed are always found.

Of these four suppositions, therefore, only the third is admissible. The choice can thus only be doubtful as between that and the view here adopted of a transcendental measure of time. From both views, however, the same inference results: as well if we attribute to the Psyche the faculty of clairvoyance,† as of ideation without the physiological scale of time, there is the same inference to a transcendental consciousness, *i.e.*, a second person of our Subject.

\* Conf. Hellenbach: 'Magie der Zahlen,' 141.
† Prevision.—Tr.

Thus if the æsthetic-psychological problem of dramatic dream is pursued to the point where it disembogues into metaphysic, these dreams at all events prove to be among the desiderated phenomenal facts which admit of being put to a better philosophical use than heretofore. In these phenomena the veil which hangs over the mystery of man is continually being lifted to some extent. The transcendental half of our being does not fall within our consciousness; self-consciousness does not illumine our whole Ego; the doctrine of the Unconscious thus receives a new confirmation, but at the same time this Unconscious appears as individualized, not universal and metaphysical. As the moon turns to us only one half of its orb, so also our Ego; but as the moon's mutation enables astronomers to observe at least the edges of the other half, so our Ego has its mutations in certain states by which the transcendental half of our being is partially visible. It is true the transcendental mode of cognition has in dream only a phantastic material to work upon, but were we confronted with the external reality with that measure of time, we should resemble Ernst Von Bär's hypothetical beings; we could see the grass grow; and whereas millions of ether-vibrations must be accumulated to be for us a beam of light, we could possibly distinguish them in their atomic detachment.

Kant has said that we cannot at all judge whether other thinking beings are subject in perception to the same conditions of time and space as ourselves,* and

* 'As for the intuitions of other thinking beings, we cannot judge whether they are or are not bound by the same conditions which limit our own intuitions, and which for us are universally valid.' The passage occurs in the subsection of the Transcen-

Malebranche supposed that there might be creatures who could think as much in half an hour as we in a thousand years. The foregoing contribution to Kant's doctrine of the ideality of time has, however, shown that we ourselves belong to this species of beings. But there are yet further characteristics apparent which must be applied to the definition of man, as the cases in which memory and imagination have been exalted far above their normal power.

The results obtained from the facts already considered are sufficiently interesting to encourage the hope of finding in other related phenomena yet further material for the definition of man. We should thence soon see reason to conclude, what has already been suggested by this investigation, that the philosophical systems of our century, in attempting to define the Kantian 'thing-in-itself,' have often only defined the Ego-in-itself. This transcendental being is characterized, relatively to the time-form of its cognition, in the dramatic dream. We have therefore to see whether in similar states reality does not offer material for cognition to the transcendental consciousness, and how the latter deals with such material.

We have first, however, another task to perform. For if the human consciousness, with its physiological scale of time, has only a relative validity, and, as experiment teaches, this scale of time is connected with an organic basis: if, further, as a matter of fact,

---

dental Æsthetic following that entitled 'Transcendental Exposition of the conception of Space,' not, as cited, in the 'Conclusion' of the Transcendental Æsthetic, which is a short paragraph added in the second edition.—Tr.

another scale of time is substituted in the dramatic dream, then this latter scale can *no longer* be connected with the organic basis. Thus the physiological scale of time is not essential to the human mind, and since to this is possible a mode of consciousness liberated from that scale of time, and thus from the organic basis, it follows that its connection with the organic body is *no necessary relation.*

Thus from the apparently insignificant facts of dramatic dreams results the weighty consequence of a transcendental being in us. But that our self should exceed our self-consciousness, that we should be more than we know of ourselves, is a paradoxical view, of which even the bare psychological possibility might by many be disputed. This psychological possibility has, therefore, first to be investigated. Thereby we shall make the acquaintance of yet a second empirical fact, which in its consequences is as important as the dramatic dreams, but, in its aspect, also just as insignificant. It can only be due to this apparent insignificance and familiarity that philosophy has not yet utilized it.

*Fig.* 1.—*Dramatic Sundering of the Ego in Dream.*

(*a*) *The Body.*—Unless dreams are to be regarded as inspirations, we must be ourselves the authors of them. Their whimsicality and beauty need not prevent our claiming them. But as in dreams we find ourselves placed in the midst of dramatically succeeding incidents, every dream may be described as a dramatic sundering of the Ego ; and the dialogues we seem to carry on in them are in truth monologues.

Again, we are not only player and spectator on the dream stage, but part of us goes to the composition of the stage itself. As the lyrick takes from himself the hue with which he overspreads nature—one calls to mind the reed-songs (Schilflieder) of Lenau, and the sea-songs of Greif—so also the dreamer. The poet produces only an illusion, that is, he only changes an already given object; but the dreamer, as he constructs the whole scene out of himself, produces an hallucination.* This dream-scene corresponds to his mood, whether that is a deposit of the waking life, or arises spontaneously in dream. Dream conjures up landscapes in wonderful conformity to our moods; and every light tone of mood is symbolized in the finest way, and all the more that in sleep our feelings have free course, whereas in waking they are more or less restrained.

This solution of the unity of the Subject, this externalization of interior processes, is, however, only possible if they are conceived by consciousness, *not as interior*, because it does not produce them, but obtains them by delivery. The question is thus of the relation of these processes to consciousness. They can only be of two kinds, either bodily or mental.

Of corporeal changes of the organism, many are under conscious control; the vegetative processes, on the other hand, the action of the heart, circulation of the blood, digestion, assimilation and separation of

---

* The distinction between illusion and hallucination is familiar to all students of these subjects; but for the general reader it may be as well to state here that an illusion is a false appearance induced upon some objective reality, whereas hallucination is the objectification of a pure construction of the mind, without any basis of external reality.—Tr.

substances, are independent of consciousness. The feelings excited by these are externalized in dream as its images. Thus if the sundering of the Subject into a plurality of persons happens, so far as this results from bodily changes of the organism, the boundary-line between voluntary and involuntary movements must be at the same time the breaking-place of this sundering. In sleep, indeed, voluntary movements cease, and only unconscious reflex-movements can occur, but it seems that we take over into dream the measure of waking [self-consciousness].*

As regards the psychical processes in the organism, physiology teaches that every thought enters consciousness only as a ready-made result, the process of its origination going on in the Unconscious. It further teaches that every sensation, every feeling, attains to consciousness only upon a stimulation of a certain degree of strength, and unless this degree is reached remains unconscious. The boundary-line between conscious and unconscious thinking and feeling is called the psycho-physical threshold; internal

* *Aber es scheint, dass wir den Massstab des Wachens in den Traum hinübernehmen.* The meaning seems to be, that in dream, as in waking life, the proper self-consciousness does not appropriate the actions of the organism which in the waking state are both involuntary and unconscious; so that when these come to consciousness in dream they suggest its secondary personalities. The muscular reflex movements of waking life, though involuntary, are of course not all unconscious, but to the finer sensibility here attributed to deep sleep, some disturbances of organic processes, which would not rise to the sensational level in the waking state, are perceptible; but only as transmuted by the symbolism of dream. Thus the measure of normal consciousness is so far carried over into dream that, when exceeded, the new accession is represented as alien—foreign to the persisting self-consciousness.—Tr.

processes which, by reason of a sufficiency of stimulation, overstep this threshold, become conscious, others remain in obscurity. If, therefore, there occurs in dream the sundering of the Subject into a plurality of persons, then—so far as psychical changes are the cause of this—*the psycho-physical threshold must be the breaking-place of this sunderance.*

Hence it is apparent, that without such a psycho-physical threshold, dividing the voluntary and conscious from the involuntary, unconscious, a dramatic sundering would not be possible; on the other hand, whenever a sundering occurs, there must be a conscious and an unconscious, and then there always happens a falling apart of the Subject into a plurality of persons at the point where the threshold is disturbed.

Dramatic sundering often occurs, even in waking, that is, when hallucinations from the Unconscious introduce themselves among the perceptions of sense. In dream, somnambulism, and all ecstatic conditions, an interior waking takes the place of the external sense-consciousness, but, being itself limited, likewise borders on the Unconscious. The two conditioning factors of the cleavage, Consciousness and the Unconscious, and the psycho-physical threshold dividing them, are therefore again present here, notwithstanding that in sleep the threshold is displaced. The state of dream first becomes intelligible with the perception that the sundering occurs at the place of rupture of this threshold. A closer examination may, however, be the more called for, as the region of the unconscious soul-life is overgrown with the jungle of superstition, because the sundering of the Subject into a plurality of persons is often mistaken for an actual plurality of Subjects.

If external or internal stimuli in sleep offer feelings to the dream-consciousness, without the latter knowing whence and how they are derived—feelings, in short, which come from the Unconscious, to which, for a sleeper, the external world also belongs—there is always thus occasioned a dramatizing of such feelings. This is very distinctly shown in the experiments for the production of artificial dreams, such as Preyer, among others, has instituted. A sleeper, on whose face he sprinkled some sprays of water, said, in dream: 'Pray take a cab; it is raining terribly!' His face being blown upon, he complained of a draught, and was sure the window was open. On a tinkling being made close to his ear, he said, 'You are breaking all the glasses,' etc.\*

The sundering of the Ego in connection with this dramatizing is still more evident when the feelings presented have their origin within the organism. This is especially occasioned by internal morbid conditions. As long as the internal organs are healthy, their functions proceed without consciousness. The perfectly healthy man knows only from books where these organs are situated. But when they are out of order we feel their functions, and in our sleep they excite corresponding dream-images. Van Erk had a patient, a girl of eighteen, who in consequence of a difficulty of breathing, always had on going to sleep the horrid dream that her deceased grandmother came in at the window and knelt on her chest to

\* Preyer: 'Der Hypnotismus,' 283.

suffocate her.* Impulses, which in waking remain unconscious, are set free in dream, and determine our actions therein, so that it was already observed by the ancients that we are more immoral in dream than in waking.†

Somnambulism is usually connected with morbid conditions, on which account it is still more apparent that every sundering depends on the projection of interior states. According to their general health, somnambules believe themselves to be in beautiful flowery meadows or in wild and terrible places. The first appearance corresponds with the depression of sensibility and abatement of pain in the somnambulic state, which by the feeling of contrast must give impression like that of redemption ; the latter, on the other hand, corresponds to the enduring remnant of sensibility. There is often a symbolical representation of the internal condition, so that, for instance, somnambules see only faded or malodorous flowers. One of Werner's somnambules constantly saw a fresh rose when she was well, a dark-coloured, evil-smelling tulip when she was ill.‡ Becker's somnambule on one occasion felt very tired, but afterwards strengthened by the sleep, and contrasted the two conditions with lyrical colouring : ' Black clouds hung to-day in my sky, and the grass in my meadow was quite withered. These were bad signs. . . . Now the grass seems quite green again, and the blades are

---

\* Van Erk : 'Unterschied von Traum und Wachen,' 28. Prague, 1874.

† Sophokles : ' Œdipus,' 981 ; Plato : ' Republic,' ix. i.; Cicero : ' De Divinatione,' i., c. 29.

‡ Werner : ' Symbolik der Sprache,' 118. Stuttgart, 1841.

broad and luxuriant, and nod to each other with the breeze as if they were intelligent.'*

If the dream scenery of somnambules is thus determined by their general health, on the other hand the actual personal cleavage seems first to occur in consequence of localized and intermittent, if not transient, feelings. This is the case especially in spasmodic conditions. Terrible human forms then appear about to seize upon the patient, while the intervals of relief are motived by benevolent guardian spirits and guides who protect and defend him. This personification extends also to the natural healing power of the organism, and even to the power of applied curatives, as in the case, for instance, of that somnambulic girl who, falling asleep by the *baquet* filled with metallic substances, saw her guardian spirit clad successively in iron and copper, by which also is represented the metallic operation of the *baquet*.†

The emergence and retreat of the 'guide' often exactly corresponds with the occurrence and subsidence of the morbid symptoms. With Magdalene Wenger the spasms and the 'guide' were concurrent; he disappeared with the sense of alleviation, and then she said, mistaking effect for cause, that he had taken away the spasms, and that she would thenceforth be free from them.‡ When the alleviation is partial, good and bad spirits appear in conflict, especially in so-called 'Possession.' In the rapidity with which such dream scenes succeed one another is reflected the skill of fantasy, whose personifications keep pace

---

\* 'Das geistige Doppelleben,' 110, 343.
† 'Archiv f. d. Thierischen Magnetismus,' x. 3, 37, 40.
‡ Perty : 'Die Mystische Erscheinungen,' i. 321.

with the quickly-changing bodily states. Every remission of pain is immediately represented by a friendly figure bringing help and chasing away the hostile demon. Selma saw in her ordinary sleep a black dog who told her he was her greatest tormentor. But in her ensuing somnambulic state she herself explained that he was only a symbolical phenomenon, signifying her spasms.\* This is so far very remarkable in that with every deepening of the sleep-life the tendency to personification should be greater; but here the case is not of the interpretation of a present feeling, but of memory, and with the possibility of comparison every change of state must bring with it a change of judgment. Schindler reports a similar case. One of his somnambules saw her deceased aunt enter, saying that the patient's life was in danger, but that with her help she would be cured. Later, however, with an exaltation of the sleep she herself described this vision as mere personification of her condition, which from an obscure feeling had been elevated into a dream-image.† It thus appears that the subjective signification of such visions is then first perceived when there is consciousness of the difference of one condition from another. In like manner we recognise the illusory character of our dreams upon awaking, though while they last they are taken to be real. The belief in their reality disappears with the change of condition. This has doubtless occasioned the error always met with in text-books of physiology, that we only mistake our dreams for real, because in dream, comparison with

---

\* Wiener: 'Selma, die jüdische Seherin,' 41.
† Schindler: 'Das magische Geisterleben,' 164. Breslau, 1857.

real things fails. This is only partially true. The deception certainly disappears in the presence of a standard of comparison; but it can also be absent in the absence of the standard. It is not only conceivable that dreams should be accompanied by the consciousness of illusion, as often transiently occurs, but with many dreamers this consciousness seems to be constantly present, without the images disappearing. Such dreamers have therefore the faculty of directing the course of the dream at pleasure, as when, for instance, they fling themselves down from a tower, only to see what will come of it.*

The standard of comparison disillusionizes; but as a rule can only be presented by the entrance of a new condition, namely, waking. On the other hand, the failure of this standard in dream is indeed the *sine quâ non* of deception; it is the condition without which the deception does *not* occur, but not its positive cause. This positive cause, which must be additional to the merely negative condition, and which, as far as I know, has not yet been sought, must be discovered if we would understand the essence of dream. But this cause is very soon to be found in accordance with what has been already said. It is the psychophysical threshold. In every condition, in waking as in every exaltation of the sleep-life, man consists, as it were, of two halves. As far as his waking or dreaming consciousness extends, so far his Ego. But he conceives as non-Ego all that oversteps the threshold from the Unconscious. Consequently the dualism of the Conscious and the Unconscious, the

* Jean Paul: 'Blicke in die Traumwelt,' § 4; Harvey: 'Les Rêves et les Moyens de les Diriger,' 16, 17, 140, Paris, 1867.

psycho-physical partition, is the common cause, as well of the dramatic sundering, as of deception which makes dreams seem real. This goes so far, that sundering and deception occur, even notwithstanding the standard of comparison, whenever that is given to us *without* change of condition. We may therefore have hallucinations also in waking, mingling subjective visions with objective things, without being able to distinguish the one from the other.

The sundering in dream often seems not quite to attain to the point of actual severance, by which is easily to be explained that enigmatical phenomenon that in dream we frequently see two characters (Wesen) simultaneously in one person. On the other hand, it may happen that, by a new sundering, *i.e.*, by a new feeling overstepping the threshold, the old one is driven away, in which case the person beheld suddenly changes form, or there is fusion of two forms. But the psycho-physical threshold is always the line of cleavage, and with the continued retirement of this threshold new lines of cleavage and new forms continually appear.

In proportion to the progress of somnambulic patients towards recovery, their guardians or guides presently declare that they will henceforth come seldom, or for a shorter time, or not at all,* quite as it must be in the projection of subjective states. To that also correspond the external circumstances under which the guides appear. A somnambule wandering through terrible regions sees the guardian spirit on the other side of a chasm, and cannot reach him; the temporal remoteness of the cure being thus spatially

* Perty: 'Mystische Erscheinungen,' i. 245.

symbolized. But as soon as the cure comes about, the guide appears unseparated by the chasm, and in a pleasant valley.* One of Werner's somnambules expressed herself still more plainly. Werner asked her how her health would be when she went on an intended journey. She replied, 'My Albert (guide) cannot be so near to me there, *because thou art not*, but he will still come and relieve me as far as possible.' Physiologically translated, and divested of the dramatic sundering, that means that she will miss the magnetic treatment, but that its after-effects will still be felt. Somnambules often remain at the stage of interior feeling, without external projection of it. Werner's somnambule 'knew positively' that her guide was always near her without seeing him. It was two months before she saw him as image, and even this only gradually became a clear perception.†

(*b*) *The Mind.*—Not bodily conditions alone are externally personified in dream and somnambulism. The spiritual Ego also can be dramatically sundered. This distinctly appears from the fact that the Ego of our dreams can make its entrance in different forms of consciousness. We either sit as spectators in the stalls, unconcerned in the scene enacted before us, or we are ourselves participant in it on the stage, or we are in both capacities at once. In the first case it is the inwardly waking dream-Ego that is the spectator, while translating into externality the feelings emerging from its unconscious sphere; it thus remains purely receptive towards the dream-images, which seem foreign to it (just as its Un-

---

\* 'Archiv,' vii. 2, 46.
† Werner: 'Symb. d. Sprache,' 106.

conscious so seems); and it regards them objectively so long as the sphere of its will\* is untouched by them. But there is an end of this receptivity and objectivity as soon as the importunate images excite the feeling and will of the dreamer, or arise therefrom; then can the dream-Ego under the illusion of reality no longer maintain its indifference, but leaps, as it were, upon the stage. In the third sort of dream, when we are at once spectators and actors, the identity of the Subject is not indeed wholly restored—the two persons remain asunder, but the spectator nevertheless knows the actors as his own doubles. Thus in this case the inner self-consciousness of the dreamer asserts itself, therefore he remains spectator; but along with it is an apparently external consciousness, whose externality is imposed by the fact that its content issues from the Unconscious, so that we stand at the same time upon the stage.

In modern dream literature one constantly meets with an attempt to distribute our dreams in different categories, according to their content and their exciting causes; but each inquirer arrives at a different and more or less arbitrary principle of discrimination. It seems to me that these attempts must be given up, and that the only useful classification is one derived from the formal rôle of the Ego, which would like-

---

\* Will is here used in the larger sense of the word, in which not mere conscious volition, or even volitional power, is signified, but that in the individual character or disposition which determines the emotional value—thus the motive force—of any mental impression or idea. The sphere of the will is all the consciousness that is coloured by feeling, or has an 'interest' for us. To be a motive force in us any new idea or impression must enter into this association at some point.—Tr.

wise give the distinction of dreams with reference to their exciting causes, as the latter are above the threshold of the dream-consciousness or below it. The cleavage-point of the sundering would therefore be also the principle of distribution.

That there can be a severance within the intellectual sphere of dream, that thus the psycho-physical threshold persists in dream, even if in some measure displaced, and that only the representations issuing from the Unconscious lead to the severance, and are transposed outwards, is distinctly proved by many dreams. It is well known that there are processes of understanding which make it eminently clear that the thinking depends on an unconscious activity, and only the final result emerges ready-made into consciousness. This is especially the case with genuine artistic productions, and generally with every fine performance; and on a small scale whenever that happens which in German is called 'einen Einfall,' in French 'un aperçu.' Hartmann speaks of this as follows; and if I premise that I do not understand the Unconscious in Hartmann's sense, as world-substance alone, but conceive it as *individual* metaphysical background of the Ego, I can in this sense fully subscribe to his words:

'If consciousness were the selector, it must be able to see by its own light what was *eligible*, which, as is well known, it is not, since only that which is *already* selected emerges from the background of the Unconscious. If, then, consciousness *were* the selector, it would grope about in absolute darkness, could accordingly not possibly *choose appropriately*, but only *take at random* what first came to hand. . . .

The reflection just made holds good of the association of ideas *in abstract thinking as well as in sensuous imagining and artistic combination.* If a result is to be arrived at, the right idea must readily offer itself at the right time from the storehouse of memory ; and that it is just the *right* idea which appears, for that the Unconscious alone can make provision. All aids and artifices of the understanding can only *facilitate* the office of the Unconscious, but never take it away.

'A suitable and yet simple example is wit, which is a mean between artistic and scientific production, since it pursues artistic aims with, for the most part, abstract material. Every witticism is, according to the common expression, a *flash* (Einfall). The understanding may perhaps make use of aids to facilitate the flash ; practice, especially in the case of puns, can impress the material more vividly on the memory, and altogether strengthen the verbal memory ; talent may endow particular persons with an ever-sparkling wit ; in spite of all that, every single witticism remains a gift from above ; and even those who think they are privileged in this respect, and have wit completely in their power, must have the experience that just when they most wish to compel it, their talent denies them its services, and that nothing but worn-out absurdities or witticisms learned by rote will out of their brain. These folk know also quite well that a bottle of wine is a far readier means of setting their faculty a-going than any intentional effort.'\*

\* Hartmann : 'Phil. des Unbewussten' [vol. i. p. 285 of Mr. Coupland's translation of the ninth edition, Trübner, 1884. I have copied the above passage from Mr. Coupland's translation.—Tr.]

Now if, as already explained, all from the Unconscious which oversteps the threshold is transposed outwards, so with regard to intellectual processes, every idea induced by involuntary association must appear as an *external* image, and every such suggestion (Einfall), every flash of wit, must be placed in the mouth of another. And so it is in fact. The whole fluidity and mutability of the dream-images depend on the conversion of abstractly associated ideas into transitory images. And since the intellectual process, whereby anything 'occurs' (einfallt) to us has its course in the Unconscious, it must in dream take on the form of the dramatic sundering. This is so much the case, that when puns and witticisms are forthcoming in our dreams, those that arrive impromptu and without trouble are placed in the mouth of another, while those which are the products of conscious thought remain our own. Thus Boswell reports an account by Dr. Johnson of a dream in which he was engaged with another in an argumentative contention, and how he was vexed by the superiority of his opponent. No wonder; for the dreamer, Johnson, was split into two persons at the line of cleavage of the threshold; the one worked with unconscious talent, the other with the conscious understanding, and therefore came off the worse.

Bertrand gives a similar example. He was asked by another in a dream if he knew the origin of the word 'dame.' He replied that he did not; but being desired to consider, he replied, after some time, that it must come from the Latin *domina*. But this derivation was denied by the other, who looked at him as if in the enjoyment of his perplexity. When at length Bertrand gave it up, the other replied, laughing, 'Don't you see that it comes from the Latin word *damnare*, because we are plunged into perdition by women?'*

Thus all processes of understanding, which have the character of sudden suggestion (Einfalls), and in which consciousness is not productive but receptive, lead in dream to the dramatic sundering of personalities. This must be the case also with acts of memory, which are often of sudden occurrence, when the recovery of what was sought must happen dramatically. Maury relates that the word *Mussidan* once suddenly came into his mind. He knew that it was a town in France, but where situated he had forgotten. Some time afterwards he met a person in dream, who said he came from Mussidan. When the dreamer asked where this town was, the other told him the Department of Dordogne, of which it is the capital. On awaking, Maury remembered his dream, looked in the map, and found to his surprise that his dream companion was better up in geography than himself.† He rightly observed that evidently he had only transferred his own recollection to the mouth of another; but how it is that first in such cases the dramatic severance happens can only be explained by the psycho-physical threshold.

There is a dream well known among students, that, years after the college 'final,' they seem to be sitting at the examination, and to be unable to answer the questions put. It is only a weaker form of this that I have often myself dreamed, after the lapse of twenty-

* Bertrand: 'Traité du Somnambulisme,' 441.
† Maury: 'Le Sommeil et les Rêves,' 142.

five years, that the examination was approaching, and that I was quite unprepared for it. Now it often happens in the examination that a schoolfellow answers the question in which we have failed. Van Goens relates :

' I dreamed I was in the Latin class, at the head of it, and determined to keep my place if possible. The tutor gave out a Latin phrase, but I remained dumb, and cudgelled my brain in vain to find the translation. I saw the boy next to me making signs of impatience to be asked—a proof that he knew the answer. The thought that I must give up my place to him nearly enraged me. But it was in vain I thought—I could in no way construe the phrase. The tutor at length passed me over, and said to the next one, ' Now it is your turn.' This scholar immediately explained the meaning distinctly ; and the interpretation was so simple that I could not conceive how I had missed it.'*

Van Goens adds that, after twenty-six years, it is still unintelligible to him how the soul, which in vain seeks something with the greatest effort, can be in one second the same soul which knows the same thing very well, while imagining itself, at the same time, not to know, but to hear it said by another.

The above theory solves the difficulty very simply. And all dreams, in which we ourselves put a question which another answers, belong to this category, and it can only be from the fact that this answer emerges from the unconscious, that it is unfamiliar to us, and is always taken for a disclosure of something we knew not.

* Moritz : ' Magazin zur Erfahrungsseelenkunde,' xi. 2, 88.

But this does not show how it happens that these questions in dream are put at all. The questioning is evidently a dramatic deliberation, as the answer is a dramatic finding. When in waking we try in vain to remember something, perhaps a name, it often suddenly occurs, quite without premeditation, hours after we have ceased thinking about it. There is therefore thinking, unconscious, yet directed to an aim, the result of which then comes into consciousness. This thinking is also possible in dream, and it explains the action of many night-walkers who perform literary work in dream. Therefore we cannot exclude even the process of unconscious consideration in dream, the conclusion of which then introduces itself as an answer from a foreign source, after a dramatic representation of the preliminary wavering and seeking. A similar wavering is apparent when we utter a word, and at the same moment perceive that it is not the right one. In this case we correct ourselves also in waking—in dream we are corrected by another. Maury, when he was learning English, spoke that language with someone in a dream, and wishing to say to him that he had called on him the day before, used the words: 'I called *for* you yesterday.' The other at once told him that this expression was wrong, and that he should have said, 'I called *on* you yesterday.' On awaking, Maury looked and found that his censor was right.*

The first tendency to this dramatic sundering can even show itself in waking, but is not developed to the point of perception (zum Bilde); as when we are vexed with, or reproach ourselves for an irrevocable

* Maury: 'Le Sommeil,' etc., 143.

act, this internal dissension expressing itself, with many very emphatically, as by striking the forehead, etc., and it is not without psychological interest that they address themselves on such occasions with the 'thou,' as though concerned with another person of their Subject.

It would be impossible that the events experienced in dream should come as from without and unexpectedly, often even occasioning us the greatest surprise —while yet we are evidently ourselves the authors of the whole—unless the soul of the dream-author and the soul of the dream-spectator were strangers to each other—that is, unless they were at least divided by a psycho-physical threshold. And so, also, those dreams which bring interchange of speech instead of actions, must be the dramatic presentation of intellectual processes, passing on this side and on that side the threshold.

We can now no longer find it strange that in the heightened sleep-life of somnambulism the dramatic sundering is so frequent, and that the somnambules have their 'guides' constantly at hand, to whom they put questions, and from whom they get answers. The literature of that subject is full of such instances. But whoever also studies the phenomena of 'possession' and insanity, will no longer doubt that in all these cases the psycho-physical threshold is the line of cleavage of the dramatic sundering.

Like the multiplication of objects by two opposite mirrors, the sundering of consciousness in dream seems always on the increase. It happens, for instance, in dream, that we are at the same time spectators and actors, when again the two cases are possible that the spectator either recognises, or does not recognise his own double in the actor. This 'double-going' is quite another case from the falling asunder of the Subject into a number of *different* persons, and is again to be distinguished from that in which we mingle and take part among the stage company without leaving our psychical centre behind in the parterre—that is, without persistence of a self-consciousness that would unite the plurality of consciousnesses.

It is to me, I confess, doubtful, whether such a subject-consciousness happens in dream. To describe it, not in the abstract but perceptibly, it must have the following character: When I am active *merely* on the stage, I see myself there, it is true, yet only so as in waking I can look down on my body and see my limbs, without my sight being an object to itself. The eye cannot see itself. But if I am at the same time sitting as a spectator, my whole form appears upon the stage, as in waking I can see myself in the mirror, and look into my own eyes. This last case is again to be distinguished, according to whether the 'double' is known as such or not, and again, whether if there is this knowledge, his proceedings are strange to me, like those of another person, or not.

Volkelt relates two dreams, from which there is at least an apparent possibility of the self-duplication of the Ego *upon the stage*. In dream he saw himself with sunken cheeks, rolling about in bed, while at the same time he was anxiously pacing up and down the room, with the idea that his second self had poisoned himself, and was near death; but, with all his anxiety, it seemed to him, also, that he would not himself be hurt by the other's death. In like manner, one of his friends dreamed that he surprised his beloved in the embraces of a strange man, and that he was about to attack the offender, but observed that the latter had his own appearance, and consoled himself with the thought that he had kissed the maiden himself.* Both these dreams prove, indeed, the double-going of the sundered personal consciousness; but they do not prove the Subject-consciousness, for, in the first case, the anxious walker in the room knew not his psychical identity with the poisoned man; and in the second, although the lover knew his identity with the offender, yet both were *on the stage.* Thus, even in these dreams, the Subject-consciousness, which should look on without acting, is wanting.

It would be very important to know if that ever happens in dream. We might thus obtain a decision on the very old problem of self-consciousness, and solve it by facts of empirical psychology of a kind not possible in waking.

All modern philosophy recognises that there can be no self-consciousness without sundering. In self-consciousness the Ego appears doubled, first as being, then as knowing. Only thus can self-consciousness contain anything: I know that I am. It therefore seems that no other explanation of this phenomenon is possible than that in analogy with dream we should take the facts simply as they are, and just say that in self-consciousness a dramatic sundering of the Ego takes place, since a single Subject falls apart into two persons, only that in waking there is no illusion of sense.

* Volkelt: 'Die Traumphantasie,' 25.

Defective and obscure as the memory of the content of our dreams often is, it is still more difficult to recollect the forms of consciousness occurring in them; and I must therefore leave here undecided the question whether a pure Subject-consciousness grasping together the personal consciousnesses which remain mutually alien is possible. Such could be represented as a larger circle, enclosing two smaller excentric ones.

But the general fact of the dramatic sundering in dream is already important enough. It gives us at least such an advantage as perhaps an astronomer might derive from the discovery that two stars together have a common point of gravity lying between them, although the further problem whether besides these two stars there is yet a third, as central sun, remains unsolved.

(c) *The Human Enigma.*—It is possible that some readers of the last chapter may censure me for refinements, satisfactory perhaps to the professional psychologist, but of no general interest. To remove this impression, and to indemnify them for their trouble, in what follows there will be deduced from the foregoing results certain consequences which may at any rate claim to be of very general interest. Philosophy has always recognised that the greatest enigma of Nature is man himself. But it is just on this enigma, whose solution concerns our highest interests, a solution upon which, according to Kant, 'depends the true and lasting welfare of the human race,'\* that the results already obtained throw an important light.

\* Kant's Werke: 'Rosenkranz,' xi. 1, 19.

The dramatic sundering of the Ego in dream will be admitted by everyone to be an indubitable fact. Now from the fact of such sunderings result two important propositions, which can the less be doubted in that they are simply the analytical dissection of the fact itself.

(*a*) It is *psychologically* possible that a subject consists of two persons, without the latter knowing their identity with each other, and with the subject. This assertion is not in the least invalidated by the objection that dreams are merely illusions. They are so indeed ; but the *psychological* fact that our consciousness can persist in such a deception remains; and it is only from the fact of this illusion that we shall now further conclude : Namely, that what in dream is psychologically not only possible, but actual, is evidently possible also outside dream ; for the consciousness which invents our dreams can neither change its whole nature, nor disappear with waking, but at most can retire for the waking man into the Unconscious. The sun still shines, even when intercepted by clouds.

Now provisionally supposing that fact of dream, the sundering, to be also a fact outside dream (only that in waking there is no perceptive illusion), then would our sensuous, personal consciousness not be exhaustive of our whole being, but would light up only a part of it. There would exist besides this sense-consciousness—our earth-face, as it were—yet another personal consciousness—an Unconscious for this earth-face—and even a comprehensive Subject-consciousness, uniting the two persons, would be possible. We should thus resemble the double star above mentioned, but of which one star would be in obscurity, and possibly in the deepest ground of our being the double star would have its central sun.

Now if our self-consciousness is not conterminous with our being, the physiological psychologists, who allow to man only his earth-face, strive in vain to solve his enigma. They do not deny the Unconscious, but they say it is in itself unconscious, and not only so for our personal Ego. But as positive assertion, this is evidently illogical, for the earth-face can pronounce only upon itself, not upon what is beyond its horizon. Were the Unconscious for itself unconscious, it evidently could not take on the form of consciousness in the dramatic sundering in dream-life; still less would the fact be explicable that in somnambulism there awakes an inner, second Ego, which speaks of the bearer of the earthly aspect as of a distinct person, naming it 'the other,' or 'the others.'

Now as this second Ego cannot possibly be produced by the magnetic sleep from nothing, but can only be awakened for our consciousness, it must exist before and after, though unconsciously for our daily Ego. . . . Thus it follows from the facts of somnambulism, that not in dream only does our Subject fall asunder in two persons, but we are always in this condition, though without the earthly side knowing of the second Ego. There may well, however, be a knowledge by this latter.

There is no objection to calling this second Ego the soul, provided we do not confound it with the popular conception of soul, which identifies soul with the sense-consciousness, and asserts the indestructibility of our earthly side; whereas upon the latter so little stress is to be laid that we could be content to expose it to the materialistic account of the physiologists, by whom, at most, would one of our persons be explained, but not the second Ego, not the Subject.

At the present day, the conception, Soul, is treated as mythical, and psychology is taught without Psyche. But from an unprejudiced study of dream we may recognise the necessary revival of this conception in a higher form, no more as wholly opposed to the body, but as identical therewith; identical, however, only in the sense in which the two persons of the dream are so in dream. Physiologists reject the soul, because they would explain man unitarily, in which they are quite right. They are for monism, not the dualism of an immortal soul and a mortal body. But as the persons of a dream in the Subject of the dream have a common centre, and as the dualism of a double star is monistically suppressed in the common point of gravity about which they circle, so also have sense-consciousness and the Unconscious a common centre, and this doctrine of the soul is not dualistic, but monistic—that is, it explains man unitarily.

It is a logical consequence of the dramatic division in dream, that the science of the future, far from giving up the conception of soul, much more probably will find itself necessitated to set up, besides the earth-aspect and the soul, spirit, or a self-consciousness comprehending them, as a third. Even if this third be not yet provable, our first inference from the act of severance in dream has yielded this result, that only in the direction indicated shall we succeed in the solution of the human problem. To proceed to our second inference.

(β) It is *psychologically* possible that two persons of a single Subject may converse with one another, without knowing their identity. Again, this is a fact of dream which as a *psychological* fact is untouched by the objection that dreams are illusions. Certainly they are, but the fact of an illusion is not an illusory fact. If in dream two persons of one Subject can discourse together as friends, there exists the logical possibility of this in waking; it is possible that we are in communication with our second Ego, without our knowing it as identical with us.

Since according to the old logical rule, principles of explanation are not to be multiplied unnecessarily, we must adhere to the dramatic severance as long as it is in any way sufficient for the phenomena to be explained. Before all must we adhere to it, while we are dealing with the sleep-life; we will therefore either set down all the 'guides' and 'guardian-spirits' of the somnambulists as wholly subjective constructions, so long as they show no other marks than our dream-figures, or explain them only from the dramatic severance of the actual man, from his double nature, when they betray signs never to be met with in the mere dream-figures. The third possibility, that the guides are actual third persons, that is, other Subjects, must remain excluded until they exhibit characteristics not to be explained by even the double nature of man. But as we do not know the faculties of our second Ego, nor, therefore, how much they will explain, this is a case which cannot easily occur.

Thus, when Tasso asserted of his visions, that

they could not belong to his phantasy, because what he learned from them exceeded his knowledge, he reasoned rightly; but it does not thence follow that these visions were foreign Subjects who inspired him, for there remains as the third possibility his own double nature, by means of which the two persons of his own Subject acted dramatically on one another.

Pure subjective illusions occur in the ordinary dream severance, as in the example already cited, in which I cannot find an answer, and it is supplied by my schoolfellow. This is merely dramatized memory; it cannot in this case be said that the one person was ignorant of what the other knew; it was only not known at first, and then it recurred. But if we add to this incident the further character, that I received an answer which had never been in my consciousness, and which exceeded its capacities, we should then be obliged to explain this severance from the double nature of man, and to admit, that by the displacement of the psycho-physical threshold in sleep, a part of my unconscious was projected into my normal Ego. The displacement of the threshold approximates to the growth of a new sense, or at least to the exaltation of the normal sensibility, wherefrom new information could unquestionably be obtained. In somnambulism that often occurs. Richard Gorwitz,* for instance, showed remarkable faculties in the magnetic sleep, but he referred them always to a black man, whom he believed himself to see. If a stranger entered the house, he was in-

* Gorwitz: 'Richards natürlich magnetischer Schlaf,' Leipzig, 1837.

formed of it by his mannikin; if he knew what remedy would be useful to him, it was this mannikin who prescribed it. If there was something he did not know, he said that the mannikin—his second Ego—had left; in general his expressions betrayed an oscillation of the psycho-physical threshold, as by saying that the mannikin only gave him information 'when he was in a good humour.'

The two results for psychology and metaphysic, which are yielded by the fact of the dramatic severance, are thus decidedly very fruitful. The one conducts us on the right way to solve the problem of man; the other enables us to reclaim a great province from the region of spirit-seeing, and to distribute it between the psychology of the earthly aspect and that of metaphysic.

The dramatic division of the Ego thus draws a thick line through half of all the stories of spirits, by explaining them from our faculty of projecting and personifying subjective conditions. And were this division, the falling asunder of the Subject into two persons, not merely incidental to dream, but the metaphysical formula for the explanation of man, many other such stories could be similarly dealt with, though there would remain the spirit, namely, our own, which indeed is first rightly proved by faculties not derivable from our earthly nature, and which are manifest in the dramatic division. That such faculties do actually emerge in somnambulism will be shown in the next chapter. Our first deduction was the existence of a soul, having a wider sphere than that of its earthly nature, but separated from the latter merely by the psycho-physical threshold, thus remaining connected with it in a monistic sense. That, however, leads to the further question, how far the soul, the Unconscious, projects beyond the consciousness. But that we do not know, and it can only be proved that the projection is very extensive. We have to distinguish between our sense-consciousness, our soul-consciousness, and the still problematical Subject-consciousness. Representing these as three unequal circles one within the other, the sense-consciousness filling the smallest, the soul-consciousness the middle one, and the Subject-consciousness the largest, the periphery of the innermost circle would stand for the psycho-physical threshold. By its displacement in the rising series to the ecstatic conditions, sleep, somnambulism, trance, apparent death, etc., the centre of the inner circle is more and more obscured; that is, the sense-consciousness tends more and more to disappear, but the circle itself is widened; that is, the consciousness extends itself more over the region of the so-called Unconscious. Already in common sleep the Ego of sense sinks; in the magnetic sleep the line of the inner circle is so far thrown back towards the periphery of the outer one that the somnambulists speak of their sense-Ego —the inner circle—only in the third person. That happens also in delirium, and is conventionally expressed by saying, 'He is beside himself,' 'He is wandering.' The *content* of consciousness in these conditions naturally retains its full reality, even when it is dramatically transferred to another person. Now there is no condition of ecstasy in which the outermost circle can be completely reached. The proof of this is easily adduced. There is no condition of sleep with ecstasy *without* visions. Visions depend on the dramatic severance, but the latter is only possible on the condition that a conscious and an unconscious, with a threshold dividing them, are both present. Whence it follows that the foundation of visions must be our own unconscious spirit, with which we are in communication, and with dramatic severance, just because the consciousness does not illuminate the whole outer circle, but an Unconscious always remains.

It thence happens that the progressive displacement of the threshold of sensibility with the deepening of sleep multiplies also the divisions of the Ego; that is, continually brings new dream-figures upon the boards without the retirement of those already present. Therefore in the crises of somnambulists the number of their visionary forms increases. So Brendel relates of the somnambule Höhne, 'The greater or less multitude of angels present determines with Höhne the different stages of her clairvoyance, indicating and expressing them; in her ordinary sleep-waking condition there are but a few guardian spirits, in exalted states they number from six to ten, in profound sleep sixteen are present.'\* This is evidently an effect of the gradual deepening of the sleep, with which continually deeper layers of the Unconscious and its faculties are raised above the threshold, giving occasion to multiplied personifications. With the insane also the fluctuation of the threshold is in the same way frequently apparent. Boismont describes

\* F. Brendel: 'Kritik der kommissarischen Berichte und Protakolle über die ärzliche Behandlung der somnambule Christiane Höhne,' 138 (Freiberg, 1840).

an insane person, who was able to place before himself his own double, conversing and contending with him, being often to his vexation refuted. The same alienist says of his patients that they often conversed with three, and even up to twelve and fifteen invisible persons. He adds that those who spoke several languages heard the strange voices the more or less distinctly as they themselves spoke the language of them well or ill: a circumstance most clearly indicating that it was their own Subject which divided itself into such visionary forms.*

But if consciousness in even our highest ecstasies does not exhaust our whole being, leaving beyond an unmeasurable fund of the Unconscious, which can furnish new divisions, then certainly man appears as a being of groundless depth, reaching with his roots into the metaphysical region, which will perhaps, however, remain always closed for his sense-consciousness, that being capable of no state in which the psycho-physical threshold could be carried back into this region. Whoever will explain visions *without* dramatic severance, thus ascribe to them reality, must conceive man as a double being, with one foot on the earth, the other in the realm of the spirits, with whom he holds intercourse. Whereas, on the other hand, if visions are explained by the dramatic severance, man is in that case also a double being, but with both sides rooted in a common stem; and even if from these visions we obtain but slight information concerning the side of our being which lies beyond the threshold of our self-consciousness, still the problem of a transcendental psychology is given, to be solved

* Boismont: 'Des Hallucinations,' 28, 583.

by later science, without abandoning monism, nor the conformity of all phenomena to law.

The double nature of man remains alike irrefragable, whether we see in the visions of ecstatics transcendent beings, or recognise in them only our own dramatized transcendental being. On this point of our double nature, thus at any rate believers in spirits and sceptics can join hands in reconciliation.

# CHAPTER IV.

### SOMNAMBULISM.

#### 1. *Natural Somnambulism.*

It is not enough for the scientific definition and characterization of a body to take account of the properties which it exhibits under normal circumstances. Rather must these circumstances be artificially altered, until they offer occasion for the manifestation of qualities usually latent. Thus the physicist and the chemist subject bodies to experiment, in the special arrangements of which the question is put to the body: What art thou? And the body answers by the way in which imposed conditions react upon it.

The definition of man, the most interesting object, but also the greatest riddle of Nature, has not yet been found, notwithstanding the thousands of years in which the question has been disputed, only because he has been almost exclusively studied in his normal condition, but not subjected to experiment by the alteration of circumstances.

That will not remain so always. Our grandchildren will pursue experimental psychology, as we experimental chemistry, and they will perhaps solve the problem of man by giving occasion, through alteration of his normal circumstances, to modes of activity usually latent, but affording us an insight into his nature.

But in what manner, by alteration of circumstances, can the psychically normal man be brought to abnormal functions? To answer this question, we must first know on what circumstances the psychically normal condition rests.

The psychically normal man is characterized, if we know what influences he experiences from the side of natural things, and in what ways he can react upon these influences. We must know his sensibility and his modes of activity. These two factors form the psychical man, and stand to one another in exact relation; the more susceptibilities, the more activities. But of the natural influences to which man is subjected, those only can come into consideration which produce a distinct impression on his consciousness. Influences which, if they occur, do not come to consciousness in him, occasion no reaction, and are therefore without concern for his psychical definition.

From the standpoint of every psychical being, Nature is thus divided into two halves: the one acting upon consciousness, the other not. Physically and indirectly, if not directly, no doubt the human organism is influenced by all things in Nature; but it is a fundamental law, that natural processes only affect consciousness when the spatial or molecular movement from them possesses a certain degree of strength. This necessary minimum of strength on the objective side of Nature corresponds on the subjective side of man to that degree of susceptibility which is designated 'the threshold of sensibility.'

This threshold is further called 'psycho-physical,' because in every affection of consciousness a physical movement of Nature, crossing the threshold of sensibility, is converted into a psychical feeling. Natural processes of insufficient strength remain below man's threshold of sensibility, do not come to consciousness in him.

The psychical normal man, the object of our inquiry, is therefore to be characterized by the possession of a normal human threshold of sensibility. But the experimental psychology, which is so highly to be desired, is only then possible if man's normal threshold of sensibility can be so displaced, that natural influences, ordinarily remaining below the threshold, may be felt. To these abnormal influences of Nature would answer, in reaction on the side of man, abnormal psychical activities. The more we learned to know of these, the more could we continually understand of the definition of man. The solution of the human problem is thus possible on the condition of an experimental psychology; but the latter is only possible if man's threshold of sensibility is alterable, can be made to shift; impossible if, on the contrary, this threshold is fixed and immovable.

But it is displaceable. Apart from slight displacements in waking life, occurring in morbid conditions, or even through mere direction of attention, the organism experiences daily a very important displacement of its threshold when it falls to sleep. In sleep the psycho-physical activity of man sinks for a while below the threshold.* Therefore sleep is accompanied by an inner waking, and to this a content of feeling

* Fechner: 'Elemente der Psychophysik,' ii. 439.

is given by the displacement of the threshold: a content which does not enter consciousness in the day-waking state, because in presence of the grosser influences of the outer world these gentle excitations cannot effectuate themselves, and therefore go on below the threshold. These excitations, for the most part arising from the inner sphere of the body, are the causes of our dreams.

Thus sleep is no mere negation of waking, but contains also positive sides. It displaces the threshold of sensibility so that the world of day disappears from consciousness; but just for this reason is the inner consciousness susceptible to influences which in waking do not overstep the threshold. So has the setting of the sun not only the negative result that darkness overspreads the earth, but also the positive one, that the weaker beams of the stars, before lost in the greater light, then become manifest.

The processes which come to the inner consciousness in sleep take place also in waking; they only remain unconscious. So sleep does not produce new influences on the organism, and new reactions of the same, but it raises over the threshold those which were below it during waking; it thus introduces to consciousness new influences and modes of reaction, which reactions take the form of dreams.

The more the threshold of sensibility is displaced, the more positive sides of sleep would become apparent, producing always new psychical reactions. Therefore would deep sleep, as connected with the greatest displacement of the threshold, without doubt afford us very valuable disclosures concerning the nature of man, if it were not unfortunately lost to memory. The question arises for experimental psychology whether dreams can be preserved before they are forgotten, or if this were not possible, whether dreamers could be brought to speech.

Both these problems will undoubtedly find their solution, which has indeed already partially happened, and that in somnambulism. Thus this condition, the clear inner waking of the deep magnetic sleep, is the natural foundation for the experimental psychology of the future. It therefore deserves to be studied with much greater zeal than heretofore. The human problem confronts us still in such gigantic dimensions that it is only a reproach to the stupidity of the materialists, who decry it by asserting that man is a mere chemical combination, and nothing more; this problem can, however, only be solved by subjecting man to experiment in the somnambulic state. For, as Mesmer said, 'The faculties of man are manifested through the effects of magnetism, just as the properties of other bodies are developed by the elevation of heat which chemistry supplies.'

The psychical faculties of man which come into play in somnambulism are simply reactions upon such natural influences as do not cross the threshold of sensibility of the normal man. Therefore somnambulism induces susceptibility to *finer* influences than are received by the senses of the waking person. Now, as the senses in waking evoke faculties the more remarkable, the more finely they are organized, so must the sense educed in somnambulism, receiving influences too fine for the day-senses, release faculties superior to those of the waking man. In fact, these faculties are so remarkable that already many a physician has been misled in his enthusiasm to declare somnambulism to be a higher condition than that of waking life, while others would see in it a falling back into the instinctive nature-life of animals.

Here, as so often, the truth lies midway. The displacement of the threshold of sensibility in the different conditions of sleep is not continually progressive, but often very wavering, and so accordingly must be the psychical faculties awakened by this displacement. Conformably to this, the utterances of even the same somnambules and in the same crisis are of very unequal value. But we must be withheld by another reason from over-estimating this condition. Somnambulism is the influence of Nature and of men in presence of a passive state; man is therein psychically decentralized, mostly in complete dependence on the magnetiser, against whom it is only seldom that a self-conscious will asserts itself. So far somnambulism is not a state of equal dignity with waking. On the other hand, it is quite indisputable that in somnambulism faculties are often revealed, if only transitorily, far superior to those of men whose outer senses stand open to the world, and whose threshold of sensibility is at the normal point.

The question is thus suggested, whether upon other planets there may exist beings of more favourable constitution in regard to this threshold of sensibility, in whom the faculties, which in somnambulism are exhibited only inconstantly and germinally, would be found in full development, and as a normal possession? Whoever accepts the doctrine of evolution will not doubt the existence of such beings standing evidently higher than man; he can, at least, not deny that such beings lie so much the more probably in the womb of the future, as man, standing at the present apex of earthly organization, prophetically announces them in the rudimentary way.

If, however, the somnambulist germinally indicates such higher beings, without belonging to them, somnambulism cannot, indeed, be considered a state superior to waking; but, regarded from the philosophical standpoint, it is more important than waking. For every intellectual advance is either merely historical, within constant limits of sensibility as determined by the threshold, or biological — that is, conditioned by a favourable displacement of the threshold. Every historical advance has, during its course, its boundaries, namely, in the insuperable threshold of sensibility, beyond which lies the solution of the deepest problems of humanity. Therefore is somnambulism philosophically more important than waking; it reaches over man as capable of development historically, anticipating his biological successor; and though this anticipation is but germinal, yet the study of somnambulism shows clearly that inexhaustible results for the doctrine of evolution are to be obtained from the impermanence of the threshold. At the same time, the claim of materialists to appropriate the doctrine of development for the support of their views is very clearly seen to be mere presumption. A doctrine which asserts that only the sensuous is actual, and which denies the world lying below our threshold of sensibility, stands in radical contradiction to the Evolution theory.

Somnambulism, just because depending on the displacement of the threshold of sensibility, offers to psychology a whole cargo of new and very weighty problems. Now, it is in the nature of man to prefer erroneous solutions to a confession of insolubility; on which account his explanations always take the form censured by Bacon : ' That which is in itself new is nevertheless usually conceived in the same way as the old.'* That has also happened in this case. Somnambulism is a phenomenon in itself new and quite peculiar, and therefore cannot be judged in the same way as what is old, that is, according to analogies of the psychical conditions of waking ; because in it we are concerned with the Psyche below the threshold, but in waking with the Psyche which is above. From this alone is apparent the perversity of explaining somnambulism, with its marked peculiarity, according to psychological laws of the waking life. The already-cited story which Livingstone relates of the negro to whom he presented a spoon, should be read by the physiological opponent of somnambulism with the addition, ' *de te fabula narratur.*'

Even the ordinary dream demands this special explanation. If we analyse our dreams, at first sight, certainly, they seem to contain merely the materials of the waking life thrown together in a disconnected, irregular state, and only the waking life which holds together its rationally-combined representations seems decentralized in dream. But, with closer observation, it is easy to see that dream also has its positive sides, for as it is connected with the displacement of the threshold of sensibility, the sleeper then first experiences influences, formerly remaining below

* Bacon : 'Nov. Org.,' 1, § 34.

the threshold, from his own interior bodily sphere; his consciousness thus obtains a new content. On these influences the Psyche reacts with faculties latent in waking life; thus the self-consciousness also receives a new content.

With the displacement of the threshold of sensibility, therefore, are opened a transcendental world, closed to the day consciousness, and a transcendental Ego. Here, again, is a proof that the normal consciousness does not exhaust the world, nor the normal self-consciousness the Ego. We must, therefore, speak of a doubled consciousness and of a doubled Ego in us, lying this side and that side of the normal threshold, and that all the more, as the two Egos only alternately appear without interchanging the content of their consciousness. The awakening somnambulist reverts, without memory of his dreams, to the point of time at which he fell asleep. Moreover, the faculties corresponding to the perceptions of the two Egos are so very different, both in form and content, that we are obliged to speak of the duplication of personalities, notwithstanding the displacement of the threshold; but by reason of this impermanence of the threshold, the dualism of persons is again monistically resolvable into the unity of a common Subject. But since, according to the figure of the two weights, the transcendental Ego awaking in sleep awakes the more clearly, the greater the loss of the day-man's consciousness, the condition of deepest sleep must necessarily be the most favourable for the distinct definition and characterization of the transcendental Subject.

That condition, however, throws us back upon somnambulism for a solution of the human problem.

Somnambulism is exalted sleep. To understand this phenomenon rightly, we must first attempt to ascertain its physiological significance for the economy of the organism. With this view an explanatory consideration of spontaneously occurring somnambulism is requisite, and it must be asked to what end Nature introduces so important a deepening of sleep.

The intensity of every sleep corresponds to the need of the organism, and is induced by physiological causes not sufficiently known, a fact which must not make us overlook the teleological character of sleep, which is shown in its effect. The more the brain-life is suppressed, and the longer it is in a condition of complete rest, the more and longer is the recuperative force active in the organism. Sleep restores the forces worn out in waking; therefore we feel refreshed when we have slept well, and the intensity of the effect corresponds either to the duration or to the depth of our sleep.

In illnesses, if the organism is much weakened, a sleep of extraordinary length is often the crisis, in which the change for the better occurs. Every physician knows the healing power of this critical sleep.

Long-lasting sleep is frequent, and its curative tendency was observed before modern times. Schubert relates, from the 'Philosophical Transactions,' the case of a boy who slept for sixteen weeks, and when at length he awoke, the disease and the desire for sleep had both departed. In the 'Acta Eruditorum' of 1707 is an account of a sleep which lasted, first fourteen days, then six months. Fiolet describes a sleep of four years, interrupted with but short waking intervals.* Micrulius reports of an aged priest in

* Schubert: 'Geschichte der Seele,' i. 245.

Stettin, who, having to read three masses on Christmas night, after the first felt the need of a little rest, and dropped in his cell into a sleep of thirteen days.\* The physician Mayo even knew of a girl of twelve years old who fell into a sleep which lasted thirteen years, so that she grew up in it from a child to a mature woman.† Similar cases, often giving rise to suspicion of simulation, have now and then been reported in our own day.‡

Now it seems to me that the physiological importance of spontaneous somnambulism lies in this, that herein the curative force of Nature sinks the organism into a sleep, the depth of which stands for long duration. If, without prejudice to physiological causes, the long sleep, and the deep sleep of somnambulists, have a teleological significance, that suggests the view that even the remarkable psychical faculties appearing in somnambulism are an extension in the same direction of this teleological principle—those, at least, which are connected with disease and its cure. Seeing with what instinctive certainty somnambules give information concerning the character of their disease, concerning its causes and development, and the requisite treatment and remedies to be applied, one is much disposed to say with Schopenhauer: 'Nature only then truly comes to clairvoyance, when its blindly-working restorative force does not suffice for the removal of the disease, but needs assistance from without, which now is rightly prescribed in the clairvoyant condition by the patients themselves.

\* Micrulius: 'Altes Pommerland,' ii. 369.
† Mayo: 'Truths in Popular Superstitions,' 107.
‡ [In fact, hardly a year passes without reports of several such alleged cases in the newspapers.—Tr.]

Thus to this end of self prescription she introduces clairvoyance. . . . Thus in the one case and in the other, it is Nature herself that kindles the light, by which to seek and afford the help which the organism needs *from without.* The application of the gift of seership of the somnambules, once developed, to other things than their own condition of health, is a merely accidental use, and even misuse, of the same.'*

This opinion of Schopenhauer's is, as said, very specious, but is logically not unavoidable. For it is conceivable, that not only the clairvoyance which is applied beyond the bodily sphere of disease is accidental, but generally that all clairvoyance is only accidental to the somnambulic state. Somnambulism would then not be the *cause from which* clairvoyance arises, but simply the condition *without which it cannot arise.* Physiologically regarded, there would then be no direct causal connection between somnambulism and clairvoyance, and even teleologically regarded, the remarkable psychical faculties of somnambulism would not lie in the direction of an extension of a teleogically acting curative force of Nature. There would, indeed, be given the causal, and at the same time teleological connection between the recuperative force of the organism—merely a collective designation for the individual organic forces co-operating—and the deep sleep introduced by physiological causes, in other words, the complete suppression of the sense-consciousness. But, on the other hand, we should no longer be directly introduced to the inner waking of the transcendental Subject within this loss of consciousness; and deep sleep would be only a condition

* Schopenhauer: ' Ueber Geisterschen.'

of clairvoyance, not its cause, just as the going down of the sun is only the condition, not the cause, of the shining of the stars.

It is the more necessary to keep in view this distinction between cause and condition, because the ordinary sleep also is not the cause, but merely the condition of the inner waking which shows itself as dream. The internal feelings which give occasion to our dream-images are present in waking also, but remain below the threshold. So, perhaps, the visions of somnambules are not newly produced, but only cross the threshold, and if the displacement of this is defective and wavering, then—as frequently happens—these visions are so also. If, finally, deep sleep is not the physical cause, but only the occasion of the inner waking, that disposes of the chief objection urged by scepticism against artificial somnambulism, that it is naturally inconceivable how magnetic passes can make anyone clairvoyant.

Schopenhauer's teleological *propter hoc*, according to which consciousness is pressed into the service of the blind curative force of Nature, may thus be changed into a mere *cum hoc*, the transcendental consciousness manifesting itself when, but not because, the sensuous consciousness is suppressed. Moreover, for the present purpose, it is quite indifferent which of the two opinions the reader will adopt; what is here to be proved being merely the existence of the transcendental Subject, and for that it does not much signify whether deep sleep is the cause or only the occasion of its introduction.

For the physician, on the contrary, this distinction is very important. For it appears that our physicians explain absolutely nothing at bottom, when they curtly put aside somnambulism as disease and hysteria. If, as to its cause, somnambulism is frequently morbid, it can yet be quite healthy as to its psychical content, as soon as deep sleep is recognised as mere condition and occasion of the entrance of the transcendental Subject. As little as night is the cause of the stars, being only the condition of their visibility, is hysteria the cause of clairvoyance. Somnambulism is not only no disease, but, on the contrary, heals the diseased, directly, through its deep sleep, indirectly, from the fact that in this deep sleep somnambules are capable of self-prescription.

That the psychical faculties of man can be exalted through disease, just because there is this distinction between cause and condition, is shown frequently also in insanity, since this is often the occasion for such functions of the transcendental Subject as have the greatest resemblance to the phenomena of somnambulism. Mesmer, therefore, seems to have been quite right when he called severe diseases of the nervous system—such as Epilepsy, Catalepsy, Insanity, etc.— an incomplete somnambulism, which could be healed if the efforts of the organism to overcome the disease were reinforced in the same direction by application of artificially induced somnambulism.

Physiologically considered, the somnambulic sleep is therefore one of the forms of the curative force of Nature ; for in waking there is heightened sensibility of the organism, in sleep heightened restorative force. The curative force of Nature therefore suppresses the sense-consciousness when the enfeebled organism needs to be strengthened by exaltation of the restorative functions. Hippokrates knew that, when he said that in mania ecstasy was good.*

But the first philosophical interest of somnambulism is certainly on account of the inner wakening introduced in the absence of sense-consciousness, when the displacement of the threshold of sensibility enables the usually insensible modes of action of natural things to be felt, and therewith usually latent faculties of the Subject to be liberated. These faculties are of such a remarkable nature that they are still always doubted by rationalistic scepticism. I must, however, reserve the account of them for a special work. Here I will only adduce two examples, choosing those which are the most violently disputed, viz., clairvoyance and the healing instinct; whereby it will appear that what calls itself scepticism is frequently nothing more than a deficiency in philosophical circumspection.

The most remarkable characteristic of clairvoyance is that time and space are therein overcome—that thus it occurs as far-seeing in space and as fore-seeing in time. The rationalist holds that for impossible. Now, it is clear, on the other hand, that as we do not know what time and space are, we have no right at all to declare their superability in certain abnormal processes of cognition to be impossible. It is only the vulgar who suppose themselves to know what time and space are; the philosopher confesses his ignorance. But should he, with Kant, hold time and space to be mere forms of our knowledge, he will, from this standpoint of transcendental idealism, find

* Hippokrates: 'Aphorisms,' vii. 5.

clairvoyance first rightly possible ; and it was just thus that Schopenhauer, as a Kantian, believed in it.

The curative instinct of somnambules has encountered still more violent attacks from physicians. Yet is it conceivable by mere reference to the analogy of hunger and thirst. These feelings admonish the organism to repair exhausted forces from time to time ; but they are quite general in their demands, that is, have no reference to any special chemical substances. Hunger and thirst are therefore gentle diseases, for which Nature suggests the remedy by an indefinite feeling in the sensibility, but not yet specialized in the idea. But if hunger and thirst attain a high degree, then is the faculty of mental representation also excited, and so arises the vision of the curative means. Thus the traveller in the desert, consumed with thirst, sees himself surrounded by springs and brooks, and Trenk, in the entrenchments of Magdeburg, had the vision of luxurious repasts. Now, if the threshold of sensibility is shifted, that is, if the sensibility is refined, then are hunger and thirst specialized, definitely directed instincts appear, as sympathy or antipathy, in different sorts of illnesses or in pregnant women, even opposed to the usual taste, and in conformity with the need of the child. Still more specialized are the needs of the organism in the highly exalted inner life of somnambules, the displacement of the threshold of sensibility being therein very considerable, and these needs attain to consciousness, though at other times they remain below the threshold, or are limited to a vague general feeling. Thus, whoever regards the curative instinct of somnambules as an inconceivable marvel, should logically also confess that the only quantitatively distinguished and less specialized curative instincts of hunger and thirst are just as inconceivable. They only appear to us intelligible, because custom has effaced their problematic character, and we confound habit with explicability. As Cicero says, we do not ask the reason of things continually seen.*

The healing instinct is not peculiar to Somnambulism alone, but belongs to other conditions characterized by the displacement of the threshold of sensibility; having indeed its foundation in this displacement; as in ordinary dream, in unconscious febrile states, etc., in madness and in 'possession,' of which an example is quoted by Horst.† The healing instinct does not merely prescribe medicinal substances. Among the 'possessed,' for instance, there is often a sudden requirement of rapid circular movement.‡ Now, this same movement appears in the so-called dance of the Dervishes, as a means of exciting the somnambulic condition; and as somnambules often prescribe the same for themselves, the reason evidently lies in the necessity for intensifying the somnambulism, that is, for deepening the sleep.

In like manner the other faculties of somnambules show themselves as only exaltations of tendencies which are weakly apparent already in ordinary dream, and even in the waking state, *e.g.*, in idiosyncrasies; so that only one who is ignorant of these preliminary stages can believe that scepticism is incumbent upon him in regard to the extreme developments. The

---

\* Cicero: 'De Naturâ Deorum,' ii. 38.
† Horst: 'Zauberbibliothek,' v. 206.
‡ Gorres: 'Die Christliche Mystik,' iv. 174.

existence of these preliminary stages is, however, another proof that somnambulism does not produce new faculties in man, but only, by the displacement of the threshold of sensibility, brings those already existing from latency into manifestation.

## 2. *Artificial Somnambulism.*

As all things of Nature can be known in their pure essentiality, if freed from their accidental constituents, their dross, as it were, and offered thus prepared to the understanding, so also somnambulism. As a natural phenomenon it enters as an incident of diseases, or of an intense emotional upheaving—as in the Christian mystic—or even under the influence of different chemical substances—as in witchcraft. But in all these cases accidental concomitants adhere, since the symptoms of these occasional causes are often intermingled with the symptoms of somnambulism. Now if physicians do not know the distinction already insisted upon, between occasion or condition, and true cause, they often take the symptoms of the displacement of the threshold in somnambulism for symptoms of those, for the most part, morbid causes, whereby the threshold is displaced.

It often happens, for instance, that the symptoms of religious ecstasy, when this supervenes—*post hoc*, but not *propter hoc*—upon hysteria, are curtly dismissed as symptoms of hysteria, or of insanity when somnambulism is induced in that condition; and as in fever morbid phantasms often occur, the visions of the somnambulism, which often follows upon fever, are also therefore described as worthless phantasms.

Now to the powers inducive of somnambulism belongs the influence which one man can exercise upon another. But because this influence can be regulated at pleasure—little as the laws of this regulation are yet known—somnambulism also may be induced as an artificial preparation, purified from its accidental ingredients.

It is true that hitherto this artificial somnambulism has been applied almost exclusively to the diseased, whose sensibility generally disappears with the disease itself; but a later experimental psychology will present somnambulism with all the greater purity, if it takes for its object, though rarely obtainable, the sound, and at the same time, sensitive man.

Artificial somnambulism takes place when a man —somnambulist—is, by another man—magnetiser— subjected to the influence of animal magnetism. This magnetic sleep is much deeper than that produced by the natural healing force alone, but essentially resembles the sleep of natural somnambulism; the inner waking, moreover, is much more complete and clear in the magnetic sleep;* and accordingly in the latter the psychical faculties, also, of somnambules are purer and intensified, though in both cases essentially alike. On all these accounts the magnetic sleep is more adapted to exhibit to us the nature of the thing than is natural somnambulism; but from the essential similarity of the phenomena we may know that in both conditions the same process, psychically and physiologically, takes place; that is to say, that it is one and the same force which is often set free in the interior of the organism, but can also be com-

* Kieser: 'Archiv für tierischen Magnetismus,' i. 3, 15.

municated by one man to another. Man can accordingly even place himself artificially in the magnetic sleep; an art of which the old Indian secret teaching in the Vedanta philosophy knew more, and even the Indian fakirs of the present day, who let themselves be buried alive, know more than we Europeans.*

Artificial somnambulism, therefore, presupposes an inner tendency, not actually produced by the magnetic treatment, but only excited to activity thereby; this treatment only facilitates the setting up of a process, which Nature frequently induces from her own initiative as a curative crisis, but it permits an arbitrary elevation and regulation of this process.

The discovery, or rather—historically expressed—the rediscovery of animal magnetism, is due to the physician Mesmer, and fell at the end of the last century. That was a time very unfavourable for the right estimation of this discovery. Materialism then already dominated the minds which were pressing on to the Revolution. Consequently, that happened, which usually happens with important new discoveries; first the facts were denied, and when they could be denied no longer, they were judged from the standpoint of the then dominant system, according to the typical case of Livingstone's above-mentioned negro. The materialistic psychology believed itself all the more justified in this judgment, that, as already said, symptoms of disease are frequently intermingled with symptoms of somnambulism arising within the disease. Cause and condition were already at that time confounded, and a causal connection was believed to exist between disease and

* Preyer: 'Der Hypnotismus,' 43-60.

the phenomena of somnambulism, and therefore somnambulism, *as to its content,* was explained as morbid, whereas only the cause of its condition is morbid.

This materialistic-physiological judgment of somnambulism naturally conveyed a wholly false conception of its phenomena, whose value can as little be expressed in terms of materialism, as pounds can be measured with an ell yard. They not only find no place in materialism, but would rather burst the ring in which its system of thought is confined.

But it would be unjust to hold the generation of that day exceptionally reprehensible. It is historically provable that at all times the representatives of science have been just those who have opposed the greatest obstructions to really new ideas. And that is natural. Goethe somewhere says that the greatest enemies of new ideas are the old ideas; and this hostile *à priori* prepossession must therefore be at its highest point among those who know the old ideas best, and who have systematised them most. The very fact of the high development of any branch of science must dispose its professors to shut out ideas which have a tendency to burst the old frames. Wholly new phenomena have no place in any system, because therein the old phenomena are already connected in an articulate whole, and it is not in the nature of systematisers to leave open spaces suggestive of imperfection. When, for example, the Paris Academy [of Sciences] received information of the fall of meteorites in France, it rejected it as superstition, and even such a mind as Goethe ridiculed in his youth the meteor of Einsisheim. Among the ancient Greeks, on the other hand, the fall of stones from the sky was recognised as a fact without any prejudice. And it is from the very advances in astronomy that this fallacy of opinion is to be explained. Greek opinion had not become shut up and petrified in a system, and could therefore more easily assimilate new facts than could the highly developed astronomy of the moderns, who accounted that to be impossible which was only indigestible for their system. Thus does the science of Nature, by the fact of its cultivation, come to be Nature's Procrustean bed.

So, also, is Mesmerism quite indigestible for Materialism, which, stiffened into a system, has lost its pliability, and instead of the system being reformed, the facts are disparaged, and we hear of hysteria, hallucination, and, finally, even of deception, only that it may not be necessary to recognise the unaccommodating phenomenon of clairvoyance. Physiologists prefer to seek the explanation of the human problem in the mangled bodies of animals, to extracting it from their own interior natures. They are people looking about everywhere for the hats which are on their heads.\*

Whoever, imprisoned in system, sets out with the presupposition that all psychology must be resolved into physiology, is logically compelled to deny clairvoyance. And if he ignores the distinction between cause and condition, he must pronounce it an impos-

\* If the scope and aim of physiological researches of this character were as ambitious as the text assumes them to be, the reproach would, no doubt, be amply justified from the author's point of view. But whatever else might be said, in the proper place, of the practices of physiologists, it seems scarcely fair to tax them with an absurdity not at all suggested by the special objects of their experiments.—Tr.

sibility for one man to become clairvoyant because another man makes magnetic* passes down his body. But this impossibility will also be conceded by every intelligent person; there is no force in the human hand to make another individual clairvoyant. But the following is quite logically possible:

With the magnetic passes which I make down another organism there streams from my hand a material agent, which is invisible to the nerves of sight, except, perhaps, in the dark. This agent is transferred to the other organism, combining with the similar agent in that organism, and in a manner not yet sufficiently explained, distributing or localising it, whereby the organism is sunk into a deep sleep.

The causal connection extends up to this point: the magnetic pass is the cause of the magnetic sleep. Now, supposing that in this sleep ordinary dream-visions occurred, the pass is not the cause of these, but the deep sleep, itself the last effect of the pass, is the *condition* of the visions, whose *cause*, however, lies in the interior of the organism, that is, in its physiological dispositions. By much less can the magnetic pass be the cause of the true visions of clairvoyance. But in the sleep thus caused occurs a displacement of the psycho-physical threshold; the line which, in waking, marks the constant division between conscious and unconscious is removed, a new material of feeling is furnished, first from the interior bodily sphere, but next from the external world, and with the new feelings are naturally introduced new cognitions and faculties. The magnetic pass is therefore

* He would of course begin by denying the 'magnetic' character of the passes.—Tr.

no cause of these faculties, which are already latent in us, but it has only by suppression of the sense-consciousness removed the obstruction to the experience of these faculties. The magnetic pass thus supplies merely the condition under which it is possible for the transcendental Subject, restrained below the threshold by the sense-consciousness of waking life, to overstep that threshold.

Not only is all that logically possible, but it is confirmed as fact by thousands of experiments. What is true of the light of the sun is thus true of the light of sense. As the one in its setting and rising neither produces nor destroys the stars, but occasions their optical appearance and disappearance, in like manner the transcendental Subject emerges from, or retreats into, the Unconscious, as the sense-consciousness goes down or rises.

To no one can even the logical possibility of clairvoyance be made intelligible, if he does not understand this important distinction between cause and condition. And yet it was understood even so long ago as by Plutarch, when he said: 'As the sun does not first shine when it escapes the clouds, but is constant, only seeming dark and invisible to us by reason of the vapours, so also the soul does not first obtain the faculty of seeing the future when it emerges from the body as from a cloud, but already now possesses it, but is blinded by union with the mortal part of us.'*

By the rediscovery of this mysterious force, which is not very aptly designated animal magnetism, the foundation is laid for an experimental psychology.

\* Plutarch: 'On the Cessation of the Oracles.'

That this discovery is still insufficiently recognised —the recent researches into Hypnotism show a tendency for the better—is easily explained by remembering the concessions which such a recognition would imply on the side of medical science. The mere definition of the thing sufficiently shows the difficulties which stand in its way. I intentionally select a definition which brings mesmerism to its most paradoxical expression, but is nevertheless correct. The magnetic treatment is a method of healing in which the patient assumes the part of the physician—he undertakes his own diagnosis and himself prescribes the remedies—while the physician, when he is the magnetiser, is the medicine. It is somewhat difficult for a physician to believe that, nor will he easily be convinced that an uneducated person in sleep understands more of diagnosis and therapeutics than a highly trained physician awake. Yet Hippokrates declared that the best medicine was dream.

The opposition is therefore natural. But that magnetism and somnambulism are healing means is irrefutably consequent upon the fact that there is a natural somnambulism introduced by Nature in many diseases as a critical and favourable symptom, just as artificial somnambulism introduces a very deep sleep, which must bring with it the recognised curative effect of light sleep in an exalted measure. But to the depth of sleep corresponds not only its physiological curative power, but also the clearness of the inner wakening, since it determines the degree to which the threshold of sensibility is displaced. By this displacement the faculty of perception extends to interior conditions and is raised to a clear inner self-inspection. This makes possible a diagnosis, the value of which is not to be less esteemed because the technical terms of science are not also at command.

But even in relation to the external world, the organism is subjected not only to influences known to us in waking, but also to others which, lying beneath the threshold of sensibility, are first perceived with its displacement. From chemical substances of the animal and vegetable kingdom it experiences influences which in waking manifest themselves only very seldom as idiosyncrasies, and it feels their useful or deleterious relation to itself, as happens also in the animal instinct. On this capacity depends the faculty of somnambules to prescribe for themselves the suitable remedies.

The remarkable faculties of somnambules are not always found united in one individual, but distributed, so that for a complete view of this condition the observation of many cases is requisite. Moreover, the individual distinctions are very important.

As to the organ of perception, and the mode of perception, of somnambules, we are still much in the dark. The brain-consciousness being suppressed in them, the ganglionic system, with the solar plexus, has been said to be the centre of perception, and so far rightly, that the psychical functions of somnambules are accompanied by parallel changes in the ganglionic system, just as there is a parallelism between sense-consciousness and changes in the brain, interpreted by materialists into a causal relation.

Let us pause here a moment, that we may not fall into the same error in our judgment of somnambulism.

Materialism confounds the condition, without which there is no mental activity, with its cause. Because the mind acts through its organ, Materialism says that it is developed from the organ. Mental activity is normal with the healthy brain, and morbid in brain diseases; from which Materialism infers the identity of mind and brain activity. But if the violin player plays well or ill according to the character of his instrument, the identity of artist and instrument is not thence to be inferred. Psychology has therefore never found a better expression for the relation between mind and cerebral-system, senses and brain, than that of Plato: 'We know *through* the senses *with* the soul.'\* Everyone would say of the relation between eyes and spectacles, that we see through —that is, by means of—the spectacles with the eye; but according to the logic of Materialism light would be a function of the spectacles.

Now, as waking consciousness proceeds parallel with corresponding changes of the senses and brain, so the transcendental-psychological functions seem to be parallel with corresponding changes in the ganglionic system, whose central seat, the solar plexus, was already called by the ancients the brain of the belly. With a somnambule of the physician Petitin, the pit of the stomach protruded like a ball.† Bertrand's somnambule said, pointing to her stomach, she had something there which spoke, and of which she could inquire. Her instinct taking on the dramatic form of dream, she bent with her face over her stomach, rubbing the latter lightly with her fore-

---

\* Plato: 'Theæt.,' 185.
† Fr. Fischer, 'Der Somnambulismus,' iii. 110.

finger, and then answered all the questions which she put herself, or which were put to her.*

A somnambule with Werner more particularly described the dualism of brain and solar plexus, as it reveals itself on the transition to somnambulism. Before her senses were suppressed, but while she was already gravitating towards somnambulism, she said: 'Where am I? I am not at home in the head. There is a strange struggle between the pit of the stomach and the head; both would prevail, both see and feel. That cannot be; it is a tearing asunder. It is as if I must send down the head into the stomach if I would see anything. The pit of the stomach pains me, if I think above; and yet down there it is not clear enough. I must wonder, and that with the head, over the new disposition of the stomach.'†

That the ganglionic system can assume the functions of the cerebral system is apparent also in the animal kingdom, as in molluscs, and such insects as have highly-developed instincts, but imperfectly developed senses.

Brain and solar plexus, the two foci of the two systems, are also just those parts of the human organism which can be most effectually magnetised. Their antagonism has already been declared in the Vedanta philosophy. It is a fundamental doctrine of the Vedas, that he, whose senses are restrained, comprehends and knows everything from the 'hollow of the heart.' Therefore is the Yogi praised who has found the union (joga) with the heart (manas).

* Bertrand: 'Traité du Somnambulisme,' 137.
† Werner: 'Symbolik der Sprache,' 124.

In general, so many parallels may be drawn between the expressions of our somnambules about their condition, and what is said in the Vedas concerning the Yogi, that it is easy to see that in both cases it is one and the same thing that is spoken of. Thus it is said: 'The self-restrained man is awake when it is night for all beings; and when all beings are awake, that is the night of the right-seeing sage.'\*

Similarly, the seeress of Prevorst: 'In this state I do not dream; it is not to be taken for sleep; it may be so for the outer world, but for the inner world it is the clearest waking.'† So another somnambule: 'This state is like nothing less than sleep, but is the brightest waking.'‡ When it is said: 'He who is united with Brahma has the eyes fixed to the middle of the eyebrows,'§ in this external mark may be recognised that by which the somnambulic state is indicated, the ball of the eye being continually turned back towards the root of the nose.

Now in this state of ecstasy there awakes, according to the Veda, the inner person (*Purusha*), which is distinguished from the waking person, the former knowing the identity of all beings (*Tat twam asi*); the latter—*Ahankara*—is described as concerned with the self-assertive Ego.‖ Even Mesmer's theory is indicated in the Vedas, for the ether of the cosmos is also within the heart. 'Spirit—*Purush*—this is

---

\* Bhagavadgita, ii. 70.
† Kerner: 'Die Seherin v. Prevorst,' i. 149.
‡ Kerner: 'Geschichte zweier Somnambulen,' 87.
§ Bhagavadgita, v. 21.
‖ Windischmann: 'Philosophie im Fortgang der Weltgeschichte,' i. 1570.

all ... who knows this in the hollow of the heart throws off the fetters of ignorance.'*

The Vedas are thus clear upon this point, that the consciousness interiorly awaking in somnambulism is other than the sense-consciousness of our Ego. But the somnambulic consciousness also demands a supporter, and since the person of the sense-consciousness, the Ego, is not this supporter, we have to distinguish between Ego and Soul, between Person and Subject; for, as Aristotle said: 'It is decisive of the question, whether the soul exists, if among the activities and emotional states of our Subject are to be found such as do not belong to the body.† Now somnambulism proves the existence of such functions in an abundance of phenomena, and therefore is the proof it affords of the existence of a soul of far more convincing cogency than all that is offered in philosophical and religious sysetms. But the doctrine of soul must assume a different form from that which it has in religious systems, where soul and Ego, Subject and person, are identified, while somnambulism proves that there is the greatest distinction between them. The religious view could naturally not withstand the attacks of materialism, which shows that the sense-consciousness, as connected with the organism, must with this be perishable, that thus the Ego is no real being, but merely a condition, a product of our organism.‡ Against that

---

\* 'Atharva Veda mundaka,' i. cap. 1.
† Aristotle: 'De Anima,' i. c. 1.
‡ There is in this passage, as elsewhere, an ambiguity in the phrase, 'sinnliche Bewusstsein.' If it is taken to include the whole normal consciousness of waking life, the concession in the text to materialism would be wholly inconsistent with the dis-

there is nothing to be urged, and even the pantheistic systems of philosophy concede it. But materialism is only victorious against the religious doctrine of soul, which does not distinguish between soul and Ego; it is powerless against a doctrine in which even the functions of the body, unconscious for the Ego, are traced to the soul; in which the soul is considered as the producer, not the product, of the body, and in which the whole organism, together with the sense-consciousness, is conceived as a transitory phenomenal form of this soul. Against this soul lying beyond our self-consciousness, and evidenced with the fullest clearness in somnambulism, materialistic arguments prove nothing, and it is also not open to the current objection of dualism; but, on the contrary, the dualism of mind and body is in it monistically suppressed.

When somnambules themselves speak of the manner of their perception, it is naturally in the language of sense; thus they talk of seeing, hearing, etc. This is, of course, only a make-shift, and perhaps one cannot conceive the far-seeing in space as if by somnambulism the sense of sight experienced a telescopic extension. It is, therefore, better to recognise in this designation of the mode of per-

---

tinction upon which the author so strongly insists, between cause and condition. And since he thinks there is good ground for believing that the consciousness which awakes in somnambulism is connected with the solar plexus as its organ, one does not see how, according to the above admission, it can any more survive that organ than the sense-consciousness can survive the brain. It must be added that in the narrower meaning of 'sinnliche Bewusstsein,' the religious doctrine of the soul is no more solicitous for the preservation of mere organic sense-consciousness than is the author.—Tr.

ception of the 'inner sense' a mere translation into the language of waking experience, rather than by literal interpretation to be misled into scepticism, or to undertake premature definitions of this inner sense. Determinately, we can only say *that*, not *how*, somnambules perceive; and since we must presuppose the universal validity of the law of causality for this state also, it is a necessary inference that there exists an organ of perception, and a regular connection between this organ and the outer world, by means of a material agent; the organ being there even in waking life, but below the threshold of sensibility, whose displacement in somnambulism makes perception possible. Could a dreamer be asked if he slept, he would say no; and this question is answered in the same way by somnambules with reference to the inner waking, and all the more rightly as what they perceive is a part of reality. Obscurely intelligible as this inner sense still is, yet in somnambulism the outer senses are so closed, that for the inner perception they are not taken into account; it is, therefore, not surprising to hear that even the born blind see in somnambulism,* as even in ordinary sleep they have dream-images.

To make intelligible the different functions of somnambules, and to dissipate the doubts in respect to them, a long investigation is necessary, and this I reserve for a distinct treatment. I must confine myself here to mere indications, the partial exposition of which in the next chapter will, however, suffice to show, that both the modes and the content of cognition of somnambules far exceed the consciousness

* Kieser: 'Archiv für tierischen Magnetismus,' ii. 1, 22.

and self-consciousness of sense. The latter form, therefore, only one of the psychical conditions possible for men, and only the half man is defined if his mental nature in waking only is considered. Not in waking, but in somnambulism can we undertake an interior diagnosis and specify the necessary remedies. An antithesis to waking shows itself also in the greater conformity of mien and gestures to the inner feelings of somnambules; their language is improved, and their memory embraces things long forgotten. Their visions are frequently allegorical, as indeed is often the case in the common dream, so that they do not usually themselves understand the meaning. Their faces are expressive of a meditation corresponding to their new condition, and of a highly elevated well-being. When their inner life rises to the highest clearness, a moral and intellectual exaltation is also evinced; the latter, however, not as enhanced reflection, but as an intuitive mode of knowledge, as happens in conditions, related to somnambulism, of instinct and artistic production, with predominant infusion of feeling and imagination. If to this is added Clairvoyance, discarding the cognitional forms of space and time—the best confirmation of Kant's doctrine—it may well be said that in somnambulism is revealed a world closed to the consciousness of sense, and an Ego closed to the normal self-consciousness. Physiological and philosophical theories of cognition have been long in clear agreement that the world is our representation, not coinciding with reality; and they recognise a transcendental world lying beyond our senses.\* This is confirmed by

\* [The author is here referring to the fact that a consciousness, or senses, in course of evolution cannot be adequate to their

somnambulism, which shows that our consciousness does not exhaust the world, since the mere displacement of the threshold of sensibility in some degree lifts the veil from the transcendental world; and the like of self-consciousness, as a special case of consciousness, our self-consciousness not exhausting our Ego, since a mere displacement of the threshold of sensibility reveals the transcendental prolongation of the Ego, and ourselves as inhabitants of that transcendental world.

Hitherto the Unconscious has only been recognised by physiology in relation to the vegetative functions of the organism, which are performed without participation of the conscious will, and in thinking, the thoughts emerging in consciousness being conceived as the final result of an unconscious process. Philosophy has made a greater advance, and Hartmann has shown this, for our consciousness insoluble, being of the Unconscious in the whole world of phenomena. This indicates a definite direction for the further development of philosophy. The first concern is a closer definition of the Unconscious. Evidently that is only possible, if there are conditions of man in which the normal threshold of our consciousness and self-consciousness is pushed back. Now, that happens in somnambulism. We know from it, that our unconscious functions are only relatively unconscious,

possible future content, which he calls the 'transcendental world.' On the other hand, it would be an utter misunderstanding to identify the transcendental world in this sense (in which it is mere future or potential phenomenon) with Kant's 'thing-in-itself,' unless we were to suppose that the biological evolution of organic consciousness could bring it to a point at which it would know immediately, without the subjectively imposed forms of space and time which characterise phenomenal perception.—Tr.]

that is, for the man of the senses, that they are, however, accompanied by a transcendental consciousness, whereby the self-diagnosis of somnambules is possible. The like is true of instinct and of the productions of genius, which are likewise accompanied by a transcendental consciousness. But because this transcendental consciousness pertains to our Ego in its transcendental prolongation, and individuality in somnambulism is by no means pantheistically dissolved, but is exalted rather, a large province must first be divided off from the Unconscious of the pantheistic system, and metaphysical individualism re-enters upon its invaded right.

The individual thus lies this side and that side of the threshold of sensibility. These two halves of our being are related as two scales of a balance: the one rises above the threshold as the other sinks below it. When somnambules awaken, their consciousness and self-consciousness shrink into the normal condition of waking life. The threshold of sensibility thus certainly effects a dualism of our being; but this is, as it were, only optically a dualism of two persons of one single Subject, as the dualism of a double star is monistically suppressed in its common point of gravitation. The doctrine of the human soul, which on account of its dualism has been given up by modern science, thus loses this objectionable character, and is monistic.

Somnambulism, therefore, forms the foundation for a doctrine of man, which may be conceived as a doctrine of his duality in unity.

Now, the study of somnambulism has certainly convinced me, that the positiveness with which I speak of its reality and high philosophical importance must seem strange to those who find among materialistic authors an equally positive denial of all its facts.

This is usually accompanied by the assertion that somnambulism has been exposed as deception by the Paris Academy. This utterly untrue assertion is repeated in good faith and belief by the opponents of magnetism, and no one takes the trouble to inspect for himself the historical documents of the Paris Academy. Büchner says : 'Already in the year 1783, on the occasion of the presence in Paris of the celebrated magnetiser, Anton Mesmer, a scientific commission under the leadership of Bailly and Arago delivered an exemplary judgment, which after careful examination described the whole thing as a swindle, resting upon hallucination, deception of the senses, excited force of imagination, and imitative tendency. The Paris Medical Academy also arrived at the same results after many thorough examinations.'* Spitta disposes of the subject with equal brevity, saying : 'The wretched swindle of magnetic cures . . . had been exposed in the year 1784 by the sentence of two commissions of investigation ordered by Louis XVI.'† In accordance with this statement, Spitta leaves the most interesting state of sleep, the magnetic, and the most interesting state of dream, somnambulism, wholly untreated, notwithstanding the title of his book, which thus no more fits the contents than a man's broad-brimmed hat a child's head ; for the title includes mesmerism, which is excluded in the contents.

\* Büchner : 'Kraft und Stoff' (1883), 361.
† Spitta : Schlaf- und Traum-zustände der menschlichen Seele' (1883), 124.

Now, I will first show that the assertion in question, which is transmitted like a disease from one opponent of magnetism to another, is untrue.

Mesmer had repeatedly applied to the Academy, which did not vouchsafe him a hearing, until directly ordered by Louis XVI. to investigate the subject. The judgments* delivered were, however, by no means exemplary, as Büchner asserts, but frivolous and unscrupulous. Two citations will prove this.

In the 'Report of the Royal Commissioners,' it is said :

'Les malades distingués, qui viennent au traitement pour leur santé pourraient être importunés par nos questions; le soin d'observer pourrait les gêner ou leur déplaire; les commissaires eux-mêmes seraient gênés par leur discrétion. Nous avons donc arrêté, que *notre assiduité* n'étant *pas necessaires, il suffirait* que quelques-uns d'entre nous vinssent à ce traitement de temps à temps.'

Not more scrupulous was the Medical Academy, as appears from the following citation from its report :

'Nous avons cru enfin ne pas devoir fixer notre attention sur *des faits rares, insolites, merveilleux,* qui paraissent contredire toutes les lois de la physique, parceque ces cas sont toujours le résultat de causes compliquées, variables, cachés, inextricable.'

No wonder that the physician Jussieu refused to put his signature to such a report.

From the last citation it is evident that the Medical Academy in no way pronounced mesmerism a 'swindle,' as Büchner and Spitta assert, for the facts, even 'wonderful' facts, they conceded, and it

---

* They are to be found in every considerable work upon the subject, *e.g.*, in Bardin and Dupuis, 'Histoire académique du magnétisme animal,' Paris, Baillière, 1841.

could therefore be only the *theory* of Mesmer which was rejected. This recognition of facts is expressed even by the Academy of Sciences in the report of the Royal Commissioners:

'Rien n'est plus étonnant que le spectacle de ces convulsions. Quand on n'a pas vu, on ne peut s'en faire une idée. . . . Tous sont soumis à celui qui magnétise; ils ont beau être dans un assoupissement apparent, sa voix, un regard, un signe les en retire. On ne peut s'empêcher de reconnaitre à ces effets constants une grande puissance qui agite les malades, les maîtrise, et dont celui qui magnetise semble être le dépositaire.'

It may be mentioned by the way that Arago, who is named by Büchner, was actually not then living. I shall speak of him further by-and-by, when I shall claim him on my side.

Whoever adduces the Report of the Commission of 1784 against Somnambulism in general, only proves thereby that he has never read this report. For in 1784 animal magnetism exclusively was in question, and it was later, *after* the appearance of that report, that the first cases of somnambulism were observed and published by a pupil of Mesmer, Puysegur. Mesmer himself, indeed, was acquainted with somnambulism, but he kept the secret. The Academies had no knowledge of it, and it was not at all an object of their investigations.

It results from the foregoing that Büchner, in order to condemn somnambulism, appeals to a judgment in which nothing whatever is said about somnambulism. But in what follows I shall show, that of another report of the Paris Academy, dealing specially with somnambulism, he has no knowledge at all. This report, ignorance of which is not permissible to a physician, is *unanimously in favour* of somnambulism, and conforms all those wonderful phenomena ascribed to it, to which also clairvoyance especially belongs.

Already in 1820-21 experiments were instituted in the Hôtel Dieu, and thirty physicians subscribed the conclusion, that the opinion of the Commissions of 1784, that the phenomena of magnetism rested upon the heightened imagination of the patients, was erroneous. The patients fell asleep also when magnetised without their knowledge, and even through closed partition doors.

Finally, on the 10th October, 1825, Froissac proposed to the Medical Academy a new investigation of the matter. After some weeks a preliminary report was read, which set forth the necessity for the investigation:

1. Parce que les expériences d'après lesquelles ce jugement (of the year 1784) a été porté, paraissent avoir été faites sans ensemble, sans le concours simultané et nécessaire de tous les commissaires, et avec des dispositions morales qui devaient d'après le principe du fait qu'ils étaient chargés d'examiner, les faire complètement échouer.

2. Que le magnetisme jugé aussi en 1784 diffère entièrement par le théorie, les procédés, et les resultats, de celui, que les observateurs exacts, probes, attentifs, que des médicins éclairés, laborieux, opiniâtres, ont étudié dans ces dernières années.

This second reason refers to the circumstance that the subsequently discovered somnambulism had not come into discussion in 1784.

There was now named a commission of eleven physicians of the Academy, who spent five years on the investigation of Magnetism and Somnambulism, and on the 21st and 28th June, 1831, their report was read by the physician Husson. The facts of somnambulism were therein unanimously recognised:

the insensibility of the magnetised; their capacity for undertaking the diagnosis of their own interior organisms and those of others, of predicting the course of their own and others' diseases, and of prescribing effectual remedies; the exaltation of memory; clairvoyance without the use of their eyes; the action at a distance of the magnetiser, etc.

In this report the Commission says expressly, that it was instructed to investigate Somnambulism, 'qui n'avait pas été étudié par les commissaires de 1784.' Similarly, Arago speaks of the more recently discovered somnambulism, 'contre lequel on n'a plus le droit d'invoquer le rapport de Bailly' (of the year 1784).

I repeat, therefore: For the rejection of somnambulism Büchner appeals to an historical document which in this respect, according to the later declarations of the Academy itself, has no validity; while on the other hand, neither Büchner nor Spitta is aware of that document, which completely contradicts the opponents of somnambulism. But that ignorance is not now allowable in either a physician or a philosopher, for the report of 1831 says even of Magnetism, that it 'devrait trouver sa place dans le cadre des connaissances médicales,' while in a theoretical regard Magnetism and Somnambulism are as important for the philosopher, as practically for the physician. In this respect, indeed, Büchner is not alone among his colleagues, for that the very smallest number of them take an interest in this study I know myself, at least as regards the city in which I live, though the facts are at hand. For there half-a-dozen magnetisers are carrying on their business, and are much resorted to.

The physicians, indeed (yet with some exceptions), talk of 'swindle,' and say that the custom obtained proves nothing. True: it proves, at least in itself, nothing for magnetism, but very much against our medical science; for the public does not desert physicians who can cure diseases.

It is the fact, as Büchner says, that in 1837 a prize of 3,000 francs was offered for the somnambule who could read without use of the eyes, and that the prize was not won. The physician Pigeaire had brought his daughter, a somnambule of twelve years old, to Paris for this purpose. In private representations before certain Academicians, the clairvoyance was established—among the witnesses was Arago; but the Academy knew how to get out of it, and in the decisive sitting there was no experiment, because the physicians declared it an insufficient precaution that the girl's eyes were bound with linen cloth, covered with cotton, and then veiled with a black velvet mask, to see through which, Arago said, was an impossibility.

But of another prize Büchner seems to be ignorant. Dr. Berna, namely, offered 70,000 (!) francs for those Academicians who could read through the masks which the Academy had rejected in the case of Mdlle. Pigeaire, with the superfluous addition that he had no objection to the sum being expended on the poor.*

Having illustrated by two examples the proceedings

* Pigeaire: 'Puissance de l'électricité animale,' 143-176 (Paris, 1839). [It might, of course, be replied that the Academicians did not pretend to be experts in this mode of deception. But what, then, will be said of the opinion formally expressed by one of the most celebrated of modern experts in similar arts—Robert Houdin —after full investigation with another clairvoyant? See *post*, p. 240. Tr.]

of the opponents of Somnambulism, I may leave judgment upon them to the reader; adopting for myself only one thing which characterises them—brevity. As against Büchner and Spitta, I add here two propositions, from which all opponents of somnambulism may escape if they can. The first contains an historical fact, the second a logical inference from it:

1. By the investigations, extending over five years, of eleven physicians of the Medical Academy in Paris, whose unanimous Report of 1831 was publicly delivered, Somnambulism, with all its so-called 'miracles,' but of which the conformity to law is not to be doubted, has been proved an incontestable fact.

2. Against these positive instances, according to the logical rule, all negative instances of ever so many experimental failures in the past and future have not the smallest weight.

Now, as this judgment of the Academy stands by no means alone, but is reinforced by an incalculable number of completely authenticated facts subsequently observed by hundreds of physicians, whoever wishes to learn the truth has only to read to be convinced; and I am unquestionably justified in declining further notice of that which calls itself euphemistically scepticism (but which is, in fact, neglect of the sources of information, and therefore ignorance) and in passing on upon my own way.

At the present time attention has been again directed to Magnetism, by the performances of the magnetiser, Hansen. The phenomena elicited by him were at first denounced as swindles, but afterwards—that the discovery might be claimed for official science—they received the name of Hypnotism. Physiologists have since become zealous students of this hypnotism, which they had neglected for forty years after its discovery by Braid, and which includes a part of the mesmeric phenomena. It is indeed not to the honour of science that it should have needed public exhibitions to incite it to the study of such important phenomena; meanwhile, it is at least no longer to be feared that mesmerism will again fall into oblivion, and if the physiologists persevere in their zeal, and will extend their experiments, it is certain that they will induce the other phenomena of mesmerism. And however sceptical they have been concerning what other observers have seen, they will not remain in that disposition as to what is not only seen but done by themselves. Perhaps the word 'Hypnotism' will still be retained, but that will be only because they are ashamed to use the term 'Mesmerism.'

Hypnotism and Mesmerism are by no means coincident in their range. Braid himself defined hypnotism as a 'result of modifying influence which fixed and intense attention directed to particular parts of the body exercises on the physical processes occurring in them, whether this attention is excited by external influence and intentionally, or from the free will of the patient, who to his concentration adds the expectation that certain changes will make their appearance.'* Now, Braid merely proved by his experiments that concentrated attention is *one* of the means of eliciting phenomena having a similarity to those of mesmerism; but he has not shown that other means of this nature do not exist. All phenomena of mesmerism may spontaneously follow upon diseases, deep

* Preyer: 'Der Hypnotismus,' 109.

trouble, religious emotion, etc., and, even if concentrated attention should be supposed in such cases, that wholly fails when sleeping persons are magnetised with success, and even with remarkable ease; which is only to be explained by the fact that ordinary sleep is an incipient somnambulism. Dupotet tried magnetising with thousands of sleepers, and proved the same phenomena in all.* So also the cautious and sceptical Deleuze says that natural sleep is the most favourable moment for influencing anyone magnetically.† Even animals can be magnetised, as is proved by the experiments of Lafontaine upon lions, hyænas, dogs, cats, squirrels and lizards.‡ From which it appears, that while in hypnotism a subjective factor on the side of the affected person is present, in Mesmerism an objective agency on the side of the magnetiser elicits the phenomena, and is taken up by the recipient organism. But should attention and imagination be supposed even with sleepers and animals, this false idea is disposed of by the magnetising of plants. Dr. Allix, in Turin, experimented on a *mimosa pudica*, which by reason of its shrinking, as if with alarm, from contact with the human hand, has also been named 'sensitive,' or *Noli me tangere*. He made it insensitive to touch by magnetising, as also by chloroform.§

If, moreover, Braid only admits the subjective factor, and were right, the magnetic agent would still not be disposed of, for the third case is conceivable,

* Dupotet: 'Manuel de l'étudiant magnétiseur,' 15.
† Deleuze: 'Histoire critique du magnetisme animal,' ii. 236.
‡ Lafontaine: 'L'Art de magnétiser,' 325, etc.
§ Fürst H. Zu Wied: 'Das unbewusste Geistesleben,' i. 140.

that concentrated attention is not of itself effectual, but liberates this magnetic agent in the organism; which would thus be a case of self-magnetising. We cannot suppose magnetisers to be a class of mankind by themselves: rather must everyone be more or less in possession of this agent; and there is no sufficient ground for doubting that one organism can impart it to another, presumably by means of the nerve-apparatus terminating the nerves beneath the skin at the finger-tips, and which is called the corpuscule of Paccini. According to the literature of the subject, this still doubted objective agent can not only be made visible in a dark room,* but somnambules see it also outside this room, as they unanimously agree, and it is even measurable.† For this reason it was a mistake to abandon so quickly the standpoint of Mesmer—who at once saw in magnetism a physical phenomenon—and to direct attention almost exclusively to the remarkable psychological phenomena of somnambulism, because this physical agent could not then be proved. Whereas the physical foundation of magnetism should first be established.

The so-called miracles ascribed to somnambulism, the conformity of which to law will be recognised in the next century, are not only facts, but also facts of the very greatest importance. In regard to both statements I can appeal to Schopenhauer, who undertook the study in the evening of his life, but unfortunately did not complete it. With reference to the actuality of somnambulism, he says: 'Who at this day doubts the facts of animal magnetism and its

* Reichenbach: 'Der sensitive Mensch.'
† Robiano: 'Névrurgie.'

clairvoyance, is not to be called sceptical, but ignorant.' And as to the importance of the thing, he says : 'The phenomena under discussion are, at least from the philosophical standpoint, of all facts presented to us by the whole of experience, without comparison the most important ; it is, therefore, the duty of every learned man to make himself thoroughly acquainted with them. . . Then, however, will a time arrive, when philosophy, animal magnetism, and natural science in the unprecedented progress of all its branches, will throw mutually a light so brilliant upon one another, that truths will be apparent which can only thus be attained.'* In fact, somnambulism offers the most convincing proof of another order of things than those of sense, and also that we men ourselves are linked with that order by the side of our Subject which for the Ego is unconscious. Somnambulism proves that Schopenhauer and Hartmann are right in laying at the foundation of human phenomena a Will and an Unconscious ; but it proves also that this Will is not blind, and that what to the Ego is unconscious is not unconscious in itself ; that, further, between us and the world-substance a transcendental Subject must be interposed, a willing and knowing being ; that thus the individuality of man avails beyond his temporary phenomenal form, and the earthly existence is only one of the possible forms of existence of our Subject.†

The science of man is therefore still unwritten. It may be that physiological psychology, the path heretofore pursued, will yet explain the earthly mode of

---

\* Schopenhauer : 'Versucht über Geistersehen.'
† Cf. Hellenbach : 'Philosophie des gesunden Menschenverstandes,' 222.

existence according to its content, but not its fact; we shall first obtain true light upon the human problem when we penetrate our Unconscious, to which somnambulism forms the single aperture; for, as the astronomer must wait for the night of the world for the observation of the stars, so must we await the night of our sense-consciousness, that the emergence of our transcendental Subject may be visible.

It cannot be said that the study of somnambulism has hitherto been carried on in the right way; rather must it be confessed that there are faults on this as on that side the walls of Troy. Against *à priori* negations on the side of opponents is to be set off enthusiasm on the side of adherents. But it may be confidentially expected that from this parallelogram of intellectual forces will be developed as resultant a period of unprejudiced study of the object upon the experimental basis, as Jean Paul has predicted: 'Of the discoveries which throw light at once upon the human double world of mind and body, scarcely any century has made a greater than that of the last in animal magnetism, only that centuries go to the education and nurture of the wonder-child, till it grows up to be the wonder-worker of the world.'*

* Jean Paul: 'Museum,' i. § 1.

# CHAPTER V.

### DREAM A PHYSICIAN.

### 1. *Dream-images as Symbolical Representation of Bodily States.*

IN sleep our senses are closed to the outer world; so that normal consciousness, depending on the stimulations of these senses, disappears with the suspension of its supply. But in sleep there is an *inner* waking, which is dream. Dream-images also must have an exciting cause of some kind, and if this does not lie in the outer world, from which we are excluded, it must be sought within us.

Thus the question arises: In what relation stand dreams to our interior? This question is evidently not solved by speaking of the free activity of our imagination. Imagination in dream can indeed be called free, in so far as no conscious will, no attention, no definitely directed consideration evokes the images; but to admit freedom in the sense of causelessness is forbidden by the universal validity of the law of causality. The course of our representations in dream as in waking must be derived from our bodily states and psychical dispositions. In other words, dream-images must contain veiled intimations concerning health and disease of the body and the soul The connection between our state of health and our dreams must further be one conformable to law, that is, definite interior conditions must also draw after them definitely coloured dreams, or at least the general direction of the dream-imagination must be determined by them.

Dream is thus a symbolical representation of interior conditions of the dreamer ; it is a symptom of health or disease. That this symptom is neglected by our physicians, everyone knows from his own experience. Perhaps none of my readers has ever met a physician who asked him about his dreams. It was otherwise, according to Aristotle's testimony, in the beginnings of medical science : ' The expert among physicians say that great attention is to be paid to dreams.' He gives the reason himself, when he says that to definite diseases correspond definite dreams.* In the following, it shall be shown that this neglect cannot be justified ; and that, notwithstanding its symbolical disguise, dream is often a finer and more reliable symptom than the beat of the pulse and the state of the tongue.

It is generally known that the physician's most difficult task is diagnosis. Most mistakes are made in reasoning from the bodily symptoms to the internal cause of the disease. Thus, for instance, a young married lady of my acquaintance was treated by an English physician in India for cancer in the stomach, and, finally, her return home was prescribed ; but on the journey the terrible cancer took the form of a sweet child, which unfortunately and naturally did not survive. Such extreme cases are, indeed, rare ; but that many errors occur in medical diagnosis cannot

* Aristotle : 'On Prophecy in Dreams,' c. 1 and 2.

be denied, and are very intelligible, as this is the physician's greatest difficulty. If he succeeds in it, his trouble is, for the most part, crowned with success; and when it is quite superfluous, the mere appearance giving the necessary information, as, for example, in surgical cases, there the profession achieves its highest triumphs.

If, now, interior states are reflected in our dreams —if dream is a symptom—regard to it is the more relevant as it may assist the physician in just his most difficult duty—diagnosis. But the task of the physician is at present a double one; he has not only to investigate the disease, but must also prescribe the appropriate remedy. Now, the following inquiry will yield the somewhat surprising result, that dream is in *both* respects a physician, that it offers indications as well for cure as for diagnosis.

Dream depends on internal feelings of the organism, which determine the general quality of the dream-images. No other cause is conceivable. It is true, the inner excitations are present also in waking, but they do not come to consciousness, the brain being then preoccupied with the energetic impressions of the outer world. As the sunlight, outshining the stars, makes them disappear from sight, so do the sensations of waking consciousness repress those inner feelings; and as, when the sun has set, the mild light of the stars is again perceptible, so also in sleep different inner excitations, unregarded in waking, attain to perception. But through the nervous system the brain is in connection with all parts of the organism, so that every internal stimulation of a part of the body is transferred to the brain, where in sleep it has its symbolical representation in a corresponding dream-image. Thus these dream-images come to be symptoms of internal conditions, and are as such the more valuable, because in waking the patient experiences nothing, or very little, of them, so that they are lost for the purpose of diagnosis. Internal feelings must be of a somewhat coarse nature to enter waking consciousness. Whereas the exalted susceptibility to inner excitations in sleep has the consequence, that much *weaker* degrees of morbid excitation attain to consciousness in dream than in waking, and therefore that diseases are announced *earlier* than they can be traced in waking consciousness. Symptomatic dreams are thus, as it were, prophetic, and while in waking we may suppose ourselves to be still in sound health, dream already betrays the first tokens of incipient disease.* Repulsive incidents in dream often depend on bodily states which in waking remain quite obscure, but are perceived by the dream imagination which represents the objective stimulation symbolically. Aristotle has already expressed the same in saying : 'Since the beginnings of all dreams are small, so also are those of diseases and other conditions arising in bodies. These must evidently, therefore, make their appearance earlier in sleep than in waking.'†

Dream is therefore a *finer* means of diagnosis than symptoms in the waking state, and betrays *earlier* stages of impending diseases, than does the other.

* [Practically, it is evident this would be of little use unless the dreamer not only remembered, but had the skill himself to perceive the import of his dreams; for the physician would not then have been called in.—Tr.]
† Aristotle: 'On Prophecy in Dream,' i. 1.

Maudsley says: 'Dreams sometimes have a truly prophetic character in regard to certain bodily affections, the early indications of which have not been sufficiently marked to awaken any attention during the mental activity of the day, or to do more than produce an obscure and formless feeling of discomfort, but which nevertheless declare themselves in the mental action of dreaming, when other impressions are shut out. When the disease ultimately declares itself distinctly in our waking consciousness, then the prophetic dream, the forewarning, is recalled to mind with wonder.'*

Every disease has its so-called incubation period, during which the patient is apparently still quite sound. At this time medical diagnosis detects no symptoms at all, these consisting in very weak excitations which do not enter consciousness, and only in dream are perhaps represented in images. Diagnosis is nevertheless facilitated by the circumstance that a property of dream is exaggeration, the inner sensations being, as it were, microscopically magnified by dream. Thus the old physician Galen† relates the case of a man who dreamed that his leg was turned to stone, and a few days later this leg was paralysed. Macario dreamed of an acute pain in the neck, but found himself quite well on waking; a few hours afterwards, however, he fell into a violent inflammation of the tonsils.‡ Teste, Minister under Louis Philippe, dreamed that he had a stroke, which,

---

\* Maudsley: 'Physiology and Pathology of the Mind,' p. 241, London, 1867.
† Galen: 'On Prophecy in Dream.'
‡ Harvey: 'Les Rêves,' etc., Paris, Amyot, 1867, p. 232.

in fact, happened to him three days later.* If Teste had related this dream to a person inclined to superstition, such an one would, from the subsequent fulfilment, have inferred the prophetic nature of our dreams in the spiritualistic sense, whereas it is evidently only in the physiological sense that this true dream is to be so described. But if, on the other hand, Teste had related his dream to an intelligent physician, the latter might possibly have been able to prevent the fulfilment.

To external impressions, also, we have often in dream that exalted sensibility to which the exaggeration of the dream-image is due. The hot bottle at the soles of the feet makes us dream that we are stepping through fire, while if the bedclothes get displaced, leaving the feet free, we dream that we are wading through a cold brook. Hervey once dreamed that his chimney smoked, yet remarked nothing of it on waking. Some hours after he woke again, when the smoke had meanwhile become very strong.†

Simon Scholzius, a learned physician, tells of one who dreamed that a tall man, dressed like a Pole, approached him, and flung a stone against his breast; awaking in alarm, he felt, in fact, a severe pain in the middle of his breast, struck a light, and perceived just there a black spot, of the size of a hand, which gradually disappeared by cupping and blistering.‡ Friedreich relates that, when a candidate for the medical profession, he once watched by a sick person who had an ulcer in the leg, which, from fear of the

---

\* Hervey, 232. † *Ibid.*, 352.
‡ Hennings: 'Ueber Träume und Nachtwandler,' Weimar, 1802, § 245.

knife, he would not allow to be opened. Suddenly he awoke from a dream, crying out that they had cut open the ulcer by force, this being found on examination to have burst of itself.*

The inner feelings are often thus dramatically motived by the imagination through events in dream. The orator Aristides dreamed in the temple of Æsculapius that a bull attacked and wounded him in the knee; on awaking he found a tumour there. Arnold de Villanova dreamed he was bitten in the foot by a black cat; next day came on the same place a cancerous ulcer. Conrad Gessner dreamed he was stung by a serpent; a few days later there rose a plague-boil on the breast, of which he died.† It was a frequent experience of Krauss that dreams of dental operations were the forerunners of violent toothaches, and that dreams of bites of a tiger or of a venomous snake indicated the parts of the skin where soon afterwards an ulcer broke out.‡ Krauss sees the symbolical expression of physiological processes not only in the representations of dream, but also in the delusions of the insane, and he thinks the exciting organ is the same in both. The close relationship otherwise apparent between dream and insanity seems to justify this inference from similar representations to similar exciting causes. Thus Maury mentions an insane man who suffered from the delusion that he was a woman, and pregnant; Maury had the same idea himself in a dream, and as he traced it to a nervous

---

\* Radestack: 'Schlaf und Traum,' 119.
† Perty: 'Die mystische Ercheinungen der menschlichen Natur,' ii. 365, 378.
‡ 'Zeitschrift für Psychiatrie, 1858 und 1859; Der Sinn im Wahnsinn.'

pain in the bowels, that was possibly also the case with the insane man.*

According to Boismont, even waking hallucinations of a dramatic nature may precede other symptoms as forerunners of diseases. A lady, going one evening to her room, was terrified by the sight of a skeleton, which drew a dagger and thrust it into her left side. During the night an inflammation settled in the same side.†

So in dreams perceptions of the general sensibility (synæsthesia) are sharpened, and those slight changes in the disposition of the organism, which escape waking perception, and whereby morbid conditions are first prepared, are often, long before the outbreak of the disease, represented in symbolical and usually dramatic form. This is especially the case when there is in the organism a chronic predisposition to a form of disease; therefore such predispositions may be inferred from frequently recurring dreams of a similar general character. It is said by the French physician, Vercy, that bloody fluxes are announced by dreams of red colour, lymphatic effusions by dreams of inundations, internal inflammations by dreams of conflagrations.‡ One dreamed of wild cats regularly before the recurrence of his chest-

---

\* Maury: 'Le Sommeil et les Rêves,' 141.

† Boismont: 'Des Hallucinations,' 248. [There are well-attested cases in medical experience which suggest a different interpretation of this instance. No doubt the hallucination was connected with a latent morbid condition; but both the character and position of the later symptom—the inflammation in the side—may probably have been determined by the shock and impression upon the imagination produced by the hallucination itself. See Carpenter's 'Mental Physiology,' c. xix., p. 682.—Tr.]

‡ I. H. Fichte: 'Psychologie,' i. 540.

spasms; another of throngs of people before his attacks of fever.* Carus reports that a man who was subject to painful and sudden spasms of the chest dreamed regularly before the attacks that he was pursued and bitten by cats; another was charged by bulls in his dreams when attacks of violent headache were impending.† In all such cases the value of the dreams for diagnosis lies chiefly in this, that they announce not only actual, but pending complaints, and can therefore be treated as timely warnings.

The association of ideas also frequently plays a part; Bonetus cites the case of a lady who could foretell her complaints quite regularly and certainly a few days before their occurrence by dreaming of her physician.‡ It is not necessary here to accept prevision; even these dreams were only symptomatic, and though not distinctly indicating the parts to suffer, yet in the heightened susceptibility of sleep an indeterminate uneasiness could be perceived, and the dream-image of the physician arise from mere association of ideas, which plays its part in dream as in waking. Hervey also relates an interesting dream of this nature. A traveller upon a journey to the sources of the Nile was seized with a violent inflammation of the eyes, which did not leave him till his return to France. Ten years later he remarked to his surprise that the scenes and events of that journey were constantly turning up in his dreams. This went on increasingly for six weeks, when finally he

* Siebeck: 'Traumleben der Seele,' 31.
† Carus: 'Psyche,' 238.
‡ Hennings: 'Ahnungen und Visionen,' Leipzig, 1777, § 214.

had another violent attack of inflammation of the eyes, from which he had remained exempt for ten years.* In this case the first beginnings of the inflammation were felt in dream six weeks before the outbreak, and awakened the associated representations of ten years before.

It has been observed that very agitated dreams precede the outbreak of insanity, *e.g.*, oppressive nightmares; and that even after recovery the conditions of insanity still make themselves felt in dream. That is the case also with other disturbances of the organism, and what we name disease extends in its course beyond that threshold of waking sensibility, on either side of which we speak of health because we only perceive the grosser symptoms. Pathological dreams which continually recur are to be placed alongside the constant delusions of the insane. Burdach mentions a man who continually raved of a general advancing and retreating with his army. On dissection there was found in the brain a hydatid, rolling backwards and forwards, whose mechanical excitation had taken a symbolical representation as in dream. Another insane person believed that he felt in his body the heads of three frogs, and on dissection it appeared that this delusion had been produced by three indurated scirrhous glands of the epiploon.†
Thus in madness as in dream, the seat and nature of the suffering can be inferred from the special character of the conscious impressions. For this reason Esquirol passed many nights by the bedsides of his insane patients, who often in sleep betrayed the causes of

* Hervey, 360.
† Perty: 'Mystische Erscheinungen,' etc., i. 61.

their disease.* We thus confound the cause with the effect, if we refer difficulty of breathing, from which we awake, to nightmares, or palpitations of the heart to fearful dreams, or explain bodily disturbances of the insane by their madness. The bodily affections are rather, on the contrary, the causes of the representations in dream and madness. Subsequently, indeed, the evoked images, by the force of their apparent objectivity, increasingly react on the bodily affections which are at the foundation of them; in this mutual action, and because the intensification is also symbolised, we have the reason that the dream-images do not remain of the same character, but are transformed as the dramatisation rises, till at length they awaken us. This wakening seems mostly to result from the fact that the excitement of the nerves of sense reaches a degree at which the system of motor nerves is also set in tension, and some muscle in motion. Even very slight tensions of the muscles immediately excite in us corresponding dreams, wherein we imagine ourselves running, flying, or falling, but they are seldom of such a degree as to occasion actual movements of limbs. Our sleep is in general motionless, only now and then the twitching of a limb, or even of the lips, betray that nerve excitations are transferred to the motor system, eliciting adequate dream-images. This is often apparent in the jerks and suppressed growls of dreaming sporting dogs. We have only to suppose a rise in this process of excitation of the motor nerves to get the phenomenon of sleep-walking. In that case there is no stopping at the mere dream-representation, but the night-walker translates his dream into action.

* Boismont, 273.

Inasmuch as our psychical affections, the feelings and dispositions of waking life, if of deep impression, always draw after them physiological changes of the organism, these are taken over in sleep, and are symbolised in dream. Dream-images thus often correspond also to our psychical conditions, and all the more that in dream they have full play, free from internal restraint. In waking we can combat unhappy moods by consideration of causes, by hope for the future, and in the worst case by religious and philosophical resignation, but in dream these rational repressive means fail us. So joyful as well as sad dispositions often manifest themselves in dream by extravagant images; dream thus offering indications for both bodily and psychical diagnosis. The material of dream is often supplied by external feelings, as a rule, however, by the internal; imagination working up this material in its own way.

As regards bodily feelings, we can sum up the foregoing in the words of Hippocrates: that in dream the soul knows the causes of disease, at least in an image. But when we comprehend this somewhat more closely, we shall gain the key to the understanding of one of the most remarkable phenomena of the somnambulic sleep, one which, although already confirmed by hundreds of physicians, still encounters doubt, because looked at by itself it is unintelligible, and which first becomes intelligible when its elementary form has been discovered in ordinary sleep, of which it is merely an exaltation.

For our dream-images not only point generally to the seat of inner feelings, but frequently represent the suffering organ itself more or less objectively (plastisch). In such dreams the spatially constructed organ of the feeling enters the consciousness of the dreamer; symbolism, it is true, still takes place, but in such images of ordinary sleep, we already find the beginning of that penetrative feeling of the body as to its morbid symptoms of which such wonderful reports appear in the literature of somnambulism.

Among later investigators it is Scherner who has taken most trouble to prove the connection between organic nerve-excitations and dream-images, whereby often the plastic, if also phantastic, representation of the organ is obtained. We have from him the following programme: ' On the nerve-excitations from the interior of the body, dream forms, in a way unattainable to waking consciousness, immediate perceptions of the inner disposition of the body; the plastic formation either enters simple and clear, or is symbolically adorned in the knowing soul. Therefore with every specific nerve-excitation, according to which the corresponding sort of dream is formed, flow into the dream the architectonic copies of the sphere of the body belonging to the nerve-excitation, and the utmost the phantasy has to do is only to paint out all the figures acceding to it in corresponding symbolism. If the nerve-excitation arises in the organ of sight, as so often happens before waking, the structure of the retina is represented perceptibly in dream; if the excitation belongs to the stomach and the bowels, one is astonished at the fertility with which the imagination excels itself in representing the great and small circuits of this organ, its windings and its longitudinal course. Springs the excitation in the heart or lungs, we are pleased with the distinctness with which the sketches of these organic movements are delineated.'

Scherner has certainly found the right point of view for the interpretation of dreams; but when he proceeds to the application, it often appears that the frame is too narrow, as other factors intervene, dream being no mere product of this inner penetrative feeling of the body. We must take into account, also, the spontaneous activity of imagination, which not only determines the modes of symbolising the material of sensibility, but also introduces foreign constituents according to the laws of association. We therefore cannot consider all the constituents of our dream-images as reflecting our bodily conditions.

Our state of health furnishes, as a rule, only the ground-tone of our dreams, giving unity of character to the images perceived, while the painting in detail seems to proceed wholly from the imagination. An interesting dream of this sort, in which the bodily condition furnishes only the general cue, and imparts unity of direction to the series of representations of the otherwise independently active imagination, is related by Volkelt:

'One evening, being in pleasant company, I had drunk more beer than usual, and therefore felt next morning a certain lassitude and leaden heaviness in all my limbs. In the intervening night I dreamed I went for a walk in the chief street of my native town, but not in my usual dress, but burdened with a black travelling cloak, the fur cap on my head, cloth shoes on my feet. I dragged myself slowly along, with the abashed feeling that this difficulty of movement came from excess in beer. Suddenly I find myself sitting on the pavement; over my feet a great heap of mantle is spread out. I turn homewards, and now carry the mantle folded up over my left shoulder. Then there approaches me an unknown maiden, who expects me to carry her rather large basket. I decline, since I had nothing to do with her basket. Then I see an old schoolfellow by me, and already my mantle has transformed itself into a small school-wallet slung on my back. On this my companion hangs something else. At length he stops my way at a corner of the street, supporting himself against the house, and flinging his hands about him, on which I awoke.

'The feeling of bodily lassitude and heaviness comes in every trait of the dream to evident expression (clothing with travelling mantle, fur cap, cloth shoes, sitting down burdened, demand to carry a basket, school-wallet, school-fellow weighting me still further, and bringing me to a stop). That feeling is certainly the incitement which gives direction to the dream, and so far forms the bond of connection; but only occultly, and *behind* the imagination. For within the dream-phantasy, which is out and out of *visible* presentation, the incitement cannot exist in its original undisguised character. It is here symbolised in that succession of images.'[*]

Now were an art of dream-signification in this physiological sense possible, that would come much in substitution of our science of life, as the process itself of life would be reflected in our dreams, while our present physiology is founded chiefly on examination of the dead body.

[*] Volkelt: 'Die Traumphantasie,' Stuttgart, 1875, § 88.

In the first place we have seen that consciousness of our bodily condition is much more extensive and distinct in dream than in waking. What in the day is either perceived not at all or only as general feeling, is in dream particularly distinguished and symbolised. Now since the desistence of impressions from the outer world, in other words, suspension of the empirical consciousness, is the condition for that more distinct penetrative feeling of the body, and the threshold of sensibility can be so displaced that a content of consciousness can emerge which for the waking man is transcendental, it is presumable that the elevation of this content is in proportion to the depth of the sleep. We should thus undoubtedly obtain valuable disclosures, could we preserve the memory of the dream-images of deep sleep, or if in deep sleep we could be brought to speak upon our condition. It is not inconceivable that experimental psychology—a science as yet scarcely born—may discover means to these ends; but meanwhile it is only in somnambulism that one of them is in some measure attained. The somnambulic sleep is much deeper than ordinary sleep, and will therefore also bring with it a clearer sensibility of the body. Somnambules, moreover, can be made to speak, and concerning their bodily health they often do so spontaneously. It may therefore be supposed that the phenomena of somnambulism will offer a valuable contribution to the proof that dream is a physician.

2. *Diagnosis in the Somnambulic Sleep.*

(*a*) *Self-Inspection.* — That inquirer is lost for science who in the phenomena of Nature seeks only confirmation of his preconceived theories, and who, confounding the horizon of his knowledge with the horizon of things, holds that only for possible which is within the first. If we approach Nature with *à priori* prejudices, we run the double risk, of either overlooking phenomena opposed to our hypotheses, or of explaining them falsely, that is to say, in the sense of our hypothesis.

Psychology is the most difficult of all sciences, and we have consequently only a narrow possession of assured knowledge in it. Here before all things is it therefore necessary that we should not allow ourselves to be blinded by the dominant common opinion, provisionally abstaining from every definitive judgment, and holding simply to the facts; for facts remain unshaken, but hypotheses are capable of development, have always changed, and will always change, till we are well-nigh omniscient. Only an omniscient person could judge *à priori* what phenomena are possible, what not; but in a province so little explored as is psychology, we must rather be prepared *à priori* to meet with the incomprehensible. Man is to us the greatest of all problems; we know not what life is, how an organism arises and maintains itself, and only from experience shall we gradually learn what forces and tendencies are latent in our soul. Wieland* says: 'Perhaps it is exactly the greatest man of science who least ventures to declare anything impossible which does not obviously belong to the class of four-angled triangles.' And in psychology especially we must follow this sound

* Wieland: 'Werke,' xxx. 97.

principle, to hold all for *possible* which does not contain a logical contradiction.

To common-sense it sounds very plausible, and even a thing of course, that a physician educated by years of study and experience should be better able to judge of a disease and its remedy when awake than an untrained person in sleep. But the plausible is not always the true, and it is not common-sense that discovers truth. The history of the sciences rather proves that every intellectual advance realises a paradoxical opinion, and intellectual development may be traced in the successive discomfitures of common-sense. There is no logical contradiction in the assertion that persons in the somnambulic state judge diseases more correctly than the thoughtful physician; the phenomenon is thus in the first place possible, and since it has already been a thousand times confirmed by physicians themselves, it is also actual. Now if these facts wholly and utterly contravene our physiological systems, one can only say, so much the worse for our systems! for in the end these must always yield to facts, not facts to them.

It has already resulted from the foregoing inquiry that dream is a means of diagnosis. Now as the somnambulic sleep is incomparably deeper than ordinary sleep, it is presumable that faculties which in ordinary sleep are only exhibited in an elementary form, will appear in somnambulism in an exalted degree.

Sleep brings with it an inner wakening, dream, and that in proportion as it excludes our senses from the outer world. This exclusion is in somnambulism more complete, the inner waking therefore clearer.

Now as in ordinary dreaming the inner material of feeling finds its more or less distinct representation, usually only in symbolical transformation, so will the clearer somnambulic dream bring with it a further, more distinct, consciousness of the bodily condition; as, moreover, persons in this sleep can be brought to speech upon their conditions, it is easy to understand that they are better informed concerning a disease which they *see*, than is often the physician, who only *judges*, that is, infers causes from symptoms.

The phenomenon of the magnetic sleep was already known to antiquity. Much that is wonderful in what the old physicians and philosophers relate of sleep, applies only to the magnetic sleep, between which and the ordinary sleep they do not distinguish. Only by observing this distinction will Hippocrates be fully understood. On the other hand, the Greek authors distinguish accurately between ὄναρ and ὕπαρ, for which our language has only the one word, dream. This is the linguistic expression for the fact that we see in all dreams only worthless phantasms, without recognising transcendental psychology; while the Greeks fell into the other extreme, and held transcendental psychological dreams to be divine inspirations.

Puységur had put a sick young man into magnetic sleep, who, waking interiorly and perceiving the seat of the disease, uttered of his own accord the words: 'I have an abscess in the head; it will suffocate me if it falls upon the chest.' The want of scientific precision in the murmured words might easily have caused Puységur to suppose them the delirium of fever. But not being prejudiced by system, he had the gift of allowing facts of a new character to avail as such; he pursued the thing further, and thus became the discoverer of one of the most important phenomena in the province of psychical knowledge.* He soon found that all somnambules, if their sleep reached the proper depth, possessed the faculty of self-inspection. With reference to this penetrative feeling and diagnosis of their own organism, somnambules can be considered their own physicians. Somnambules may be compared to the stethoscope in regard to the investigation of the interior organism.

In magnetic sleep, therefore, as in ordinary sleep, there is an inner waking, but it reaches a higher degree of clearness. It seems that in this deep sleep the inner organs are no longer seen in the form of phantastically transformed symbols, but in actual plastic representation, parts affected by disease being particularly discerned in this perception. The ordinary dream is occupied much less with the sound organs than with the diseased ones; the latter are those which repeatedly obtrude themselves in the images, and impart to these their constant character. But whereas the symptomatic dream-images give only indirect information of the causes of disease, the magnetic dream represents perceptibly the causes themselves, and the inner machinery of the organism. This fact is mentioned by Hippocrates in his treatise on dream: 'When the soul by sleep is released, not indeed altogether from the body, but from the gross service of its parts, it retreats into itself as into a port for protection from storm; it then sees and

* Puységur: 'Recherches physiologiques sur l'Homme dans l'État de Somnambulisme,' Paris, Dentu, 1811, p. 45.

knows all that goes on within, painting this condition in different figures and colours, and explaining distinctly the state of the body.' In his third book, 'On the Habits of Life,' he says also: 'All that passes in the body, the soul sees even with closed eyes.' The same condition is evidently referred to when it is said in the Vedas: 'When the soul reaches that hidden chamber in which Brahma resides, then the gross body quakes, and the soul with searching glance sees through this dwelling (the body), which is the house of the man.* Still more briefly in another place: 'In its body it goes about as it pleases.'†

The self-inspection of somnambules is in no way dependent upon an abstract knowledge, but merely on an exalted faculty for internal sensations, developing itself to perceptive presentation, and plastic reproduction of the inner sphere of the body, as according to Scherner can happen even in ordinary dream. The clearness of these presentations reaches very different degrees, but rises by habit, and whereas somnambules at first do not get beyond an account of mere internal feelings, their utterances frequently attain to the exactitude of anatomical descriptions, such as a layman without abstract knowledge would give from mere perception. Frau von U., magnetised by a clergyman, described her ear, saw four little knuckle-joints, one like a hammer, another like a stirrup, the third round, the fourth small, in a tube of water.‡ A cataleptic patient said to Petetin: 'A

* Windischmann: 'Philosophie im Fortgang der Weltgeschichte,' i. 1358.
† 'Kommentar des Sankara über Brahma-Sutra,' iii. 2, 3.
‡ Kieser: 'Archiv für den thierischen Magnetismus,' vii. 1, 73.

physician would think himself fortunate if he had my disease for a quarter of an hour; Nature would reveal all her secrets to him, and if he loved his science he would not wish, as I do, to be soon well again.'\*

This self-inspection being without abstract knowledge, the anatomical descriptions of somnambules naturally leave much to be desired in regard to learned exposition. The same would be the case with a medical student, if early in his course he had to report upon a section with his still defective knowledge. The utterances of somnambules are therefore not to be suspected on account of this defect in their description. Sleep can exalt the capacity for internal feeling, and that can lead to a representation of the organs concerned; but it is in no way apparent how it can awaken abstract knowledges not formerly in the mind. When the physician Deleuze put one of his colleagues into the somnambulic state, the sleeper spoke of his internal disease in quite scientific phraseology.† It would be in the highest degree suspicious were all somnambules to speak like professors, but the anatomical and physiological blunders which occur so often in their utterances are not so.‡ But these utterances become deceitful just when their own reflections get mixed up with their perception, and this danger is especially near when they are plied with questions which cannot be answered from self-inspection.

\* Petetin: 'Electricité animale,' ii.
† Deleuze: 'Histoire critique,' etc., i. 168.
‡ Instances are to be found in Morin's 'Du Magnétisme et des Sciences occultes,' Paris, Baillière, 1860, p. 196.

Reasonable physicians, therefore, adhere to the rule of waiting for the spontaneous utterances of the somnambules, which then are usually given with definitude. That indicates the moment when the internal sensibility has risen to the point of self-inspection. It is just then that the magnetising physician may, with advantage, direct this inspection by skilful questioning. Premature questioning cannot awaken the self-inspection, and there is not only the danger of the somnambules seeking for answers which must be false, because not arising from self-inspection; but also, owing to the peculiar rapport in which they stand with the magnetiser, that the latter's ideas and reflections may get transferred to them, so that they become the mere echo of the physician. Much, therefore, depends on the intelligence with which the physician puts his questions. Van Ghert's somnambule said that she saw very distinctly into her body when the physician himself saw with her and helped her by his thoughts; all was then clearer and more distinct.* Another praised the influence which the physician's questions had on her perceptive faculty; when he desired her to look at her lungs or any other organ, everything opened before her eyes.† Another saw only the diseased organs of her body spontaneously, the sound ones only when the magnetiser placed his hands over them.‡ The celebrated Hufeland adduces three different cases of self-inspection, illustrating its partial character. One of his

* Kieser: 'Archiv,' ii. 1, 69.
† *Ibid.*: 'Archiv,' ii. 1, 86.
‡ Dr. Fischer: 'Der Somnambulismus,' iii. 201.

patients saw her bowels quite spontaneously and suddenly, when she laid herself on her bed; when she stood up the vision ceased. Another time she awoke suddenly in the night, crying out that she saw her brain and spinal marrow. A second saw only those parts of her interior organism lying near places touched by Hufeland. And a third saw the interior flesh and veins of her arm immediately she touched a magnet, and this she carefully avoided doing, the sight being disagreeable to her.\*

Very remarkable is the faculty which somnambules possess of knowing the future course of their diseases. This was known to Hippocrates, who said that there were dreams in which the diseases of the body were predicted. Much as the sceptic may be inclined to doubt such a faculty, it has nevertheless been confirmed by a very large number of physicians with great certainty. It may suffice here to refer to the judgment of the medical faculty of the Paris Academy. The physician Delpit reports of an epileptic who during an attack predicted the time of her recovery to a minute.† In Bertrand's 'Traité du Somnambulisme' are mentioned more than sixty convulsive attacks of a dangerous character which were foreseen, and their occurrence and duration determined to the minute by somnambules. The same physician reports the case of a somnambule, who announced a delirium of forty-three hours, fourteen days before, knowing nothing of it in the interval.‡ Dr. Bendson's somnambule gave out the time exactly when she should

---

\* Hufeland: 'Ueber Sympathie,' 200, 202, 155, 199.
† 'Bibl. Med.,' i. 6, 308.
‡ Dupotet: 'Traité,' etc., 440.

be relieved from a worm, and even its exact length.\* Even the prevision of death occurs with somnambules without their having any memory of it in the intervals of waking consciousness. Souvages treated four persons who rightly predicted the day and hour of their death, and a man of sixty years of age, who predicted his death a month before, and who died of a frost-fever.†

On the other hand, prognostications of death, even with otherwise reliable somnambules, are frequently erroneous. Deleuze renounces even the attempt to explain, and says it is one of the darkest points in this province. It seems to me, however, that the thing explains itself, if we remember that somnambules do not foreknow by reflection what is to happen to them, but see all in images as every dreamer does. Now, if there is presented the image of a very dangerous crisis, or deep swoon, that would have the greatest resemblance to dying or even death. And Deleuze himself indicates the right explanation, for he admits that the crises which the somnambules had taken for death were always very alarming and dangerous.‡

The organ of dream is still the formative imagination, even if it must be allowed that it is not the imagination we have in waking, and which is then not approximately equal to the faculty as it exists in dream. Therefore, such predictions will not enter consciousness as abstract knowledge, but as image, although that may seem to be contradicted by the often

---

\* Kieser: 'Archiv,' xi. 1, 161.
† Souvages: 'Nosologie,' ii. 738.
‡ Deleuze: 'Instruction pratique,' etc., 422, 426.

extraordinary exactness with which time is fixed. A somnambule who predicted the point of time of a severe spasmodic attack, added : 'I see myself now run off to bed.'* They see not only the interior of the body, but even future events in images. 'What I say of myself is quite as though I saw it . . . and so I see my different postures this day quite clear as in images. It is just as if pictures hung before me, in which my postures had been copied, and so I can describe them beforehand.'†

Thus, as in ordinary dream thought does not remain in the abstract, but immediately passes into the representation of things, so also with somnambules. A further proof that there are only differences of degree between dream and somnambulism is to be found in the fact that in both the forms of the images frequently agree, being often allegorical, and often, as it were, with a dramatic severance of the individual, because we place thoughts, awakened in us in dream, in the mouth of another—thus exercising in dream a sort of ventriloquism—and all dream-representations, though having their seat within ourselves, are forced upon us always from without. The allegorical picture-form runs through the whole history of the widow Petersen's disease. She foresees different situations which she is to encounter in her illness; but this knowledge is pictorial and allegoric; a dove accompanies her, either as an indication of her relation to the future, or as actually speaking to her, or as holding a letter in its beak.‡ In this dramatic self-

* Kerner: 'Geschichte zweier Somnambulen,' Karlsruhe, 1824, § 100.
† Ibid.: Op. cit., 67.
‡ Kieser: 'Archiv,' xi. 2, 82; xi. 3, 67.

determination are often introduced the guides and guardian spirits of somnambules, giving occasion to manifold superstition.

As somnambules foresee in images the future development of the disease, and with that can often determine what advantage they will derive from the magnetic treatment, so also they are frequently able to see in the same way what would have happened without that treatment. Thus one patient declared that, but for magnetism, apoplexy, from the bursting of one of the larger vessels in a violent congestion, would occur, putting an end to her life within a year.* Another saw that she would have died in eighteen months, because without the magnetic treatment five incurable tumours would have arisen.† Obviously, the truth of such deliverances cannot be established, and they are therefore of but small value. Not only the effects, however, but also the causes of their diseases are known to somnambules in different degrees of clearness. Often there arises in them only the instinctive feeling of the cause, often they see in their interiors an irritant object foreign to the organism. Thus Kerner's somnambule saw a piece of mother-of-pearl, which years before she had inadvertently swallowed, grown into her stomach, and how, in the course of further treatment, it was gradually forced out, showing seven fissures, the thing coming, in fact, to view after a purge.‡ Somnambules often discover the occasion of their illness by a long retrospect, as in the case of one who referred the headaches

* Kieser: 'Archiv,' xi. 1, 22.
† Puységur: 'Recherches,' etc., 171.
‡ Kerner: 'Geschichte zweier Somnambulen,' 94.

from which she had long suffered to a fright she received fifteen years before, when her brother fell through into a hidden well.*

Now, if anyone wishing to dispense with the hypothesis of actual clairvoyance, should still conclude that the knowledge of somnambules is in the abstract, supposing that by means of their exalted sensibility they obtain indications enabling them to reason from their present condition to its past cause and future effect, he would not thus attain his object; for the predictions of somnambules often extend to events not prepared in the organism, even when concerning their own persons, but resulting from external accidents. Meissner's somnambule dreamed that she was floating on a wave, and struggling with the greatest energy against drowning; the next day she fell into the bath in a swoon, and, being alone, was in danger of being drowned.† Another saw in dream a man approach her saying: 'How long has she been ill?' and then make magnetic passes from her head to her feet. Three days later she was called into the parsonage-house, where this second sight was fulfilled.‡ Hortense, a somnambule, had predicted in dream that at a certain hour she would fall down. To prevent this her husband and the physician were present at the time named, and when she had to leave the room her husband took her under his arm. But suddenly a rat sprang past her, and she sank with a scream on the ground.§ Something similar is reported by Klein

---

\* Kieser: 'Archiv,' vii. 1, 100.
† Ibid.: 'Archiv,' x. 2, 101.
‡ Werner: 'Die Schutzgeister,' Stuttgart, 1839, p. 316.
§ Champignon: 'Physiologie, Médicine et Metaphysique du Magnétisme,' Paris, 1848, p. 344.

of the somnambule Auguste Müller. On the 14th January, 1817, she disclosed to her magnetiser that on the 12th of February, between three and four in the afternoon, she would swallow a pin unless she was prevented. On the day named, therefore, she was not let out of sight, and all pins were removed. It happened, however, that she got up, and turning her back to those with her, conveyed the pin of her gold brooch to her mouth. Slipping through her fingers, it was indeed thrown up again by coughing, but left a small scar in the uvula.* Such cases, which could be multiplied indefinitely, sufficiently prove that the utterances of somnambules rest on actual clairvoyance, and have nothing to do with operations of the understanding. With many, however, it seems that this clairvoyance remains confined to the development of disease, and does not embrace events which are due to accident. This was the case, for instance, with the somnambulist observed by the physicians of the Paris Academy, who predicted a succession of his epileptic seizures, of which only the first in fact occurred, the last being prevented by the accident in the meanwhile that he was killed in attempting to stop a runaway horse.†

It is a hint given to us by Nature herself, that the spontaneous utterances of somnambules have almost always exclusive reference to their disease. The physician should therefore be contented with bringing to their consciousness only that which lies, so to speak, already on the tongue, as Socrates considered

* Meier und Klein: 'Geschichte der hellsehenden Auguste Müller,' Stuttgart, 1818, p. 96.
† Dupotet: 'Traité,' etc., 144.

himself as only an intellectual midwife to his pupils. If he compels answers of another nature, he will find that his own ideas are unwittingly transferred to the somnambules, or he will excite in them an ingredient of reflection, foreign to their condition, and quite unadapted to the discovery of the desired information. Such attempts may even lead to the mental disorganisation of the somnambules.

But restricted as this clairvoyant insight remains, in general, to the internal sphere of the body and the course of disease, and though the utterances of somnambules cease to be reliable in proportion as they overstep this sphere, yet attempts have always been made, both in modern and ancient times, to make prophets of somnambules, or to obtain from them elucidations of metaphysical questions, which must be regarded as wholly worthless, as they do not spring from natural instinct, but from reflection, containing therefore only presentations of the religious conceptions in which the speakers have grown up, with phantastical additions.

That the self-inspection and clairvoyance of somnambules in relation to disease is in fact only a natural instinct, not produced, but only excited and unfolded by the magnetic treatment, is best proved by the fact that this capacity is not exhibited only in artificial somnambulism, but often in a still purer form in the natural somnambulism which in the course of disease is often spontaneously induced and suddenly developed. Such a case is related by a Florentine physician, Antonius Benevenius: A young Florentine, named Gasparo, being wounded by an arrow, tried to draw it from his breast, but the iron point remained in, leaving the wood in his hand. Soon afterwards he began to prophesy; he named the persons who came to visit him long before their arrival, and designated the hour of his recovery; but said that later on he should travel to Rome and should there die. Benevenius assures us that at the hour appointed the point of the arrow came out, the prophetic gift then ceasing, and, further, that Gasparo in fact died afterwards at Rome.*

Thus, in waking, our healthy organs perform their functions imperceptibly for our consciousness, and we are sensible only of those which are morbidly excited. In ordinary dreaming this inner sensibility is exalted, especially in relation to diseased organs, and the exciting cause is represented in symbolical images. Finally, in somnambulism, self-inspection is among the most constant phenomena, inclining likewise especially to the diseased organs, often without any symbolism. But as the ordinary dream often dramatises the internal feelings, and a severance of the dreaming subject occurs, so is it also with somnambules when the result of the self-inspection is imparted to them by seeming guardian-spirits, or by a deceased person with whom the mind is much occupied. Even the process by which the disturbed organic forces seek to restore their equilibrium often takes on the form of a struggle between a good and a bad genius. There is no reason to attach importance to this form, and to infer from it the actual existence of such spirits, which have no more reality than the personalities into which our Ego dramatically sunders

* Colquhoun : 'The Secret Sciences of all Times and Peoples,' German edition, Weimar, 1853, p. 233.

itself in the common dream; but just as little reason is there, because scepticism objects to this form, on account of it 'to shake out the child with the bath,' and deny the capacity of somnambules for self-inspection. This fallacy, of laying the accent on the form, and holding the nature of the thing to be inseparable from this form, has been very destructive in the history of somnambulism, because among the old Greeks, in the dramatic sundering of the somnambulic sleepers Apollo and Æsculapius made their appearance, and the Christianity which succeeded, having deposed these gods, believed it necessary to give up the whole institution of the temple-sleep.

It may be well to pause here, and introduce an attempt theoretically to explain the facts of somnambulism which have been considered up to this point; for as in what follows we shall meet with even much more remarkable things, the sceptical reader might easily want patience to peruse a succession of phenomena which he holds, *à priori*, for impossible, unless he is first provided with a standard by which to judge of them, and their possibility is made clear to him.

We see that in the inner wakening of somnambulism there is a knowing and a willing, while our normal experience disposes us to see in knowing and willing functions only active in waking life, and connected with certain changes in the nervous system and its centre, the brain. Now since in deep sleep, as a matter of fact, this central nervous system has no relations with the external world, while nevertheless an inner wakening occurs, and the soul of the sleeper experiences influences, first from the sphere of his internal organism, but often also from beyond its limits, it follows immediately from this fact, that the cerebral system of nerves is not the soul's only means of connection with the outer world, but that we stand in conjunction with Nature by yet another, and, as it were, subterranean way. Now if we do not forthwith adopt the Psyche, free from body, of the Spiritualists, but even for this subterranean connection would seek an organ of material mediation, physiology directs us to the system of so-called sympathetic nerves—named also, on account of its multiplicity of nerve-cells, the ganglionic system, a still very mysterious structure, of which not much more is known than that it governs the vegetative-life process of the organism. As the cerebral nerve-system has its central seat in the brain, so the ganglionic system has its centre in the solar plexus. This is a collection of combined nerves, larger and smaller, mutually connected in the cavity of the chest, near the pit of the stomach, behind the stomach. The functions of these two systems of nerves, brain and ganglions, go on quite independently of one another; heart-action, digestion, secretion of bile, etc., are not subject to our conscious will, and continue in sleep. Externally, to the eye of the anatomist, this mutual independence of the two nerve-systems appears as an almost complete isolation from one another.

This visible independence must certainly be in some way grounded in the inner nature of man, and the fact of his inner waking in sleep requires, indeed, that to this sympathetic nerve-system not only sensibility, but even capacity for consciousness[*] should

---

[*] That is, that it should be able to take the place of the brain as the apparent centre of consciousness. All sensation is, of course, consciousness, but the distinction implied in the text is thus explained.—Tr.

accede. Such an opinion is decidedly not arbitrary. After the experiments of different investigators with decapitated frogs, and that of Pflüger upon the sensorial functions of the spinal marrow, there remains no doubt that a capacity for consciousness must be attributed to every nerve-cell, and we shall have the less hesitation in this, as in our time physics and chemistry, impelled by the facts of Nature herself, have had to throw overboard the conception of dead matter, and to ascribe even to atoms a capacity of sensibility, thus the rudiments of consciousness.

Now, if material changes in the system of sympathetic nerves are accompanied by a ganglionic consciousness, that is nevertheless independent of our brain-consciousness. Physiology has introduced the conception of the 'psycho-physical threshold,' to indicate the boundary line between those material changes in the organism which are felt by us and attain to consciousness, and those changes which proceed without an accompanying consciousness. Whether the first or the latter is the case, depends on the force of stimulation of these processes on the central nerve system. This psycho-physical threshold thus limits merely the sphere of brain-consciousness, and such stimulations as remain below this threshold may nevertheless be accompanied by a ganglionic consciousness. That this is in fact the case, is proved by sleep, and particularly by somnambulism. The fact of inner waking affirms nothing else than that processes of the organism which in waking remain unconscious, are then perceived. But this fact is explicable by two hypotheses. Either this inner waking has nothing whatever to do with the brain-system of nerves, and then the ganglionic system must be regarded as the supporter of consciousness; or the system of sympathetic nerves in sleep conducts the excitation received to the brain, and there elicits a response, and in that case, at least, the psycho-physical threshold must necessarily be displaced in sleep, and all the more, the deeper the sleep is. Many phenomena of somnambulism appear to testify to the occurrence of both processes, and that in sleep the isolation of the cerebral nerve-system from the ganglionic partially ceases.

Man summarises in the word 'I' all the feelings which lie on this side the psycho-physical threshold of sensibility, because he refers them to a single supporter, and makes his *personal* consciousness dependent on them. Excitations below the threshold remain unconscious. That such excitations take place, we know positively; and that fact of itself already obliges us to distinguish between our person and our subject, between consciousness and soul, in so far as subject and soul project beyond the limits of our personal consciousness. The thread which binds together the individual feelings, and thereby makes a personal consciousness possible, is memory; without memory no identity of person. Now, if it can be proved—and somnambulism proves it manifestly—that even the unconscious nerve-excitations are held together by an individual supporter, and are connected with one another by the thread of memory, then the consciousness accompanying them will be likewise a personal consciousness, but this consciousness will be other than that of the cerebral consciousness which is composed from the nerve-excitations lying above the threshold of sensibility. Our Subject, our Soul, falls asunder, therefore, into two persons, not, indeed, different in themselves, but divided by the threshold of sensibility. If the memory which connects the successions of feelings of each single person severally also connected those of the two, were there no threshold of sensibility marking off one person from the other, both persons would flow together in one, identical with the Subject comprehending them; consciousness and soul would then coincide. This, however, is only the case in Somnambulism; but we awake from this state without memory, and then the bridges of connection, by which the two persons could communicate, fails.

Medical-Councillor Klein says of his somnambule, Augusta Müller, of Carlsruhe, that whenever she meditated on her own condition or the disease of another, respiration ceased. She then resembled a marble figure, all colour left her face, and no other sign of life could be remarked than a weak pulse in the hands.* Thus we see here very distinctly the retreat of the diurnal life as reverse of the inner waking. But the sayings of somnambules unanimously point to the ganglionic system as the material supporter of the interior sense. They often speak of the stomach as the seat of their presentations, so that many reporters use the term 'seeing with the stomach.' But of a seeing in the physiological sense it is not here allowable to speak, though the presentation which takes place in the inner waking has either really the form of a perceptual image, or at least somnambules employ that mode of

* Meier und Klein: 'Geschichte der hellsehenden Augusta Müller,' Stuttgart, 1818.

expression in describing it. An analogy with physiological seeing is also so far given, that the organ of the inner sense cannot be at the same time itself the object, as the eye sees all but itself. Kerner's patient said she saw all parts of her body except the stomach (that lying too near the focus of sight); most clearly of all she saw the marrow and the blood, as through a glass lying on the pit of the stomach, now appearing clear, now obscure.* Another somnambule, on being asked what parts she saw, answered: 'All that I will, except the stomach and part of the forehead above the nose, with which the ray of perception proceeding from the stomach is in connection.'† Nevertheless, even the stomach is also frequently an object for the inner sense, and with the Seeress of Prevorst even the solar-plexus; she describes it as a sun moving slowly, she sees its nerves shining, and delineates the course of several of them with complete anatomical correctness.‡ This inner sight, concentrated in the region of the stomach, is very frequently referred to in the sayings of somnambules, and must therefore have a real foundation of some sort.

The solution of our external personality by the transcendental in the somnambulic state, also very well explains that the disease is quite differently conceived, not only as to its quality, but as a fact, and in regard to the fate of the individual. While the transcendental consciousness expects a cure with the greatest assurance, despair of it remains in waking. A patient who, waking, was always much

---

* Kerner: 'Geschichte zweier Somnambulen,' 75.
† Kieser: 'Archiv,' iv. 2, 172.
‡ Kerner: 'Die Seherin von Prevorst,' 82, Stuttgart, 1878.

troubled and spoke of dying, in the magnetic sleep was quite cheerful and laughed at the fears by which she was tormented when awake.\* Another in waking thought herself lost, but was always full of hope in sleep.† Somnambules, however, insist on an energetic combating of the evil by the physician, not feeling the fear with which in waking they anticipate his methods; they warn him against mild proceedings from false pity.‡ It can only result from complete solution of the sense-consciousness by the transcendental, from the dualism of two persons of one Subject, that a somnambule spoke of her approaching death in her twenty-fifth year in the same cheerful tone as of other things.§

This solution is not always complete; there is often in somnambulism an opposition between the sensuous and the magnetic Ego, then reflected in the dramatic form which the self-inspection takes on. A French idio-somnambule (that is, one with whom somnambulism occurs spontaneously, without magnetic treatment) was irritated with the violent pains which she suffered in the stomach, as by another person assailing her, and continually bade the same to be silent and to go away ‖ Yet more distinctly was this the case with the already-mentioned Widow Petersen, who dramatised her self-inspection by a symbolical dove. Light is thrown upon her utterances, which sound like senseless phantasms, when they are looked upon

---

\* Kieser: 'Archiv,' ii. 1, 101; Reichel: 'Entwicklungsgesetz des magnischen Lebens,' 107, Leipzig, 1829.
† Aubin Gauthier: 'Histoire du Somnambulisme,' ii. 359.
‡ Kieser: 'Archiv,' ii. 1, 174.
§ 'Archiv,' vii. 2, 38.
‖ Ibid. ii. 2, 199.

as representing that tension between the magnetic and anti-magnetic Ego. The self-inspection had not yet attained to clear perception when she said: 'There comes the dove with a sealed letter, which it will open.' Then the curiosity of the sense-consciousness prevails, when she continues: 'Ah, now I see a second smaller dove, picking the seal with its beak.' The magnetic Ego again comes forward in the words: 'Get back, says the larger one; that cannot be. I see for the patient; thou hast not the power. Is not that humiliating to the small dove, which means as well by me as the large one? But the old one remains immovable; she thinks it out thoroughly, and is therefore steadfast. Now the dove has three letters, one in the beak and one under each wing. . . . In eight days I shall learn the contents of one, later of the second; the third will be opened on New Year's night.'* Thus the self-inspection took place later, as on this occasion the transcendental consciousness had not sufficiently emerged to succeed.

Self-inspection is only thinkable on the principle of a changed relation of our consciousness to the organism, by displacement of the threshold of sensibility. As we thereby obtain knowledge of our interior parts, which fails us in waking because the nerve-excitation giving the information remains below the threshold, it follows that our sense-consciousness does not embrace the sensibility of our whole Subject —in other words, the normal consciousness does not exhaust its object, the soul. A doctrine of Soul which is restricted to the analysis of our conscious representation and thinking is therefore incomplete,

* Kieser: 'Archiv,' xi. 3, 67.

and will never succeed in solving the human problem. We must study all those conditions of man in which the sphere of consciousness extends itself. That happens in ordinary sleep and in somnambulism, first in reference to the interior of the body, and especially the diseased parts of it, as in waking, indeed, the sound organs are unfelt, but the diseased ones immediately become objects of consciousness. But since in the inner self-inspection the living active organism is observed, and the process, by which the curative power of Nature seeks to restore the disturbed equilibrium of the organic forces, is represented in symbolical images, and often dramatically, the study of somnambulism promises much more valuable conclusions concerning man than can result from reports of dissections, even if in addition we subject half the animal kingdom to vivisection. Vivisectors can therefore only believe their method indispensable, because they are wholly ignorant of somnambulism, and in general hold the materialistic explanation of life to be the only possible one. On the other hand, all physicians who have studied somnambulism are agreed that from it alone can valuable conclusions respecting the economy of the organism be obtained; and thus they can see in vivisection nothing but useless cruelty.*

Notwithstanding obscure points connected with this fact of self-introspection, the experience already gained enables a general theory of the phenomenon to be sketched. Here, as throughout the whole province of transcendental psychology, the necessity of distinguishing between consciousness and soul,

* Deleuze: 'Instruction pratique,' etc., 440.

Ego and Subject, is imperative. In the development of the body the Ego has absolutely no active part, our vegetative functions are for it unconscious. But somnambulism teaches that for the soul they are by no means unconscious; for if somnambules know disorders in the organism as disorders, and even preferably concern themselves with these, they must necessarily possess some kind of standard of comparison, a representation of what ought to be. To see through a disorder as such, the healthy normal condition must be known. It follows that the normal process of life, also, and not only its disturbances, must go on with a transcendental consciousness, which can only be, if the soul, the supporter of that consciousness, is identical with the organising principle in us. Darwin himself is, indeed, disposed to admit that the struggle for existence aims only at the adaptation of organisms to the conditions of existence, so that the higher developments of species from one another would still require an impulse of organic formation. That this formative impulse is provided with consciousness, is shown by self-introspection, and that to the supporter of this consciousness a will must be ascribed, is proved by the functions of the natural curative-force, which, as it can only be regarded as a continuation of the organising impulse, must participate in the consciousness of the latter.

The prognosis of somnambules leads us to the like result. When somnambules predict in detail the course of their disease, often to the extent of months, that implies some sort of knowledge of the laws of the inner life, which again is only possible, if the subject of the prognosis is identical with the organising principle.

(*b*) *The Diagnosis of the Diseases of others by Somnambules.*—As our visible body is the nearest object of our sensuous consciousness, but also mediates the relations of the latter to the external world, so also is the interior of the organism merely the nearest object of the somnambulic sense, which, however, likewise stands in manifold relations with the external world. This is not the place to inquire how far the inner sense can go beyond the sphere of the body, and what modifications our perceptive forms, time and space, thereby undergo. Here we are only to show that, and how far, dream is a physician, and only that extension of the inner sense beyond its own bodily sphere shall at present be investigated, which occurs in the somnambulic diagnosis of the diseases of others.

According to the experience of physicians who have concerned themselves with this subject, it is the rule that somnambules with the faculty of introspection can also see through foreign organisms. As regards the fact of this capacity, I will first refer again to the already-mentioned report of the Medical Academy in Paris, wherein it is said: 'The magnetised person, sunk in somnambulism, judges the diseases of those with whom he puts himself in *rapport*, determines the character of the disease, and indicates the remedies.'

It will contribute somewhat to the elucidation of the subject to point out here that even in waking we can exceptionally experience influences from without not conveyed to us by the normal sensibility of the senses, and which must therefore depend upon a slight function of transcendental consciousness. There is, for example, the case of so-called idiosyncrasies, the best known being the insuperable repugnance of certain persons for particular animals, most often cats, a repugnance frequently evinced when the proximity of the animals is unknown. But I must reserve the treatment of this subject for another occasion, contenting myself here with the remark that such idiosyncrasies occur in an exalted form in somnambulism when the object is kept at hand—a proof that these waking antipathies depend in fact on a slight awakening of the transcendental consciousness.

It seems that even the capacity of determining the diseases of others is already exceptionally apparent in the waking state. An elementary form of it perhaps insinuates itself even into professional diagnosis, which does not always solely depend on reflective judgments and logical reasoning from the symptoms to the cause of the disease, but often upon an intuitive glimpse, especially when there is a great affection between physician and patient, from which results a relation similar to the somnambulic *rapport*, and to that which is often observed between mother and child. As, however, in all arts and sciences reflexion and intuition are mutually more or less exclusive, and only in genius come to an ideal equivalence, physicians with a predominant tendency to abstract understanding attach but small value to this sort of half-instinctive diagnosis.

The oldest instance of it is, nevertheless, that of a physician. Galen (who, from his own statement, appears to have owed much of his practical knowledge to observation of the sleep life) is reported to have defined the course of approaching diseases with such remarkable exactness, that we are reminded of the magnetic clairvoyance of somnambules. To the Senator Sextus, then apparently quite well, he predicted that in three days he would be attacked by a fever, which would leave him on the sixth day, would return on the fourteenth, and would disappear on the seventeenth after a crisis marked by a general perspiration, as events proved. Another physician having recommended bleeding to a young Roman in fever, Galen forbade it, saying that a bleeding from the left nostril would occur of itself, and then the patient would recover.* For the benefit of those who would still ascribe such diagnoses to Galen's extraordinary professional skill, other cases may be mentioned. Des Cartes believed that two hysterical young girls had predicted each other's crises.† In the *Mercure de France* (September, 1720, and June, 1728) there is an account of two Portuguese ladies, who appear to have enjoyed great celebrity for their diagnoses. One of them was in great estimation with the Queen of Portugal, and received a large yearly salary. She saw into the interior of the human body, the circulation of the blood, and the digestive process; and discovered diseases which had escaped the most skilful physicians.‡ In a later time, Ludwig von Voss writes to Dorow: 'Do not

* Puységur: 'Recherches,' etc., 319, 322; Colquhoun: 'The Secret Sciences,' etc., 113.
† Dupotet: 'Traité complet de Magnetisme animal,' 440.
‡ Le Brun: 'Histoire critique des Pratiques superstitieuses,' i. 58 (Amsterdam, 1733).

laugh if I tell you that I can feel where one has been sitting on a sofa or a chair half an hour before, especially in the case of men of much vitality; that yesterday I felt that one had come from far, and was tired; that I knew with my whole person, by his influence on me, he must have been occupied, particularly in the afternoon, with calculations and with mental strain in them. . . . In my person has been developed the strange unhappy faculty of knowing in the quietest condition all the sufferings and infirmities of men, and even the slightest fibre set in activity in another's brain by thinking. In the street I have to get far out of the way of people, especially of those who are ill. On first entering a room, I know immediately what is the matter with everyone.'*

To what a degree of clearness this insight into foreign bodies can attain, remarkable instances are related by the English physician Haddock. He says of his somnambule Emma: 'When patients will allow themselves to be personally examined by Emma, as a rule I request them not to inform me of their symptoms before the clairvoyante has undertaken the examination and has described the internal condition and the symptoms; and it not seldom happens that they express their astonishment when they hear Emma exactly describing their symptoms, and indicating the suffering parts so rightly, or naming the time of day at which periodical attacks recur; all without a word having been said either to her or to me. . . . On two or three occasions Emma has shown the seat of the disease of insane persons,

* Clemens: 'Das Ferngefühl nach Zeit und Raum,' Frankfurt, 1857, p. 28.

who were not actually present, on her own head, and from these indications I have ventured, on phrenological grounds, to say what would be the principal symptom of intellectual disturbance in those cases, and the physicians of those patients have confirmed my account.'*

Even cases in which the accuracy of the diagnosis has been established by subsequent dissection are not rare. Naturally such diagnoses, given from mere perception by the inner sense, without any abstract knowledge of anatomy and the physiology of the human body, have not the scientific, or even verbal, precision which belongs to professional reports upon sections. Nevertheless a skilful physician will draw useful conclusions from such statements. Frau Lagendré, a somnambule who had been magnetised in order to obtain her opinion upon her mother's condition, gave the following diagnosis: 'The right lung is shrivelled up and compressed; it is surrounded by a tough glutinous membrane; it swims in a quantity of water. The right lung no longer breathes, it is dead. There is some water in the cavity of the heart.' Now after the death of the mother, which, according to the prediction of the somnambule, occurred the next day, the dissection was undertaken by Dr. Drousart and Moreau, secretary of the Royal Academy of Medicine, and entirely bore out the above statement.†

As the self-introspection depends on the feelings experienced by the somnambules of organs of whose functions normal consciousness is unaware, so the

---

\* Haddock: 'Somnolism,' etc., 192, 193.
† Gauthier: 'Histoire du Somnambulisme,' ii. 363.

vision through foreign organisms presupposes a still greater displacement of the threshold of sensibility and emergence of the transcendental half of the being. Now, on the doubtless correct assumption that such perceptions depend upon material influences, as of perhaps a subtle emanation, this clairvoyance would thus appear to be quite a natural capacity, which can only not be awakened in the ordinary condition because the foundation of a feeling is then wanting. The transcendental Ego stands in another relation to the outer world than the empirical Ego; it is as it were only the prolongation of the latter, the root of our being, whose connection with the external can then first be felt when the life is drawn down from the stem above ground, and its summit, the sense-consciousness, into the root. To denote this altered relation the term 'magnetic rapport' has been adopted. The magnetic treatment is, however, far from being the only means of introducing this rapport, that is, this displacement of the normal relation to the external. And it cannot be too much insisted upon, that it is not the whole Subject that is pushed into another relation with the external, but merely the person of day-waking consciousness; the rapport is not first produced by somnambulism, but exists for the Subject before and after it; only not for the person of consciousness. This person knows only of five connecting threads with the outer world, it has only five senses; while our Subject has at its disposal further threads of connection, whereof some are sensible in the condition which we call somnambulism. The number of these threads we cannot at all determine *à priori*, experience alone can inform us on this point; but even had no somnambule ever been observed, there could be no doubt whatever of the existence of such threads of the Subject, that is to say, of unconscious relations between us and things. This is not only a logical consequence for the pantheistic conception of the world, but even materialistic monism, by reason of the Evolution theory, cannot escape it, though the books of materialists prove that Logic also belongs for them to the Unconscious.

The relation of man to Nature will never be understood, as long as we conceive the Subject to be absorbed in the person of consciousness, nor will the definition of man ever be reached if the Ego above the threshold of sensibility is held to be alone existent, and the delusion survives that an exhaustive account of man can be given by a physiological psychology. Man is like those stars (*e.g.*, Procyon) which with an obscure companion are united into a double star, and describe an ellipse about a common point of gravity. Now if one only holds the clear star for actual, and recognises only those lines of gravitation which bind it to the centre of attraction of the Milky Way, its motion becomes a mystery, which is first solved when one admits also the further lines of gravitation which are directed to the dark companion-star. So also he, who will be a monist, who will conceive man and Nature together, must take into consideration the dark companion of our conscious Ego, the Ego which lies beneath the threshold of sensibility. It is the insight that between us and Nature there exists a more comprehensive rapport than that of the five senses, that first puts us on the right foundation for seeking the solution of the human problem; but whoever neglects our occult companion, and pursues physiological psychology, resembles an astronomer who would explain the motions of Procyon by the central sun.

The rapport of Somnambules with the outer world is first directed to their magnetiser, through whose body they appear to be able to see with especial ease. Van Ghert's somnambule fell to crying when she compared her own inner state with that of her magnetiser, whom she declared to be sound in all his organs.\* But the rapport next extends itself to persons with whom they are connected by sympathy and affection; they concern themselves willingly with friends, whom they endeavour to inspect in order to help. Finally, it is in the power of the magnetiser to extend this rapport also to indifferent persons, and when this happens through bodily contact or through a material vehicle, *e.g.* hair, we have another proof of an actual material influence exciting the clairvoyance. The rapport must be dependent on some sort of material agency to which the normal man is not susceptible. Van Ghert's somnambule fell into rapport with every patient who touched a string extending from her at any distance; she even herself felt the disease of the person thus in connection with her, and could declare the evil he suffered from, its cause, and former treatment, quite correctly and particularly.† Professor Mayo says: 'From Boppard I sent to an American friend who was staying in Paris a lock of hair, which Colonel C., whom I was then treating, had cut from his own head, and

\* 'Archiv,' ii. 1, 80.
† *Ibid.* iii. 3, 49, 70.

had wrapped up in notepaper from his own desk. The Colonel was quite unknown even by name to the American, who could have not the slightest indication of the person to whom the lock of hair belonged. His commission, which he punctually executed, was to give the paper containing the hair into the hand of a Paris somnambule.' The deliverance of the latter, which was correct, was that the Colonel suffered from a partial paralysis of the hips and legs, and that for a complaint of another nature he was accustomed to use a surgical instrument.\* In the Saltpetrière in Paris, a somnambule was put into the sleep for the purpose of determining the disease of another person. She fell into violent agitation even before the patient had opened the door, and then refused to make the diagnosis in his presence. When he had withdrawn, she contradicted the medical opinion that the disease was in the chest, asserting that it was heart disease, and predicting a violent hæmorrhage on the fourth day, and death on the tenth ; as in fact happened, the correctness of the diagnosis being also established.†

An interesting diagnosis is that of a somnambulist celebrated in his time, Alexis, on the occasion of a meeting with the famous prestigiator Houdin, who had come to Alexis on the supposition that he had to deal with an expert in his own art, and thinking to expose him. He brought to him some hair of his son, whose age Alexis rightly declared, with the addition that the son had pains in his right side. But he immediately contradicted himself, saying that

\* Mayo : ' Truths in Popular Superstitions.'
† Mirville : ' Pneumatologie,' i. 32, Paris, 1853.

it was Houdin himself who must have these pains, which he perceived because his son's hair had been touched by him. The son, on the contrary, Alexis declared to be perfectly sound, and when Houdin denied this, he said that the little swelling on the right eye, about which the father was very uneasy because the physicians feared Amaurosis, was not at all dangerous.* The whole report of the meeting of these two men should be perused, the celebrated conjurer finally declaring, after many experiments, that there was not in the whole world a conjurer who could by his art imitate the capacity of Alexis.† It may be said that the judgment of a conjurer has no value, and only a professional man of science could decide in this case.‡ But that is just the question, who is here the expert? It is only now for the first time that the ground-lines of a transcendental psychology can be sketched, and the laws of somnambulism are as yet little known to us; official science from Mesmer's day, thus for a whole century, has notoriously held aloof from these phenomena, declaring them to be *à priori* impossible;§ so that this science has really

---

\* Mirville.

† [This declaration Houdin put into writing, signed, and sent to the Marquis Eudes de Mirville, who transmitted it with a memorandum to the French Academy of Sciences. The text of Houdin's letter is given in Mirville's 'Pneumatologie,' vol. i.—Tr.]

‡ [That could not well be said, at least in this country, where the testimony of well-known men of science to phenomena usually discredited is always met by the objection that the professional conjurer, and not the man of science, is the right person to expose the trickery which may deceive observers not specially trained in such arts. (When the conjurer in his turn gives testimony, it is said that he is not the right sort of conjurer.)—Tr.]

§ This *disposition* is no doubt the reason why the evidences have never been fully and fairly entertained; but it is doubtful

no experts at all. Nor will it soon be otherwise; official science having been but just awakened from its dogmatic slumber by the performances of the magnetiser Hansen. For the rest, whoever looks on clairvoyance as an impossibility, and therefore as trickery, by this very assertion designates the conjurer as the professional expert in this province; and thus for a sceptic the declaration of a Houdin must carry as much weight as that of a professor.

To cite a case of correct diagnosis in very recent times, even a decided sceptic will have nothing to object against the judgment which the president of the Upper Consistory at Münich, Dr. von Harless, has passed from his own experience. When a lady in Leipzig was suffering from a critical spine disease, his friend Professor Lindner—without the knowledge of Harless, who was averse from such things—consulted a somnambule in Dresden upon her condition. 'On his return he imparted to me the following statement. He had asked the somnambule if she could transport herself in spirit to a neighbouring town (known to her), and into the room of a sick person there residing? She replied in the affirmative, on condition that some indication was given her by which to distinguish the house in question from the

---

whether in England any well-known man of science, (with the single exception of Faraday in a possibly inconsiderate sentence), has ever *explicitly* committed himself to a judgment of *à priori* impossibility. The scientific countrymen of Bacon have learned to be cautious in their language, if not to be really free from the unphilosophical prejudice in question. Indeed, the latter is so far from being the case in relation to these phenomena, that the result has been a not very candid pretence of general amenability to evidence, coupled with a practically absolute refusal to consider it.—Tr.]

neighbouring ones. It was answered that the house might easily be known by two signs, for first it lay obliquely opposite the choir of a church; and secondly, there was a pump—the only one in the street—just in front of the house. The somnambule seemed satisfied, and after some time she said she had found the house, and the room in which the patient was, and that the latter was just then suffering again from paroxysm, and sat or lay upon a sofa; whereupon she described the room and the dress of the patient. The indications, so far as the questioner knew, agreed. He then asked if the patient could be helped. The answer was that this was very easy. The illness was the result of a violent chill.'*

When astronomers refer to the ether as the material mediating agent between the eye of a man and a star a hundred billions of miles distant, that does not strike us as mystical, and we believe it on his word. But when such a rapport of somnambules is spoken of it sounds mystical, because our physical apparatus cannot trace the agent, and because we do not reflect that there are many more threads of connection with the outer world for our Ego below the threshold of sensibility than for the conscious Ego.

The fact that this rapport is mediated by a material agent, which is only mystical just at present, but for which the discovery of the corresponding spectroscope is merely a question of time, is inferred from various observations. Puységur reports of a somnambule that she merely went round a patient unknown to her, of whose name even Puységur himself was ignorant, and then gave a completely

* Harless: 'Bruchstücke aus dem Leben.'

correct diagnosis.* But every doubt of this material agent disappears before the frequent experience that, with this intuitive inspection of other bodies, the symptoms of the disease can be transmitted to the somnambule, and a community of feeling of it be set up. For this reason a distinction has been made between intuitive and sensitive somnambules, but they evidently differ only in degree. Szapary says of a somnambule: 'In order to investigate a disease and judge of its curability, the seeress had always to go herself into the diseased individual, and take upon herself in spirit all the patients' infirmities and sufferings. In this condition she then saw the morbid processes of others in her own body, compared them with healthy conditions, and prescribed the necessary dietetic course and the corresponding remedies. Such ingressions, however, always weakened her, and the more, the more painful and offensive the disease, but she nevertheless made the sacrifice willingly. . . . Later on she went into the sleep again, when she began to cough, and continued doing so more and more violently, and complained very much of spasmodic pains in the chest. It was clear to me that this phenomenon was derived from the disease of the physician who stood in rapport with her, which he confirmed, for at the same time, ten miles off, he was in a similar condition.'† Faria, who was much experienced in these things, thence explains the unwillingness of somnambules to undertake the diagnosis of infectious diseases, and he asserts that if the image

* Puységur: 'Recherches,' i. 365.
† Szapary: 'Ein Wort über animalischen Magnetismus,' 110, 142, Leipzig, Brockhaus, 1840.

of the sick person can be impressed on their memory during the sleep, they will recognise him when accidentally meeting him.*

This sensitive participation in a disease, usually only during the continuance of the rapport, is confirmed also by Werner, the magnetiser being there the intermediate link between the diseased person and the somnambule: 'Every attempt of mine during the illness of R—— to magnetise another, was known to her immediately in the next crisis, and painfully felt. A relative on a visit to me suffered fearfully from headache. I laid my hands on her forehead and on the crown of her head, which considerably relieved her. Next day R—— complained that through my hand she had contracted some of the headache. And, in fact, even after the crisis, she complained of headache all day.'†

As, with many somnambules, diagnosis is of this sensitive character, in certain cases they resist undertaking it. Consumptive patients are not willingly examined by them,‡ and from contact with the epileptic and syphilitic they turn with horror.§ Puységur relates the evil consequences following upon the diagnosis of an epileptic girl, the somnambule who undertook it declaring that in proportion as these consequences to herself increased with further contact, the sick girl would be relieved and cured.|| This reminds us of the well-known mediæval *transplantatio morborum.*

---

\* Faria: 'Du Sommeil lucide,' 240, 460, Paris, 1819.
† Werner: 'Die Schutzgeister,' 297.
‡ Pigeaire: 'Electricité animale,' 244.
§ Deleuze: 'Instr. pratique,' 447, 453.
|| Puységur: 'Memoires,' ii. 155, 165.

The most remarkable somnambule in existing records was undoubtedly Frau Hauffe, the 'Seeress of Prevorst.' Of Dr. Justinus Kerner's book it may be predicted that it will be among the most read in the next century, though in our own the journalism representing pretended enlightenment has succeeded in placing it and its author under the ban of mysticism, which has not, however, prevented five editions of it from appearing. Now as to the reproach of mysticism, that can at most apply to Kerner's explanatory attempts, which may be contested, but not the facts he reports, to which many other observers, laymen, physicians, and philosophers, are committed. Kerner's opponents should therefore have offered better explanations than his, instead of acting as if by this reproach the facts themselves were dismissed from the world. But experience shows that the reproach of mysticism always marks only the point at which the understanding of the 'enlightened' censurer comes to a halt, and he finds himself under the necessity of flinging his gun at the mark. But understanding, as we know, comes to a halt with each at a different point, and so everyone carries about a sack, the repository of all that is 'mystical' according to the horizon of each. The largest sack of this kind, whose capacity is always in inverse ratio to the understanding, is that of the savages. Our reflective verbs and the genders of our nouns still give us information of this condition, since all natural phenomena were animistically explained. Even now we can see by our peasants, that Telegraph and Railroad appear mystical to them; and with our so-called learned the size of the said sack and thereby the narrowness of the corresponding understanding is accurately expressed in the use of *à priori* judgments, in which the subjectively impossible, that is, the not understood, is translated into the objectively impossible. The frequent or rare use of the word 'impossible' is therefore the surest gauge which is offered by the speaker himself for the estimation of his intellectual capacity.* The less cultivated a man is, the more of an à-priorist is he; the more cultivated, the more circumspect, and that not only in believing, but also in disbelieving.† The King of Siam declared the Dutch ambassador mad when the latter mentioned the fact that in winter in his country water became so firmly frozen that one could go upon it ;‡ and even Pliny somewhere uses these, in this respect, significant words: 'Who would have held it possible that there were black men before he had seen a negro?' As long as we have still anything to learn from experience, and we have certainly still most to learn, there is only one *à priori* judgment which is justifiable in the mouth of a mortal: the logically self-contradictory is impossible. Everything else is possible; if it contradicts our former experience, it is this ex-

---

* [Except when, as is usual in this country, by a sort of intellectual cunning, this word is studiously avoided, while the conception it denotes is still predominant, being evinced by the habitual assumption that no unfamiliar phenomena can rest upon good evidence.—Tr.]

† [An observation which is much needed in this age. Culture, or rather intellectual acumen, has long been associated with the rejection of popular beliefs, and so we have come to confuse the accident of an intellectual epoch with the essential character of intelligence and progress.—Tr.]

‡ Wallace: 'Die wissenschaftliche Ansicht des Uebernatürlichen,' 3, Leipzig, 1874. [See Hume's 'Essay on Miracles,' for the same story.—Tr.]

perience that was defective; and if it contradicts the laws known to us, there are then unknown laws, suppressing the known ones, as the magnet suppressed gravity before anything was known of magnetism. This digression seemed to me necessary, because I am about to cite the thoroughly honest Justinus Kerner, which in these days needs some courage. For at present most men derive their intellectual knowledge exclusively from the daily Press. Of the quality of this knowledge one may get the best idea by considering that the State still unfortunately admits just anyone to the business of journalism (*Press-handwerk*) without requiring from him any sort of intellectual preparation.\* From this cause phrases and catchwords get planted firmly in men's minds, and are devolved without being subjected to any examination; and thus also the name of Justinus Kerner has become a bugbear suggestive of superstition, and people who have never read a line of him are seized with a shudder of imaginary enlightenment when they hear him mentioned. But I am now concerned only with the facts reported by Kerner and others, and I do not myself altogether approve of his way of accounting for them.

As a sensitive somnambule Mrs. Hauffe was extraordinarily distinguished. 'For the ailments of others she had so acute a sense that upon approaching

---

\* [However true it may be that the people are educated by the daily Press, it is more than doubtful whether the State could advantageously insist on the education of journalists. In any such attempt the standard could only be the established culture—the old ideas, which, as Goethe said, are the greatest enemies of new ones—and as the result the influence of journalism would be more than ever unfavourable to conceptions subversive of the dominant modes of thought.—Tr.]

a patient, and even before contact, but still more after it, she at once experienced the same feeling and in the like place as the patient, and to the greatest astonishment of the latter, could exactly describe all his sufferings, without his having given her any previous verbal information. Usually, she felt the mental condition along with the physical, thus the momentary disposition of grief or joy, etc. The physical state was transferred to her body, the psychical to her soul. . . . One evening there came to us a Mrs. Burk (who was wholly unknown to us), from Göppingen. She desired me to let her be felt by Mrs. Hauffe, in the latter's waking state, on account of a pain in the region of the liver, but otherwise she told me nothing whatever of her state of health. Not to seem disobliging, I brought her to Mrs. Hauffe. The latter felt the lower part of her body, became very red,* and said she felt palpitations of the heart and pains in the region of the liver; but what was very distressing to her, that she had suddenly almost lost the sight of her right eye. Mrs. B. was astonished, and said she had for many years been nearly quite unable to see with her right eye, a defect of which she had said nothing to me, because she knew it was an old and incurable ill. Without close investigation the defect of the eye could not be discovered, since it was a paralysis of the nerve. The obscurity in Mrs. Hauffe's eye continued for several days, and the pupil had become quite insensitive, as by a cataract. Only by degrees, by people with sound eyes looking fixedly for several minutes together into the darkened eye,

* [Presumably indicating a sudden transference of the patient's sensations to herself.—Tr.]

did the latter recover its power. . . . On the 5th September, 1827, I gave into Mrs. H.'s hand a ribbon, on which the name of a sick lady (quite unknown to me, as was her complaint) was sewn, probably by herself, and which she had touched or worn before sending it. The name was that of a Mrs. M. in U. Scarcely had Mrs. H. held this ribbon in her hand for a few minutes than she experienced a great disgust, choking, and the most violent sickness. Then she felt pains, particularly in the bone of the left foot, uneasiness in the breast, and extreme irritation in the uvula. Loathing and a terrible choking continued; she required the hand which had held the ribbon to be frequently washed; but nothing availed. At length she fell into a state of catalepsy and apparent death. . . . At six o'clock in the evening, when I received the Swabian *Mercury*, I read in it a notice of the death of the lady to whom the ribbon had belonged. She had been several days buried before the ribbon was put into Mrs. Hauffe's hands. . . . Van Helmont relates the case of a gouty woman who always got severe attacks of gout after sitting on a sofa on which her brother, who had been dead five years, was wont to sit.'\*

The inspection of other bodies is, like self-inspection, critical, the cause of the disease and its later course being frequently known. A somnambule, being asked by a father about his insane daughter, said that the latter had fallen from the top step of a ladder twelve or thirteen years before, which was the original cause of her complaint; the father could not remember

\* Kerner: 'Die Seherin der Prevorst,' Stuttgart, 1877, pp. 113, 115.

the incident, but learned at home that in fact it so occurred.* Bertrand's somnambule said to a patient who was brought to her that the wound on his head proceeded from a ball which had entered through the mouth, smashed the teeth, and gone out at the back of the neck.† Alexander Dumas relates in the thirteenth book of his 'Memoirs'—and the same narrative is given by Dr. Foderé in his 'Pneumatology'—the case of a young lady who was put into somnambulism to discover the disease of her mother. She thereupon became pale, and tears were in her eyes as she said that her mother would die the next day. She described in detail the state of the interior organs, lung, liver, bowels; and as the mother in fact died the next day, the complete correctness of the diagnosis was able to be established by dissection. Two members of the Academy were present at it; but to one of these gentlemen even a proof so striking did not suffice, and he preferred to call the girl a deceiver, the limit of his own understanding being for him the limit of things.

Thus, if our theories are not to lag behind the facts, we must recognise that the Ego below the psycho-physical threshold, the so-called unconscious, is only relatively unconscious, from the standpoint of the Ego above the threshold of sensibility, not unconscious in itself. This transcendental half of our being, lying beyond the sphere of our normal consciousness, stands in other relations to things than does the man of five senses, and has other modes of perception than his, and in these also the scale by

---

\* 'Archiv,' xi. 2, 42.
† Gauthier : 'Hist. du Somn.,' ii. 303.

which we measure time and space in the day-consciousness undergoes a change. When, however, this transcendental Ego comes forth in dream and somnambulism, its perception often takes on allegorical and symbolical forms, or even the form of the dramatic sundering of the Ego, and then, indeed, we should decline to superstition should we take this mere form of knowledge for real.

### 3. *The Curative Instinct in Dream.*

We can now proceed to the somewhat difficult question, whether dream, which in relation to diagnosis and prognosis can be termed a physician, is so also as regards medicinal science. If this question related singly to sleep, there would be no difficulty, for that in sleep occurs the process by which the organism is recuperated, and that it has a natural restorative force, has long been known. But our question concerns dream, the inner wakening, and we do not ask if restorative processes, but if conscious ideal processes, related to medicinal science, occur. Now since that, which in the inner wakening emerges as clear idea and clear will, often already in the external waking state makes itself felt as obscure presentiment and impulse—and, therefore, all instincts have their root in the transcendental half of our being, and depend on a breaking through of the isolation of the two nervous systems—and since, further, the instincts which are directed to the healing process are only to be regarded as a continuation and modification of the natural curative force, it is with this that our inquiry must begin.

Man passes about a third part of his life in sleep. As to the causes of sleep physiology is not yet clear; but it is incontestable that we require this periodical suspension of our conscious life, and that regular and sound sleep is one of the chief conditions of bodily well-being. Man can therefore be even killed by artificial prevention of sleep. I believe that the punishment of death by sleeplessness formerly existed among the Japanese. It occurs also as *Tormentum insomnii* in the witchcraft cases in Germany, England, and the States of the Church, the witches being kept continually awake; they were driven round unceasingly in the prisons till their feet were disabled, and they fell into a condition of utter despair and imbecility.*

Accordingly, the opposite proceeding, the placing a sick person in the deepest possible sleep, by which the restorative force is intensified, must be highly conducive to health.

This proceeding is that of Nature in spontaneous, of the physician in artificial, somnambulism; but in both cases it is found that the natural curative force is more energetic than in waking and in normal sleep. Nature takes a critical sleep as curative means into her service in very many diseases; and as it has been observed that even plants grow more quickly in periodical conditions resembling sleep, so also somnambulism evinces an exaltation of the restorative process. The somnambule Julie renewed teeth which had been extracted within a few weeks,† and

---

* Soldan: 'Geschichte der Hexenprocesse,' i. 263.
† Strombeck: 'Geschichte eines allein durch die Natur hervorgebrachten Magnetismus,' 144.

Wienholt reports a case in which the diseased teeth of a somnambule were restored during a six days' sleep.* Braid, also, the discoverer of hypnotism, has observed that the latter, as distinguished from ordinary sleep, effects extraordinary cures in acute diseases, and improvement in chronic ones.†

The like is the case also with artificial somnambulism. As a condition of deep sleep, it is already a very real remedy, able to cope with even surgical cases by the mere exaltation of the natural curative force. Many are the declarations of somnambules concerning the special benefit of the magnetic sleep. A consumptive patient once in the somnambulic state desired her physician to place her in a nine days' trance (*Scheintod*), during which her lungs enjoyed complete rest, so that she woke entirely cured.‡

If there is a healing force in Nature, the secret of medicine can only consist in strengthening and guiding it. Maxwell, the forerunner of Mesmer, knew this. From his proposition: 'There is no disease which is not curable by the spirit of life without help of a physician,' he draws the right conclusion, and continues: 'The universal remedy is nothing but the spirit of life increased in a suitable subject.'§

Now it is this mode of cure which Mesmer rediscovered. He wished to heal the diseased organism by the forces inherent therein, which he only excited to activity and directed. This is effected by magnetism. Modern physicians are nearer to this stand-

* Wienholt: 'Heilkraft,' etc., iii. 3, 30.
† Preyer: 'Die Entdeckung des Hypnotismus,' 144.
‡ Schopenhauer: 'Parerga,' i. 275.
§ Maxwell: 'Magnetische Heilkunde,' ii. Anhang.

point than they often know themselves. With every year they are more averse from treatment by drugs, which not only proceeds from the false materialistic assumption that man is only a chemical problem, but even in regard to the effects is only a driving out of the devil by Beelzebub. To this mode of treatment applies the saying of Petrus Poterius concerning the physicians of his time: 'That instead of healing disease sooner than Nature could do without them, they often so manage that Nature is obliged to fight disease and physician at the same time.'* Maxwell expresses the same when he says : 'They do not know much, who, to cure a disease, see themselves obliged to make a worse one.'† And Montaigne, when his friends advised him to call in a physician, used to answer that they should let him first recover his strength, so that it might be able to resist the attack.

In modern medicine the opinion has been more and more gaining ground that Nature and not the physician cures, that the art of the latter consists only in supporting and directing the curative force of Nature; that is to say, by medicaments to offer Nature the means of attaining her aim. By this conception, which is now that of every physician, the doctrine of remedies is brought into very close relation with the curative force of Nature. But now, if it is asked in what connection the capacity of somnambules to find the remedies advantageous to them stands to the natural curative force of their organism, it is evident that this question refers only to a special case of the

* Poterius: 'Opera omnia,' 604.
† Maxwell: 'Magn. Heilkunde,' ii. 4.

more general question of the relation of Nature and mind, the unconscious and the conscious, Will and Idea. Everyone will answer differently according to his philosophical standpoint, but this is not the place for a philosophical discussion of this question. It may therefore be enough to remark that *every* doctrine of Monism, be it pantheistic or materialistic, is already compelled upon logical grounds to regard spirit, consciousness, idea, as natural continuation of the process of organic development. Conceived from the standpoint of biology or of physiology, in both cases consciousness appears as the natural flower of the organic life-stem, the prolongation, as it were, of the organic. Mind is drawn from Nature, and since the law of development prevails in Nature, it prevails also in history. To the account of this relation the Darwinian philosopher Spencer has devoted the best of his works.*

Thus only when we recognise the dependence of our sense-consciousness upon the mother-stem of the organism, is it intelligible that, as Zeising has proved, the rule of the golden section, as formative principle, governs not only organic Nature, but even the ancient Greek and the Gothic temple architecture;† that further, as Kapp has shown, in the discoveries of technic art organic models are unconsciously imitated, as, for instance, the eye in the *camera obscura*, long before any scientific analysis of this model.‡ This idea of Kapp's is so fruitful that it affords a clue to the solution of the seemingly insoluble problem of the

---

\* H. Spencer: 'First Principles.'
† A. Zeising: 'Neue Lehre von den Proportionen des menschlichen Körpers,' Leipzig, 1854.
‡ Kapp: 'Philosophie der Technik,' Braunschweig, 1877.

nature of the inhabitants of the planets.\* The study of the four works named is not required of my present readers, but to eventual criticism it is indispensable ; for the relation of mind to Nature is of fundamental importance for the following inquiry, and it is here that the critic who would subvert the further results must take his stand. To anyone adopting my solution of this question—and, I repeat, it is the only solution for the Monist, even if a materialist—this and the following chapter will appear quite naturally intelligible.

If the realm of mind is only the natural prolongation of that of Nature ; if their histories, as biology, are to be conceived in the sense of the doctrine of development, so that Hegel and Darwin are mutually complementary; if Idea is related to Will as flower to branch ; if the same force that forms the brain also determines the functions of brain, then is it self-evident that whatever acts in nature must assert itself in consciousness ; but then it is easy to see in the curative instinct, and in the involuntary idea of the remedy, only a natural continuation of the curative power of Nature. And if even the waking consciousness adheres to its organic stem, that is still less strange in the case of dream-consciousness, since in sleep, the sounder it is, the deeper we are sunk into the organic impulse of Nature. Thus, if there is an objective curative force of Nature, from the standpoint of monism there must also be a subjective curative idea, which in waking announces itself only as instinctive craving, but in sleep as vision of the remedy.

\* See the author's work : 'Planetenbewohner,' Leipzig, 1880.

So that dream, which has already appeared as physician in regard to diagnosis and prognosis, is one also in regard to the remedy. Waking, ordinary sleep, and somnambulism, are members of a series. Sense-consciousness is at the highest in waking, disappears in proportion to the depth of sleep, and in somnambulism is suppressed to the point of insensibility. But the inner waking is proportional to the abstraction of the sense-consciousness, and is most clear in somnambulism. Whoever, therefore, will study the abnormal capacities associated with the inner waking, must follow them *through all three conditions*. Already in waking he will meet with its most elementary forms; will find them more distinctly in sleep, and still more so in somnambulism. In this way the phenomena of each condition throw light upon those of the other, while they remain unintelligible when considered apart.

Accordingly, it is in waking that we have first to seek the psychical faculty of discovering remedies, though in this condition it can only appear as unconscious instinct. I cannot, however, dwell long upon this stage, and it will suffice to adduce two well-known facts: the instincts of animals in regard to their nourishment, and the remarkable inclinations of pregnant women, who often reject customary food and express the strangest longings — such as for broken points of lead pencils. I have lately seen a lady in this condition who disliked being kissed by her husband when he had just been smoking, but a few days after the birth of the child this smell became again as agreeable to her as it was before the pregnancy. These phenomena are evidently of a kind with those health-instincts which survive with somnambules long after their magnetic condition has ceased. One of Kerner's somnambules said that an inner impulse to take a certain remedy remained with her a long time, even without her going into the sleep, and informed her what was good for her or the reverse.* Another said to Kerner: 'Since I was magnetised, foods most of all disgust me which are unsuitable to my state, *which now is the ordinary one.* Flesh and pastry disgust me; milk and apples are the only things right for me.'† Now, when Kerner himself used the remedies prescribed to him by somnambules, he acquired, he says, a disinclination to the foods which aggravated his complaint, chiefly meats; whereas he had the greatest appetite for things which he formerly disliked, as vegetables.‡ Thus the nutritious instinct here got transferred to the magnetiser.

It is one of the constant effects of magnetism that it excites inclination to beneficial, and dislike to deleterious foods.§ According to Reichenbach, the sensitives always and instinctively observed a pure diet, and it is only another expression for the displacement of the threshold of sensibility, when he says, that with them 'Nature with her vegetative power prevailed more strongly.'‖ A patient of Wienholt's was seized with an insatiable voracity for indigestible things, such as codfish, meat-puddings, yellow peas,

---

\* Kerner: 'Geschichte zweier Somnambulen,' 259.
† *Id.*, 380.
‡ *Id.*, 362.
§ Kluge: 'Derstellung,' etc., 87. Heineken: 'Ideen und Beobachtungen, tier. Magnetismus,' betr. 51. Hufeland: 'System der prakt. Heilkunde,' i. 41, etc.
‖ Reichenbach: 'Der sensitive Mensch,' i. 386.

brown cabbages, and often ate them against his will. That lasted four months, and always with the most wholesome effects.* Bonetus tells of a man who never could eat bread, but in an attack of fever had a desire for it, and before the next attack ate a quantity voraciously. The fever was then stopped; but after the cure the disinclination for bread returned.† Brentano mentions that the famous nun, Catherine Emmerich, when she was a child, brought health-plants, known only to herself, from a distance, and planted them at home, and also extirpated the poisonous herbs for a long way round.‡ Similar things occurred with other religious ecstatics, concerning whom modern rationalism is still ignorant that they were merely somnambules with a religious colour.

Thus it cannot be doubted that the healing force can penetrate into the waking consciousness as instinctive impulse. But we are concerned with the question, whether it also extends into the subjective world of ideas, and this has to be proved for the dream state. Anciently it was not at all doubted that dreaming persons could discover appropriate remedies for diseases. Hippocrates, Aristotle, Galen, Aretœus, Pliny, Cicero, and, in later times, Tertullian, Lord Bacon, Montaigne, and many others, asserted the possibility of vision of remedies in dream; and it is only now that one is obliged to re-inspect the

* Wienholt: 'Heilkraft,' etc., i. 366.
† Muratori: 'Ueber die Einbildungskraft,' ii. 258.
‡ 'Die Tyroler ekstatischen Jungfrauen,' i. 119 (1843). The anonymous author is the Prussian State-Councillor, Wilhelm Volk.

evidence instead of saying that the thing is 'notoriously' so.

There are two considerations well calculated to suggest the possibility, and indeed the necessity, of such indications of curative means occurring in dream, and thus to deprive them of their marvellous character, and I mention them to procure a better reception for what follows. They are, first : that a blind healing force is really far more wonderful than the production of an ideal representation of the means ; and second, that with sleep is associated the displacement of the psycho-physical threshold, whereby a new material of sensibility is introduced, and the suggestions obtain a wholly material foundation—indeed, are in some measure necessitated.

By referring the curative instinct in sleep and the prescription of somnambules to the curative force of Nature, the problem is only, indeed, pushed back ; but it is pushed back upon a fact which is subject to no doubt, and which has at all times excited the admiration of thinking physicians, and so much is already gained.

If we consider the perverse modes of life led by most, especially in civilized countries, the crowding of population in our great cities, which are hot-beds of all possible insanitary conditions, and further reflect that, in the country especially, most sick persons either subject themselves, or are subjected, to an irrational treatment, even non-professional persons must allow that the curative force of Nature has in fact no small task laid upon it, and in so far as, notwithstanding all, it is equal to it, we must feel the greatest respect for its capacity of performance. Still more striking to a layman is the activity of this force in cases of external injury, cuts, bullet-wounds, fractures, etc., because here it is particularly apparent that the physician is only the assistant of nature. But it is the physician himself who will most admire the curative power of nature in diseases, when he follows her strenuous efforts for the restoration of health. The more he understands this, the more will he also recognise that nature alone can help immediately, the physician only mediately, through nature. The physician outside can indeed support the one within, which governs every organism, but cannot supply its place. Modern medical science is even disposed to see in diseases themselves only crises, brought about by our internal physician, the curative force of nature, to overcome the life-threatening mischief by means of the peculiar tendencies of organic activity.

Carus, speaking of the curative force of nature, says : 'The mere simple self-closing of an injured vessel, and the stoppage of bleeding, is in this regard a highly important process. How gradually the stream of blood into the injured vessel takes another direction, and thereby relieves the pressure upon the wounded parts, how the coating of the vessels gradually draws itself together, how by coagulation of the blood the peculiar form called the *thrombus* arises, and how now peculiar processes of vegetation are set up, by the influence of which, without anything of all this coming to consciousness, the closure of the wound is finished, while at the same time wholly new conduit vessels are formed, and the course of the blood, perhaps quite interrupted in the injured part, is in this way perfectly restored, invite the most multifarious reflections . . . and in saying that it is the highest commission of science to penetrate consciously into the depths of the unconscious soul-life of the world, I may add that it is particularly the task of medical science to follow these unconscious curative movements, and to bring them to the clearest knowledge, that they may be as far as possible intentionally furthered, in suitable cases imitated, and especially occasioned.'*

In fact, the curative force of nature is to be compared with the organic process of growth. As we can consciously bring the material of nutrition to the organism, but it is nature's part to dissolve, distribute, assimilate, and partially to reject ; so the physician can indeed support the healing process, but he must always leave the principal office to nature.

Now, unsignificant and ill-defined as this phrase, the curative force of nature, may be, it cannot be asserted that this force, real as an objective fact, is an impossibility in the world of subjective ideas. That could only be asserted on the supposition of an insuperable boundary line between nature and mind. But monistically regarded, mind is only the continuation of nature, and therefore the curative force of nature must be able to proceed into the world of ideas. What else is man than a piece of nature, and one, too, in which nature has attained to self-consciousness ? It thus needs only the further consideration, that by displacement of the psycho-physical threshold in sleep, a new material of sensibility attains to per-

* C. G. Carus : 'Psyche,' 101.

ception, to see that nature makes use of the organ of perception produced by her so far for self-knowledge as to make self-inspection possible, and to view objectively the activity of the organic process and of the curative force. As all the unconscious proceedings of life, the formative impulse of the organism, the nutritious instinct, selective affinity in the assimilation of food, the sympathies and antipathies of the soul-life, of which we can give no account, come to consciousness in somnambulism, so also the curative force of nature ; and if this inner physician awakes in us, he can also, by reason of the material of sensibility brought to him by the displacement of the threshold, obtain ideas related to the healing process.

As by displacement of the psycho-physical threshold a whole new material of sensibility is afforded, it can be presupposed that this change of our relation to the things of nature makes possible influences of the same important to the healthy state, so that unusual longings or aversions, unknown to the normal condition, are awakened. To show that this conjecture is correct, a whole succession of experiments could be cited, of which two must be here noticed.

The celebrated chemist, Bezelius, in association with Reichenbach and the bath-physician, Hochberger, instituted highly instructive experiments at Karlsbad in 1845. They went to a so-called sensitive, a Fraulein von Seckendorf, before whom was laid a large number of chemical compounds wrapped in papers strewed upon the table. Being asked to pass the inner surface of her right hand lightly over them, she felt herself very differently affected by the different packets: many were quite without effect upon her; others exercised a peculiar attraction on the hand. She was now desired to separate the packets into two sets, according to this difference. 'The creator of the electro-chemical system appeared not a little struck on perceiving on the one side, that of the substances which had attracted her, exclusively electropositive; on the other, that of the non-attractive ones, merely electro-negative bodies. Not a positive showed itself among the negative, not a negative among the positive; the partition was perfect. . . . That which had been brought about in a century at the cost of infinite diligence and acuteness, the electro-chemical classification of bodies, was accomplished by a simple sensitive girl in ten minutes by merely feeling with her empty hands.'*

It can only be remarked here, by the way, that this sensitiveness of certain persons is a somnambulic faculty surviving into the daily life, as in the above case Fraulein von Seckendorf told her visitors before the experiment 'a series of wonderful somnambulic occurrences which she had experienced.' Suffice it to observe that this sensibility applies also to organic substances. Kerner gives many remarks of a somnambule on the subject: 'Whenever in this sleep I take a plant in my hand, and hold it for awhile, I so penetrate it, that from the small veins or form of the leaves I can read, as it were, what qualities and powers they possess.'† It is therefore not surprising, if sensitives and somnambules feel the effects of substances,

---

\* Reichenbach: 'Aphorismen über Sensitivität und Od.,' 7, 8; Wien, 1866. 'Der sensitive Mensch,' i. 706; Stuttgart, 1854.
† Kerner: 'Geschichte zweier Somnambulen,' 376.

that they know more of their qualities than the normal man, for whom these feelings remain below the threshold, and that those in whom the curative force of nature comes to consciousness know the peculiar tendency of these substances, and whether they further or disturb the curative force. The seeress of Prevorst reacted so finely on the contact, and even on the mere proximity, of minerals, plants, and animal substances, that she immediately felt their medicinal effects. Siemers experimented on a somnambule with about two hundred medicinal substances, which she touched with the tips of the fingers of her right hand, often also putting some of them on her tongue. If she was unwell she had a finer sense. Many substances he gave her in extract, powder, decoction, tincture, or raw root, and yet she could identify them. This somnambule saw sometimes in Siemers' house bulbs of crocus, amaryllis, hyacinths, and tulips, and, with few exceptions, correctly indicated the colours of the future flowers, and whether they would be single or double.* It is related of the scullion of an English consul in Egypt, that, being magnetised by the consul for his cough, he asked for sugar of agrimonium from the medicine-chest of an Italian who was present, and found the right bottle by touch.† Similar influences affect many persons, even in waking, as so-called idiosyncrasies. Many have the St. Anthony's fire from eating strawberries or crawfish. Goethe had an antipathy to garlic, as Schiller had to spiders. It is related of Tycho Brahe that he trembled at the sight of a hare, and Platen, as

---

\* Perty: 'Die mystischen Erscheinungen,' i. 263.
† 'Archiv,' viii. 2, 127.

my father, who saw it, told me, when at school, would spring up in horror from his desk if he saw a spider.

Thus as the organic formative impulse comes to consciousness in the interior self-inspection, so also can the curative force of nature come to consciousness in the inner waking in sleep and somnambulism. Sanitary-Councillor Schindler says : 'If we follow the processes set up by the organism to neutralize poisons introduced into it—as the conversion of metallic oxides into the less injurious sulphide ; the processes by which foreign bodies are removed by suppuration, capsulation, absorption, and expulsion ; those which the body effects to remove by empyrosis a broken-in bone ; intestinal processes by which the passage of the bowels is restored ; if we follow the cicatrising of wounds, the production of new nerves, muscles, and bone-masses, the restoration of circulation by the new formation of a collateral network of vessels when a large vessel has decayed ; if we consider those which occur every day in inflammation and fever, which are only to be looked upon as vital processes to save the individual from foreign influences ; we must confess that no physician could proceed with more circumspection, and that a physician can only act with advantage when he has sought out the healing method of nature—when he has become her servant. But where now is the health-artist ? is he not within us ? and is not the whole of medicinal science derived from our exploration of the curative method of this internal physician ? When, therefore, we call medicine an empirical science, we have only to reflect that healing is older than medical science, and that the physician in us healed long before there was a science of healing. This physician in us is quite like the instincts of animals . . . Instinct comes to consciousness in the somnambule, who gives it words, and seeks the remedy, as the conditions of recovery.'*

Now since the bodily organs of the outer as of the inner waking, brain and ganglionic system, can only be anatomically and physiologically explained in connection with the whole organism, and the blood only as product of the whole vegetative life, so in principle it is quite self-evident that we cannot detach the functions of these organs from the general natural activity of the organism. Nature and mind are thus inseparable, and materialism, which in all mind sees exclusively the function and secretion of bodily organs, can certainly not escape this consequence. But if it concedes this, it must admit the conscious representations of the dream-life in relation to the healing process as a necessary inference from this conception; and the following instances cannot appear to it impossible marvels, but as entirely natural things; and it must then contest and deny the curative force of nature itself, and that finger-cuts heal of themselves. Materialism has thus only itself to understand—and that is little enough—to concede the possibility of health-dreams. But if one speaks of these things to a materialist, he feels them as an injury to his understanding, and rejects them as superstition—another proof that with this sort of natural philosophers logic is not to be found.

* Schindler: 'Das magische Geistesleben,' Breslau, 1857, p. 247.

For every monism, since it is logically forbidden to regard nature and mind as merely mosaic fragments in juxtaposition, the health-dream is only the latest issue of organic activity. Now materialism is monism, and it connects nature and mind, will and idea, body and soul, in the sense of conceiving soul as mere effect of body. This is only *partially* true: the sense-consciousness is attached to the functions of the nerves and brain. But were it *wholly* true, from the fact of *the healing force* materialism must all the more infer the possibility of *the healing idea*. To the materialist, therefore, it can at most appear striking that Cabanis, who has had the greatest influence on the development of materialistic conceptions, raises no objection to this opinion, confirmed as it was, moreover, by his own experience.

'L'on voit dans quelques maladies extatiques et convulsives, les organes des sens devenir sensibles à des impressions qu'ils n'appercevaient pas dans leur état ordinaire, ou même recevoir les impressions étrangères à la nature de l'homme. J'ai plusieurs fois observé chez les femmes qui sans doute eussent été jadis d'excellentes pythonisses, les effets les plus singuliers des changements dont je parle. Il est de ces malades qui distinguent facilement à l'œil un des objets microscopiques, d'autres qui voient assez nettement dans la plus profonde obscurité pour s'y conduire avec assurance. Il en est qui suivent les personnes à la trace comme un chien, et reconnaissent à l'odorat les objets dont ces personnes se sont servies ou qu'elles ont seulement touchés. J'en ai vu, dont le gout avait acquis une finesse particulière, et qui désiraient ou savaient choisir les aliments et même les remèdes qui paraissaient leur être véritablement utiles avec une sagacité qu'on n'observe par l'ordinaire que dans les animaux. On en voit qui sont en état d'appercevoir en elles-mêmes dans le temps de leurs paroxismes, ou certaines crises qui se préparent, et dont le terminaison prouve bientôt après la justesse de leurs sensations, ou d'autres modifications organiques attestées par celle du pouls et par des signes encore plus certains.'*

---

* Cabanis: 'Rapports du physique et du moral de l'homme,' ii. 35; Paris, Musson, 1855.

Thus, without speaking of somnambules, Cabanis concedes half the somnambulic programme, and can do so, since these phenomena do not contradict monism, even of a materialistic sort. It may be incidentally mentioned that Cabanis was one of Mesmer's earliest pupils, a fact which seems not to be sufficiently known, but which has been proved by the physician Mialle.*

The second form of monism is pantheism. This sees a soul-principle ruling in the organic activity of the body itself, and thus can still less object to the possibility of health ideas, since the curative force and the curative idea are inseparably connected. This conception has been developed most completely by Hartmann. For him organic growth, the replacement of lost parts of the body, the healing force of nature, are connected with ideas which he ascribes to the Unconscious — that is, to a metaphysical world-substance.† On this account he has been violently attacked from the side of the men of science, and so far rightly, that exact science can explain the life-process only from the organism itself. But if Hartmann is read without any prepossessions, it will soon be found that he has a very sound kernel. He analyses the organic processes very acutely, and in so doing cannot escape the inference of an unconscious idea.‡ Now, if the sound constituents of the scientific, and of this philosophical conception are combined, we find ourselves compelled, as if accord-

---

\* Cf. Deleuze: 'Faculté de prévision,' 141.
† Hartmann: 'Philosophie des Unbewussten,' Abteilung A.
‡ In opposition to Schopenhauer, to whom the Unconscious, the 'thing-in-itself,' was exclusively Will.—Tr.

ing to a psychical parallelogram of forces, to locate every idea connected with the unconscious or instinctive tendencies of the organism in the individual psyche, in the transcendental Ego lying beneath the psycho-physical threshold. Not for this do these organic processes go on unconsciously, though truly they do for the Ego above the threshold. This third sort of monism unites the sound constituents of materialism and pantheism, dropping the unsound ones of both, and seems best to correspond with the facts. It is also that which can least of all dispute the possibility of health-dreams, since, according to its own conception, the possibility of such dreams has only one condition, the displacement of the threshold of sensibility, which is a known fact of dream.

After these introductory observations, we can turn to particular examples of health-dreams; and I will begin with one which shows the necessity of cautious judgment. A Colonel B. was shot through the head, and otherwise injured, at Leipzig, in 1636. After long sufferings, there appeared to him by night the form of a lady, who enjoined him to throw away a gold tube which had been placed in the head to carry off the discharge, and said that he would thus be healed. The physicians declared that his death would infallibly ensue, but the dream being repeated still more impressively the next night, the colonel obeyed, and in the morning the physicians found the wound healed.* Like every foreign body in a wound, this gold tube must naturally have occasioned a troublesome irritation. Now, as such irritations in dream often even lead to reflex movements to get rid of

* Hennings: 'Ahnungen und Visionen,' 317.

them, this one could easily have been the provocation of a dream-image in which the removal of the tube would be dramatically enjoined; and as it is certainly allowable to assume that the tube was no longer necessary, that explains the self-closing of the wound, without adding this case to the class of health-dreams, to which it has much resemblance.

The rationalistic explanation may be more difficult in the case of a dream, connected with dramatic prognosis, which Bautzmann relates of a young girl: The dream announced to her the impending illness, its duration, and all its particular incidents; there appeared to her two men, who enjoined her to mark in the calendar the days and weeks on which this or that should be the case with her. Among the rest, the men recommended bleeding, which, however, the physicians and her parents would not permit, till she herself opened a vein in firm trust in her dream, whereon the violence of the disease immediately abated.*

As there is a danger of proving nothing when one would prove too much, it is advisable to exclude all those dreams in which an action to be performed *upon the organism* is recommended or commanded, since such dreams may always proceed from local irritation, which may either occasion an actual reflex movement for relief, or a dream-image, motived by what has already occurred.

But the rationalistic explanation is excluded, if there are dreams, as Hippocrates in his book on dreams affirms, in which are seen the kinds of nutriment that are advantageous for the body, or the

* Perty: 'Mystischen Erscheinungen,' i. 112.

remedies of the latter are represented in consciousness. Such a vision is recorded by Bourdois, of the Medical Academy of Paris: A man began to rave during a violent attack of cholera, and Bourdois thought he heard the word 'peach.' Respecting the instinct thus uttered, he had that fruit procured, and the sick man ate it eagerly. This desire, which, had it occurred in waking, would have been describable as unconscious instinct, was thus for the transcendental Ego connected with an idea, that came to consciousness by the displacement of the psycho-physical threshold.* In the course of the night the patient ate some thirty peaches with the greatest avidity, and the day after he was well.†

Melancthon suffered from a painful inflammation of the eyes, which would yield to no treatment. He once dreamed, as Camerarius states, that his physician prescribed to him white Eye-bright (*Euphrasia officinalis*), and by the application of this remedy he was cured. A similar case, in which the health idea took on a dramatic form, is given by Ælian in his 'Miscellaneous Stories.' The celebrated Aspasia, who afterwards became Queen of Persia, had in her youth a swelling in the face, by which she was much disfigured. The physician who was called in de-

---

\* That is to say, in the normal waking state, the definite desire for the definite thing, peach, would have remained below the threshold, and would have come into the consciousness above the threshold only as an indefinite craving, to which no name could be given. By the exaltation of the sensibility, called the displacement of the threshold, in an abnormal condition, the sub-physical consciousness of the idea, the exact dictate of nature, became psycho-physical—that is, could take on the sense-expression in the image, peach.—Tr.

† 'Dict. de Médecine,' v. 190.

manded a fee which her father could not afford, so that she had to forego his aid. Aspasia was therefore inconsolable; but there appeared to her in dream a dove, which soon took the form of a woman, and said: 'Be of good courage; despise physicians and their physic. Powder one of the roses which adorn the statue of Venus, and are now faded, and lay this rose-powder on the swelling.' The maiden followed this counsel, and the swelling went down. The essential thing in this dream was the dramatic health-instinct. The form in which such dreams are clothed is always taken from the ideality of the subject, and therefore appears in space and time. In our days, this Aspasia would have taken roses from a statue of the Virgin Mary, or the prescription would perhaps have been brought by a messenger, as a telegraphic despatch. It would be wholly fallacious, on account of such forms, to fling away the kernel of the thing, as Ælian would perhaps have done, because he regarded Mariolatry as superstition, or as a Catholic would do, because he rejected the belief in a goddess Venus. It would be equally fallacious to take this external form of dream into account. Dream very frequently takes on the dramatic form; it is a sort of ventriloquist, or, better expressed, a verbal intercourse between the Ego above the threshold and the one below. Thus regarded, all that somnambules and the modern spiritists say of their guardian spirits and guides is perhaps dissolved into vapour; but modern scepticism has not the least right to throw away the kernel also on account of the form.

Avicenna relates, that one who had an inflammation of the tongue dreamed he should hold in his mouth the juice of the lettuce, by doing which the complaint soon abated.* Even the phenomenon, very frequent in somnambulism, in which the place is seen where the remedy is to be found, seems to be a possible incident of ordinary dream. A boy of five years old having sustained an injury to a bone, giving rise to gangrene, an amputation was about to be performed. In the night he saw himself transported into the apothecary's shop, where was a vessel for salves with a Latin inscription, which on awaking he could still remember; the salve was tried, and he recovered.† It is related of a sleep-walker, that during her illness she dreamed that the water of a neighbouring spring would make her well. She drank much of it, and when they once tried to deceive her with other water, she knew the deception.‡

That a similar instinct can be exalted into vision even in waking, has the proof, among others, of the numerous instances of fainting travellers in the desert, who see images of oases and springs. A negro who had lost his way, as I have read somewhere, having been for sixty hours without food and drink, saw around him clear springs of water, by which he thought to refresh himself, wherein this Tantalus was naturally disappointed. Mungo Park, in a nearly fainting state on a journey in Africa, dreamed incessantly of the richly-watered valleys and pastures of his home.§

So Trenk, tormented by hunger in the trenches of

* Nudow: 'Theorie des Schlafes,' 139; Konigsberg, 1791.
† Splittgerber: 'Schlaf und Tod,' i. 141.
‡ Fischer, 'Der Somnambulismus,' ii. 80.
§ Schubert: 'Geschichte der Seele,' ii. 205.

Magdeburg, saw himself surrounded by luxurious banquets ; and George Back, one of Franklin's first expedition, when near starvation from frightful privations, constantly and regularly dreamed of rich repasts.* The need of the organism comes thus to be an object of vision. The self-prescriptions of somnambules follow the same law, need and vision in their case being only much more detailed.

In the ' Frankfurter Konversationsblatt ' of 25th of August, 1842, there is an account of an English officer who had fallen ill of fever in war. During a sleepless night he had the vision of a venerable man, who said to him that he could only be cured by cold washing in the court at daybreak, after which he should dry himself, and return to bed. He followed this dramatized instinct, and recovered.

The Jewish seeress Selma, of whom Dr. Wiener gives an account, had numerous dreams of this nature, as to which it is questionable whether they should be ascribed to ordinary or to somnambulic sleep. She once dreamed that someone offered her a roll of bread smeared with hog's-lard, saying, ' Eat, it is hog's-lard !' On awakening, she felt ravenous for hog's-lard—an inclination which, as a religious Jewess, she strove to conquer. She kept her dream from the physician, fearing that he would counsel her to obey the craving. But when next night the dream repeated itself, and she believed she could no longer resist the desire, she told her physician, who, as he said, would long ago have prescribed something of the sort, had he not been withheld by her religious

* Mayo: 'Wahrheiten im Volksaberglauben,' 101.

scruples. It was, perhaps, an after effect of just such a dream and a surviving obscure instinct, that made her complain one day that she had an appetite for a certain food, but, in spite of all reflection, could not specify it. In the evening, however, when she was in the somnambulic state, and was asked if she had not a particular appetite for something, she named fresh pigeons' eggs and a fieldfare.*

It would be mere verbal contention to claim this faculty of prescription for instinct, instead of recognising in it a somnambulic capacity becoming free even in ordinary dream; for, in the first place, the word 'instinct' tells us nothing, and is only a name for something unknown, and, secondly, there is no justification for the distinction. If we would attach some definite meaning to the word 'instinct,' we must admit that, for the Ego below the psycho-physical threshold, which in dream shows itself movable, it is connected with ideas; while, if it succeeds in overstepping the threshold in waking, it drops the idea, and only expresses itself still as obscure impulse. Thus in sleep the healing-force of nature acts in the sphere of ideas; in waking, only within the sphere of will. But were it only blind will, as Schopenhauer thought, it could not show itself in somnambulism in connection with idea.

The relationship of the health-dream with somnambulism appears also in this, that many dreams are reported in which the remedy for the diseases of others is seen. All these reports show that on the part of the dreamer the pre-condition is a deep internal

* Wiener: 'Selma, die jüdische Seherin,' 22, 35, 40; Berlin, 1838.

agitation through trouble concerning the disease, in general, a sympathy of the soul, whereby a like relation appears to be produced, as in somnambulic rapport, so that it is questionable whether this phenomenon does not already belong to the province marked off, by a fluid boundary line, as somnambulism.

A dream of this nature, which has classical celebrity, is that of Alexander. He fell asleep by his friend Ptolemaus, who was dying of a poisoned wound. In dream he saw a dragon who held a plant in his mouth, and said that with it he would heal his friend. On awaking, Alexander specified the exact colour of the plant, and the place where it was to be found, and was sure that he should know it when he saw it. The soldiers who were sent found the plant, which not only soon healed Ptolemaus, but also many other soldiers who had likewise received arrow-wounds.* Pliny relates of a mother who dreamed she was to send her son, who was in the field, the root of a wood-rose which she had seen the day before; and her son, who had hydrophobia from the bite of a mad dog, was cured.†

Remarkable is the dream of the physician, Christopher Rumbaum, of Breslau, which excited in his time an extraordinary sensation. It is to be found, with assurance of its historical truth, in the Breslau Collections (April, 1718); it was cited by most writers of that time, and by many was held to be purely supernatural.‡ Rumbaum had under his

---

\* Curt. Rufus, ix. 8; Cicero de Divin., ii. 66; Diodorus, xvii. 103; Strabo, xv. 2-7.
† Plinius: 'Hist. Nat.,' xxv. 11.
‡ Conf. Horsb.: 'Deuteroskopie,' ii. 122.

treatment a friend to whom he was much attached, but whom he saw no way of helping, and despairing of his restoration, he fell asléep, disturbed in mind. In dream there appeared to him a book in which was especially described how the cure was to be effected; he applied the means thus indicated, and the patient recovered. So far the dream might be explained by dramatized health-instinct and rapport. But we are expressly assured that first, some years later, a book appeared in the press, wherein this method of treatment was to be read on the same page on which Rumbaum had read it in the dream. Now, unless anyone will explain this part of the dream as a mere accident—which was not the opinion of the better informed contemporaries—he must admit the phenomenon of prevision. This is not the place to speak of that; but it may be observed that Kant has conclusively shown time and space to be intuitional forms of our sense-consciousness. In the chapter, 'Dream a Dramatist,' it appeared that our transcendental consciousness has a completely different measure of time, which already suggests the possibility of prevision.

The clear ideas of dream often leave behind them after waking an obscure presentiment or impulse, which need not, however, originate in sleep, but can occur spontaneously in all waking conditions connected with a displacement of the threshold. Physicians know that in nervous diseases, fevers, pregnancies, scurvy, etc., definite nutritious instincts often occur, with the knowledge of what is advantageous in the apparently hurtful. Hunger itself is such an instinct, so that dream directed to a particular nutriment may be explained as a specialized hunger, which has obtained its content as idea by the displacement of the threshold. Now, as also dream directed to a particular remedy is properly only the specialized healing-force of the organism, which has received its representative (ideal) content from the transcendental region of consciousness, these health-dreams offer no difficulty whatever to the understanding. If it is considered further, that somnambulism is a deeper sleep, in which the complete suppression of sense-consciousness is accompanied by a proportionately clearer waking within, that thus in this sleep also, the capacities of ordinary dream are present in an exalted degree, there is no longer anything unintelligible in the advanced phenomena of somnambulism with reference to the healing instinct.

### 4. *The Health-Prescriptions of Somnambules.*

The health-prescription of somnambules is the last issue of the sanative power of nature, and is rooted in it. In the sanative power nature works herself, and directly, in the health-prescription indirectly, determining, to functions in her interest, the organ of ideation which she has created. It is not from the brain, the reflective activity of understanding, that the health-prescription flows, but from the organ of inner waking, the ganglionic system. This, as already noticed, experiences influences not accessible to the waking brain-life, from earthly substances; and it is therefore explicable that it may be able to feel the utility or hurtfulness of these substances. If, however, an idea must be thought in all circumstances as a brain idea, still the first excitation to it must be sought in the ganglionic system, which in sleep is less isolated from the cerebral system, and could awake there an echo of its own feelings in the form of ideas.

Schopenhauer says: 'Nature properly only permits clairvoyance (of which somnambulism or speaking in sleep is the prelude), when her blindly working sanative power does not suffice for removal of the disease, but needs remedies from without, which are then rightly prescribed by the patient himself in the clairvoyant condition. To this end of self-prescription she brings forward clairvoyance, for "*natura nihil facit frustra.*"' Schopenhauer has presented this important point of new departure, which somnambulism reaches in clairvoyance, in the clearest light by comparing it with the similarly important point of new departure in the biological process, when Nature makes the step from the plant to the animal. With elevation in the organic scale, the needs must be more complex, and to seek out and select their objects the organ of cognition must arise, for which the sight of things comes to be the motives of action. Schopenhauer continues: 'Thus, in the one case as in the other, Nature herself kindles a light by which the assistance needed by the organism *from without* can be sought and obtained.'* Thus, according to Schopenhauer's theory, somnambulism repeats on the small scale what happens in the process of nature on the large one, and is a special case of the latter. Now, if, instead of seeing, with Schopenhauer, the

* Schopenhauer: 'Parerga,' i. 276.

substance of man in a blind universal willing, I seek this substance in the transcendental willing of the individual, this will being, for me, not absolutely, but only relatively blind (namely, for the man of the senses), if I thus substitute a representing and willing Ego for a merely willing and blind 'thing in itself,' every parallel of Schopenhauer can be accepted, and so far I can adopt his theory of somnambulism. The health-prescription is thus in the line of prolongation of the sanative power, which makes use of this consciousness for the search for external remedies.

Two sorts of somnambulism are to be distinguished, the natural and the artificial; not, however, according to the content of their phenomena, but according to the exciting cause. Nature herself introduces somnambulism in the course of many diseases as a beneficent crisis; artificial somnambulism ensues upon magnetic treatment, which does not actually produce this state, but only awakes the predisposition to it residing in the organism. The magnetic physician is therefore, like every other, merely the assistant of nature. Now as Nature of herself can introduce somnambulism, and as both sorts are by no means always connected with health-prescriptions, it follows that this condition has *in itself* a sanative power, which explains why the health-prescriptions of somnambules insist in the first place upon magnetic treatment, which should come to the aid of the natural disposition and develop it. That is very obvious, for as common sleep exalts the vegetative life-processes of the body, this must be much more the case with the deep somnambulic sleep, and to these vegetative functions belong also all sorts of the natural sanative power.

Further incidents of common sleep are the disappearance of sense-consciousness, and the incipient inner waking in dream. These also are both exalted in somnambulism, and since in the inner waking that faculty is brightened, which even in the outer waking state emerges as instinct for a particular nutriment or remedy, there result perfectly definite health-prescriptions, the fruit of which is the strengthening of the somnambulic disposition by magnetic treatment, this state being in itself one of sanative power, quite apart from the fact that it often converts the dreamer into a self-prescribing physician.

The magnetic mode of treatment is at present unfortunately, but quite accountably, in great discredit. Owing to the great difficulty, even apparent impossibility, of explaining the very strange phenomena of somnambulism, science has hastily flung its gun at the mark, and has confounded the impossibility of explanation with the impossibility of the thing, although the decision of the question of the magnetic sanative power has nothing to do with the possibility or impossibility of a theoretical explanation. We cannot explain mineral magnetism, and yet we use the compass for navigation; we do not know what electricity is, yet we apply it. Under these circumstances healing magnetism is now more in the hands of ignorant laymen than of scientific physicians, and is overspread with all possible superstitions. But it is not for Science to find fault with that for which she herself is responsible, since she has parted with the control of the subject. Recently scientific attention has again been directed to it ; literary contributions to it are constantly on the increase, and it is no longer to be feared that this most important of all phenomena will again fall into oblivion. A time is thus coming when magnetism will triumph, because it will be applied at the right time, not first with patients who are given up and have already exhausted every other resource, and further, because it will be exercised by physicians, or at least under their control. Even then we shall perhaps know no more of the nature of this mysterious force than at present; but physicians will not on that account abstain from the application of it, and will confess that they could prescribe few of their medicaments if experience of their effects were not enough to dispense with preliminary explanation of their mode of action.

Somnambules thus prescribe magnetism for themselves, and in many cases see in it the only remedy advantageous to them. At the same time they lay the greatest stress, not only upon particular hours of treatment, but even on the number and kind of magnetic passes they are to receive.* They show the magnetiser the movements of the hand which he has to apply in his treatment,† and they know this instinctively, even if in waking they are ignorant of magnetism. The physician Koreff knew a somnambule, who, in waking, had no acquaintance with the subject, and yet instructed her physician, who was

* 'Archiv,' vii. 2, 55; Reichenbach : 'Der sens. Mensch.,' i. 324, 331, 469.
† T. d. M. (Tardy de Montravel) : 'Journal du Traitement magnétique de la Demoiselle N.,' 118; Londres, 1786. 'Suite du Traitement,' etc., 130. Wienholt : 'Heilkraft,' etc., iii. 3, 168.

likewise ignorant of it, the number of magnetic passes to be given.* Experience, in fact, teaches that the different manipulations which occur in magnetic treatment bring with them also important different modifications of the somnambulic state. Tardy's somnambule lived in two totally different conditions, according to the magnetic treatment to which she was subjected; the content of her consciousness changed, as to that of another person, when she was magnetised in one way in the morning and in another way in the evening. She said to her magnetiser: 'I feel that my sleep quite changes its character, I now again see everything which ' appears to me in the usual morning sleep, but nothing more of that which I see besides in the evening.'†

It is very remarkable that even the auto-somnambules see in magnetic passes a means of exalting the natural somnambulism. Possibly the historical origin of animal magnetism in ancient India may be thus explained, for it may easily be that the first application of it was directed by an auto-somnambule.

Now what in the organism is excited by magnetic treatment is not at all a new force, strange and mysterious to it, but are simply its own active forces, exalted and moved to livelier activity. What the organism is doing in every moment of life to maintain the balance of inner forces and outer disturbances, it does in common sleep in a higher degree, and with still more energy in the magnetic sleep, which thus merely sustains a natural activity of the organism.

* Deleuze: 'Instruction pratique,' etc., 400.
† Tardy: 'Suite du Traitement,' 117, 118.

This natural effort of the organism to remove morbid disturbances is always proportioned to the mischief to be combated. Thus only is to be explained the always recurring phenomenon, that as the health is restored, sensibility to magnetism is lost. When the patient is restored he cannot again be placed in the magnetic sleep. 'I laugh,' said a somnambule, 'to think of the vain attempts you will make to-morrow to put me to sleep. You will not succeed, for I shall be well.'*

It is therefore one and the same force which forms the organism, sustains the life process, and repairs injuries; its activity is greatest in the magnetic sleep, but it discontinues this when the aim is attained. And, again, it is the continuation of this same natural force which in waking produces hunger, and the instinct for definite food, which in ordinary sleep, acting representationally, elicits the vision of the remedy, and which, when the inner waking reaches its greatest clearness in somnambulism, is exalted to the stage of self-prescription. As these organic forces form the body according to a definite type, so they restore it after this type in their health-functions.

Whoever holds in earnest the monistic conception that mind is only the continuation of nature, will not find it difficult to recognise continuity in the succession of formative impulse, natural sanative power, nutritive instinct, and health-idea; indeed, to such a monist, it might even be suggested *à priori* that instinctive health-ideas *must* occur. The organic formative impulse is related to the natural sanative power, just as the interior self-inspection to the health-

* Tardy: 'Essai,' etc., 60.

idea, and as the sanative power requires for its explanation that already the formative impulse is schematised by an idea, so also the health-idea is only explicable if the interior self-inspection is already a critical one. Self-inspection is not in all cases connected with health-ideas, and even when these occur, they first develop gradually from an obscure feeling to clearness. But that health-ideas are not only rare exceptions is shown in the fact that their simplest forms occur already in ordinary sleep, and can therefore appeal to an unbroken succession of observers of this phenomenon. Hippocrates, who constantly recommends physicians to have regard in diseases and dreams to the 'divine,' by which the transcendental psychological capacities are to be understood, says concisely: 'In dreams are seen the nutriments which are good for the body.' Similarly speak Aristotle, Galen, Aretæus. Cicero says, the qualities of different plants are shown by dream.* Later, it is the physician Abdallah-Abnusina (Avicenna) who cites health-ideas in dream.† Then follow Ficinus,‡ Janitsch,§ and others, down to the most recent time.

In citing cases of health-ideas I shall not divide them into those in which the somnambules prescribe for themselves and those in which they prescribe for others, a distribution which would belong rather to a book of reference, but shall adopt a principle of division which will advance our understanding of

\* Cicero: 'De Divinatione,' i. 10.
† Avicenna: 'Can. Med.,' viii., s. 2, c. 15.
‡ Marsil. Ficinus: 'De Immort. Animæ,' xvi. 5.
§ G. Janitsch: 'De Somniis Med.,' 1720. Th. Quellmalz: 'De Divinationibus Med.,' 1723. M. Alberti: 'De Vaticiniis Ægrotorum,' 1724.

the matter, that is, will discover the source of the prescriptions.

For there are only three sources from which these prescriptions of somnambules can logically flow : (1) The instinct of somnambules elevated into the ideal sphere; (2) The reflection of somnambules; (3) The reflection of the physician transferred to the somnambule. That the first of these is the true one will now be shown; the proof being further strengthened by the refutation of the others.

*(a) The Prescriptions of Somnambules are Instincts.*

The use of the word 'instinct' can here no longer mislead the reader, who already knows that instinct for me is connected with the idea which lies below the psycho-physical threshold, and belongs to the consciousness of the inwardly waking transcendental Ego. The excitement of this idea depends on the material of sensibility accessible to the transcendental consciousness, and only in so far as sensibility and idea remain below the threshold can we from the standpoint of the sense-consciousness speak of an *unconscious* instinct.

The proof that the prescriptions originate from such an instinct can only be derived from the way in which they come, and from what they contain.

They come in the deep sleep of somnambulism, and are the more definite the more the sense-consciousness is suppressed, that is, the deeper the sleep and the clearer the inner waking.

The physician Wienholt therefore advises that only in their deepest sleep should somnambules be asked about remedies, and he assures us that he had never then received a direction that was not to the purpose, though often, indeed, one more heroic than he would himself have ventured.* Still more is the instinctive character of the prescriptions betrayed by their coming from the insane and 'possessed,' in which case every other source is excluded, a proof how rightly Mesmer and Puységur judged, when they called the insane ill-regulated somnambules. Strombeck saw a person in an insane state who gave out categorically how she should be cured; no attention was paid to it, and she became completely mad.† Even bodily ill-usage, which somnambules, like the insane, inflict upon themselves, may be referred to instinctive impulse. A somnambule of Petetin, if she got an arm free, could inflict violent blows on her stomach. The region of the stomach was also the chief object of such attacks among the convulsionaries of St. Médard at the beginning of the last century. The three-volume work of Carré de Montgéron, which is full of official documents, is one of the most remarkable accounts of these occurrences, which excited all Paris during thirteen years, but remained so little understood, that all the copious polemic to which they gave rise turns on the question whether these phenomena were to be ascribed to God or to the devil.‡ The maltreatment of themselves by these convulsionaries calls vividly to mind the cruelties inflicted on their own bodies by Indian penitents, of

* Wienholt : 'Heilkraft,' etc., 1, § 14.
† Strombeck : 'Geschichte eines durch die Natur hervorgebrachten animalischen Magnetismus,' 144.
‡ Carré de Montgéron : 'La verité des miracles operés par l'intercession de M. de Paris, etc.,' Cologne, 1745.

whom Windischmann speaks,* adding that he has seen many phenomena of this sort, arising from confused somnambulism, in madhouses, where the treatment of such individuals was not understood, and which impressed one like an assembly of Indian penitents, in which everyone was busy in his own way.

To such ill-regulated somnambules belong also those 'possessed' persons of the middle ages, who were brought under the description of witches, just because medical science had no category for somnambules. So indications of somnambulism in prognosis and health-prescriptions are found in the 'possessed' children of Annaberg, of whom it is said: 'The children began to rage violently, with frightful distortion of the limbs and whole body. . . . Their breath has been often taken away, and they have devised and demanded remedies for themselves, which have been of immediate service. . . . They have known beforehand how they would be tormented, and when it would cease.'† With the possessed nuns of Unterzell, also, whose abbess, Maria Renata, was burned as a witch in 1749, the prescription of remedies occurred.‡ Tertullian, too, was aware of this phenomenon of possessed persons speaking as physicians, and as, according to the spirit of his time, he could only ascribe this to demons, he arrived at a very artificial explanation: 'When demons cure diseases, it is because they have themselves caused

---

\* Windischmann: 'Philosophie im Fortgang der Weltgeschichte,' i. 1481.
† Hauher: 'Bibliotheca Magica,' iii. 28-47.
‡ Horst: 'Zauberbibliothek,' v. 206.

them; they prescribe effectual remedies, and then it is believed they have driven away the disease, because they have ceased to cause it. (*Quia desinunt lædere, curasse creduntur*).'*

Self-prescriptions occur, moreover, with those somnambules who have the faculty of self-introspection and of diagnosing the diseases of others, and must therefore be regarded as a prolongation of these instinctive faculties, thus as the latest flower of Nature's sanative power.

One of the most remarkable cases of this sort is the history of the disease of Frau Marnitz, who was treated in vain for heart disease by more than twenty physicians for years, but then, becoming spontaneously a somnambule, knew her disease, defined its course, and restored herself by her prescriptions.†

As the introspection is no abstract knowledge, but intuitive representation of the interior, so also the health prescriptions. Instinct passes over into the perceptive sphere, producing dream-images; that is, the somnambules have a vision of the remedy. Professor Ennemoser knew a somnambule whose representation of her remedy took the form of a large nut filled with milk; she described it as big as a head and covered with fibrous flesh. Her exact description of the tree suggested a cocoanut, which was procured from Hamburg, and the patient improved daily.‡

Thus, while there is seldom an abstract naming of the remedy, the description of it, and of its medicinal

\* Tertullian: 'De præscr.,' c. 35.
† Dr. A. Schmidt: 'Bericht von der Heilung der Frau Marnitz,' Berlin, 1816. (Cited in Perty's 'Mystische Erscheinungen,' i. 307.)
‡ Ennemoser: 'Der Magnetismus,' 140; Leipzig, 1819.

qualities, are often so definite as to afford the physician a sufficient clue. But if there is a doubt, the somnambules will frequently take in their hands the drugs between which the uncertainty exists, and find the right one by tasting;* for the influences, which for the normal man remain below the threshold of sensibility, come to consciousness in them, and awaken instinctive inclination or repugnance. Wienholt's somnambule said of a remedy that it was to be prepared from a plant growing in a boggy place outside the city gate; she described its form and size, and desired that it should be cut small, boiled, and then drank with milk. Of a necessary condiment she could only say that they were grains, larger than anise, brown, with a shrivelled appearance, and a taste like pepper. Different seeds being laid before her, she chose *grana paradisi*. In another case, no one knowing the plant she asked for, she desired that when awake she might be persuaded to take a walk on the rampart, that in a later sleep she might be able to indicate the place where it was to be found.† The physician Billot tells us of a somnambulist who had prescribed a plant for a sick lady; he indicated its place in a wood, four hundred metres from a certain house, at the foot of an oak. He was taken to the wood, where he did not find the plant, but then lay down and went to sleep; on awaking, he directed them to a north-easterly search. The distance from the house was measured, and at the foot of the oak the plant was found.‡

\* Kluge: 'Versuch einer Darstellung,' etc., 165.
† Wienholt: 'Heilkraft,' etc., iii. 3, 26, 45, 47, 75, 188.
‡ Billot: 'Recherches psychologiques,' etc., ii. 317.

This further pursuit of the perceptive representation, by which the place is found, often occurs.

A somnambule of Puységur prescribed for herself a vegetable which she could neither name nor properly describe. She now proposed to her magnetiser that he should presently go with her for a walk in the garden, where she would see it and feel an instinctive impulse to pluck it. When she awoke she had forgotten everything—as is commonly the case, for the reason that the idea is below the threshold—but in the garden she plucked a plant, without being able to allege any other motive than her caprice, till she had collected enough for the prescribed medicament.* Another somnambule specified the place where the remedial herb was to be found at a distance of a mile, knew no name for it, and could only say that it was bitter.† To another, after awaking, Puységur repeated his own (the somnambulist's) prescription, mentioning where the plant was to be found, a league off, at which knowledge of the magnetiser the patient was surprised.‡

A somnambule of Reichel indicated a white case in a certain row in a druggist's shop which she had not entered for eight years, as containing her medicament.§ Römer's somnambule prescribed everything for herself. Once she required a drug from the shop, and gave the colour of the case and its number in the row, from right to left and the reverse. There being

* Morin : 'Du Magnétisme,' etc., 200.
† Puységur : 'Recherches,' etc., 81.
‡ *Id.*, 145, 147.
§ Reichel : 'Entwicklungsgesetz des magnetischen Lebens,' 67 ; Leipzig, 1829.

some scruple about compliance, she was displeased, till the physician went to the shop, and, as the drug seemed to him proper, allowed its use. Another remedy she saw in a porcelain case covered with dust and cobwebs, in a shop she had never entered. The physician brought her two medicaments wrapped in paper, but she knew by the smell the one she had prescribed. She also prescribed for another patient a remedy out of the same shop, from the third case of the sixth row, of which she could only further say that it was thick and black.* A similar case is vouched for by Carus.†

In degree as the inner waking is clearer, the idea of the remedy gets defined from general signs to particulars. Dr. Hanak reports the case of a somnambulist who prescribed for himself root of Angelica, and a certain black herb with long leaves; he could not name it, but only the mountain on which it would be found. It was *Gentiana Amarella Linnæi*, and when it was brought to him he recognised it immediately as that which had appeared to him in the magnetic sleep.‡ A patient of the physician Bende got the idea of musk powder, so that she saw the, to her unknown, musk, from whose body the drug that was to heal her fell. She first described it as bright brown, and of the size of a small roe; in a later vision the image was more distinct, and she saw the bag from which the powder fell, but in waking spoke

---

\* Römer: 'Historische Darstellung einer höchst merkwürdigen Somnambule,' 17, 19-31; Stuttgart, 1821.
† Carus: 'Lebensmagnetismus,' 93.
‡ Hanak: 'Geschichte eines natürlichen Somnambulismus,' 86, 91. From the Latin, Leipzig, 1833.

of it as of a plant.* Even the treatment to be applied by the physician is frequently seen in image. A somnambule saw ten leeches at work on her chest, and suggested this to the physician, who followed her counsel.† Another dreamed that her physician, to cure her of her deafness, magnetised her feet in a warm bath, and the hint was adopted with complete success.‡

Haddock's somnambule, Emma, was very remarkable in this, as in many other respects. There came once to Haddock a gentleman whose daughter suffered from a brain disease defying all medical treatment; to mediate the rapport, he left behind him merely a paper with pencil sketches by his daughter. Haddock gave the paper to Emma, and asked her if she could find the person who had made the sketches, and could state her condition of health. She soon found the young lady, described exactly the external symptoms, and her own perceptions in relation to the internal state of the brain, to which organ she referred the whole cause of the disease. After recommending different mesmeric passes, she exclaimed, pointing to the ceiling of the room: 'There is what, with mesmerism, will cure the young lady.' She then described small bottles and bowls in a workshop in Manchester, in the window of which stood a bust. Haddock now recollected a homœopathic apothecary's shop at that place, with a bust of Hahnemann; he procured a case of those medicaments from there, and put it, sealed, into Emma's hand. She indicated exactly the

* 'Archiv,' xi. 3, 37, 40, 87.
† Dupotet: 'Manuel,' etc., 73.
‡ Champignon: 'Physiologie,' etc., 324.

position of the remedy, which was ipecacuanha. They gave her a globule, and she described its composition (lactine, flour, with spirits of wine diluted with tincture of ipecacuanha), saying that the real medicine was mixed with two other things and with something sweet. The remedy was completely successful.* Now, that Emma could perceive the substance in homœopathic dilutions shows the high degree in which the threshold of sensibility was displaced with her; but it also shows, quite apart from the success of the cure, that though the actions of such dilutions may remain below the threshold of sense-consciousness, while allopathy has a more perceptible influence, this is far from being a reason for rejecting homœopathy. To say more here upon this point is, indeed, superfluous; for from the very important work of Professor Jäger on 'Neural Analysis'—notwithstanding that it is systematically ignored—every reader may be irrefragably convinced that the human nervous system immediately reacts upon the most attenuated homœopathic doses, a fact which Jäger has exhibited in a very striking way by experiments with a Hipps's chronoscope.†

The opinion that the health-prescriptions proceed from the transition, into the sphere of ideas, of the sanative power of Nature herself, receives very important confirmation from the fact that the vision of the remedy commences with undefined images, and gradually becomes clear. For if already ordinary sleep exalts the vegetative functions, and if the magnetic treatment, in deepening the sleep, did nothing else

* Haddock: 'Somnolismus,' etc., 183, 187.
† Jäger: 'Entdeckung der Seele,' 3 Aufl., 2 Bd.; Leipzig, 1884.

than further exalt the sanative power of Nature, it follows of necessity that the excitement of ideation by the sanative power is a gradual process in course of magnetic treatment, and the therewith connected exaltation of the sanative power, and thus that the vision of the remedy can also become gradually more distinct. The inner waking and the distinctness of the vision is just proportional to the deepening of the sleep and the displacement of the threshold of sensibility. Auguste Müller prescribed a medicament to a patient, but remarked that she should 'dream the way to use it on the following night.'* The perception proceeds from the general to the particular. A clairvoyante with Wolfart received first the representation of water containing earth and salt; by little and little the image developed into that of an alkali and carbonate health-spring with the most definite characteristics of the immediate neighbourhood, and finally the name Ems was uttered.† It is very often the case that somnambules know of no remedy, but feel that they will find one in a later sleep.‡ Thus there here takes place within the dream-life an exaltation similar to that which is frequent in waking, from a mere indefinite presentiment to distinct vision, as is perhaps also the case in second sight. There are also somnambules who in the ordinary somnambulic state can find no remedy, but discover it in the exalted condition called trance (Hochschlaf).§

It often happens that somnambules later on correct

* Meier und Klein: 'Geschichte der Auguste Müller,' 9.
† Wolfart: 'Jahrbücher,' ii. 2, 69.
‡ 'Archiv,' ix. 2, 126, 127.
§ Dupotet: 'Traité complet, etc.,' 256.

their own statements and prescriptions. The reason of this may be twofold. If they have been disturbed by premature questioning, before the moment of spontaneity has arrived, their statements do not flow from the pure spring of instinct, but are adulterated by reflection or memory. The difference of two statements may also be due to the inconstant depth of the sleep, with which, as has just been said, the definiteness of the instinct, and the clearness of the idea proceeding from it, also change. There is thus no reason for interpreting such corrections in the sceptical sense. Deleuze refused a somnambule a medicament she had demanded, and succeeded in dissuading her from it; two weeks later she was glad that she had not taken it, its application having been properly delayed till now, which was the right time for it. The insufficient depth of the sleep on the first occasion was, therefore, the cause of this fallacy in regard to the time. But if the sleep is at once deepened, the correction can follow immediately. It is therefore desirable to repeat former questions, in the case of such deepening. A somnambule of the physician Koreff pronounced herself incurable, and was perhaps right, so far as she measured the disease by the force hitherto applied by her physician in combating it. But when the latter, by the greatest effort, had placed her in a deeper sleep, she awoke so strengthened, that the incorrectness of her prognosis was apparent. It would have been very instructive, had the physician repeated his question before the awaking, when it is likely it would have received an answer differing from the first statement. Koreff even cited the case of a somnambule who corrected the self-prescription of another somnambule, and succeeded in dissuading the latter from it, and in inducing her to adopt the true remedy.* But it could only exceptionally happen that the judgment of another's disease should be truer than the patient's own.

The instinctive source of prescriptions appears also in this, that they frequently borrow from dream-life its well-known form of dramatic self-sundering. The somnambules in that case do not see the remedy, but learn it from an inner voice, or it is imparted to them by a visionary person, as in the already-mentioned dreams of Aspasia and Alexander. Such cases often occur, and have given occasion to superstitious conceptions, because their explanation by reference to the similar and familiar phenomenon of dream-life has been neglected. The reality of the adviser has been believed, which might have been prevented by the simple consideration that in that case the reality of the dragon in Alexander's dream, and of the symbolical doves which play so frequent a part, must be also accepted. The transcendental subject in the individual betrays itself as the source, when the somnambule only hears a voice, but sees no person.† Even these voices are at first only heard faintly, as from a long way off; but afterwards, especially after long operating on the pit of the stomach, always more distinctly.‡ The physician Heineken reports the following remarkable answer of a somnambule, whom he had questioned concerning the mode of her introspection and prescriptions: 'All

---

\* Deleuze: 'Instruction,' 1, 130, 426, 424.
† Werner: 'Symbolik,' 121.
‡ 'Archiv,' x. 3, 303.

my limbs are as if penetrated by a stream of light ; I
see the interior of my body—all its parts seem transparent; I see the blood flowing through my veins ;
*I observe exactly the disorders* which are in one part
or the other, and think attentively on the means by
which these can be removed ; *and then it seems to me
as if someone called out to me,* You must employ this
or that.'* It thus appears that the remedy first presents itself as a sudden suggestion in the course of
introspection. It appears further—quite in agreement with what was said in the chapter on 'Dramatic
Self-sundering in Dream '—that this suggestion necessarily assumes the dramatic form, because its overstepping the threshold of sensibility is emergence
from the unconscious. Now, if this explanation of
dramatic health-prescriptions is correct, we are led by
it *à priori* to the hypothesis, that when the deepening
of the inner life fails of the necessary degree, the
suggestion is left out, and, therefore, that there must
be somnambules possessing only the gift of introspection, without that of prescriptions. Now this is very
often the case, which is only explicable if the above
theory of dramatic sundering is correct. Such somnambules, in whom the latent faculty for prescriptions
remains unconscious, often get the physician to suggest
different medicines ; and if he mentions one that is
appropriate, they know it to be so. This is again a
proof that the faculty for prescribing is not essentially wanting, but is only retained in the unconscious.
Our unconscious memory often follows the same
psychological rule. If, for instance, we cannot recall

* Heineken : 'Ideen und Beobachtungen,' etc., 128.

the name of a place, the unconscious existence in us of the name nevertheless enables us to determine critically among successive suggestions made by someone else, rejecting them till the right name is mentioned, when we recognise it at once.

St. Augustine makes mention of a boy who often had visions, lay without feeling, and with eyes open saw nothing—evidently a case of somnambulism. He affirmed that he saw two boys who announced to him the cause of his illness, and he was finally cured because his physician adopted the treatment prescribed by these visionary boys.* This dramatic sundering occurred also with the Jewish seeress, Selma, already mentioned. She saw her guardian spirit and an old man ; the first prescribed linseed oil, the second olive oil. Later on the dream recurred in a different form ; she now saw her sister, who went with her into a shop and asked for linseed oil ; the shopkeeper considered olive oil more to the purpose, but tried in vain to persuade the sister. It is remarkable that this sister, who was in good health, had a similar dream the same night.† In this dream is evidently reflected the still present indistinctness of vision.

Another form of prescription appears in visionary writings. The Petersen somnambule saw Roman letters forming themselves large and bright, as if gilt.‡ The particular form of such visions appears to be often involuntarily determined by the magnetiser ; for Bertrand mentions one, all of whose patients had similar visions of the remedy, by seeing themselves

---

\* Augustinus : 'De gen. a. I.,' vii. 17.
† Wiener : ' Selma,' 149, 151.
‡ 'Archiv,' xi. 1, 95.

in a waste place, which, when they were questioned about the disease, became over-grown with the remedial plant proper for each case.* So also are allegorical and symbolical forms borrowed from the dream-life. A patient saw her condition symbolised as a flower adorned with all its leaves, but with a dark spot on the side of the calyx, to signify her chest complaint, from which she foresaw long years of suffering.† Another saw in the stalk of her symbolical plant a worm eating through the pith up to the flower, which then fell off.‡ The somnambule of the Medical-Councillor Klein saw in vision a mountain-journey, the scenes of which represented the physical and psychical struggles connected with her magnetic cure.§

Finally, the instinctive origin of the prescriptions may be inferred from their singularity. This is especially observable in such instinctive actions as are adopted to deepen sleep. If, for example, the long-continued rotatory movements customary among the Dervishes are intended to excite the somnambulic condition, the imitation of this proceeding by somnambules can only have the deepening of the sleep for its object. It deserves mention that, according to Reichenbach, this rotatory movement occurs in connection with the phenomena of the Od light.‖ Chardel knew a patient who put herself into somnambulism, and was clairvoyant, by turning round till

---

\* Bertrand : 'Traité du Somnambulisme,' 420.
† Werner : 'Schutzgeister,' 202.
‡ *Ibid.* : 'Symbolik,' 141.
§ 'Archiv,' v. 1.
‖ Reichenbach : 'Der sensitive Mensch,' ii. 165, 166.

she was giddy.* A patient of Deleuze suffered on a journey, away from her magnetiser, a dislocation of the thigh-bone, which she herself set in an access of somnambulism; and whereas before she could not endure the least touch, she now stood up, went round the room, and made rotatory motions without any trouble.† The like was also observed among the convulsionaries of St. Médard. One of these passed from one to two hours daily for several months in these rotations, making about sixty in a minute; he stood on the tip of one foot, the other describing a circle in the air. Another, a woman, confined herself to motions of the head, so rapid that her features could scarcely be distinguished.‡ We already find the origin of this method of exciting clairvoyance in India. Thus it is required of the Brahmanic novitiates to turn round twelve times twenty-four times, and, if strength suffices, twenty-four times forty-eight times.§

But the medicinal remedies also betray their instinctive source by their strangeness. Comparing the counsel given by the Delphic Pythia to the epileptic youth, Democrates,‖ and the prescriptions given in the temple-sleep which are preserved upon some votive tablets,¶ with the mediæval ones of Paracelsus, and those of somnambules, so striking does the relation appear between the whole series of

* Chardel: 'Essai de Psychologie,' 254.
† Deleuze: 'Instruction,' etc., 439.
‡ Carré de Montgéron: 'La Verité,' etc., ii. Art. Kath. Bigot. und Schlussartikel, 143.
§ Agrouchada-Parakchai, ii.
‖ Theodor Puschmann: 'Alexander von Tralles,' i. 568; Wien, 1878.
¶ Conf. Sprengel: 'Geschichte der Medizin,' i. 162.

these phenomena, that the hypothesis of their common source in somnambulism spontaneously suggests itself.

If the prescriptions of somnambules are rooted in the sanative power of nature, and are of an instinctive character, it is antecedently to be expected that they will show a relationship to the remarkable instincts of animals. Already in antiquity these instincts excited such surprise in observers that it was thought that animals must participate in the divine soul, and even later inquirers are inclined to ascribe infallibility to those instincts that relate to the provision for offspring. This infallibility is also claimed by many magnetisers for the prescriptions of somnambules. That in this they have gone too far is apparent from the fact that the prescriptions are frequently phenomena of a mixed character, and it is often difficult to decide whether the utterances are free from constituents of the waking consciousness, reflection, or fancy. This danger, and the further one, that opinions of the magnetiser himself may be transferred to the somnambule, are particularly to be apprehended when the prescriptions are elicited by much questioning, and hence the spontaneity of the healing-vision is desired as an indication of instinct. Puységur relates that a somnambule often intentionally concealed her vision, fearing the inquisitions and experiments of the bystanders, which interfered with her self-inspection.* Faria commends the suddenly arising visions as especially to be relied on, preferring them to others which are gradually developed,† and in this

* Puységur: 'Recherches,' etc., 190.
† Faria: 'Sommeil lucide,' 349.

he seems so far right, that the latter more easily admit the false stimulations above referred to.

True instinctive prescriptions, therefore, never present themselves as an abstract knowledge in the somnambulic consciousness; they have the external forms peculiar to dream-life : intuitive perception, dramatic sundering, and symbol. The danger of foreign influences is at its least in auto-somnambulism; in this, therefore, when it rises to the stage of prescription, we see the most perfect form of the sanative power of nature; and in such prescriptions the somnambule appears as little subject to deception as the natural sanative power itself. Kerner says of one of his somnambules, that what she prescribed for herself acted 'with mathematical certainty,' but her prescriptions for others were of less avail, his explanation being that the patients did not closely observe the hours prescribed for the remedies, a point much insisted on by somnambules,* who explain failures, and also the alterations they make themselves in their prescriptions, by the imperfect execution of their directions.

As the prescriptions cannot depend on theoretical knowledge, and therefore the assurance of success can only have the form of a firm belief and trust, all utterances containing theoretical explanations and reasonings must be regarded with suspicion. Even in the rest there is still danger of deception, for the images of the exalted dream-phantasy in somnambulism have the freshness and vivacity of really instinctive visions, and are indistinguishable from these,

* Kerner: 'Geschichte zweier Somnambulen,' 373.

as with some insane persons products of imagination are indistinguishably mingled with real objects. It is therefore easily explicable that somnambules are convicted of mistakes, and that they even withdraw them themselves.* The influence of rapport with the physician further accounts for the observation which has been made that German, French, and English somnambules often only echo the medical theories prevailing in their countries.† But though particular cases may be referred to these two sources of health-prescriptions, in general they can be excluded—a further indirect confirmation of the view that prescriptions are instinctive.

(*b*) *The Prescriptions of Somnambules do not issue from Reflection.*

Independence of reflection is the characteristic sign of all instincts, and is therefore found in the health-prescriptions of somnambules. This is apparent from a whole succession of phenomena. It is first of all to be mentioned that, according to experience, the most reliable prescriptions are those given by somnambules who are quite ignorant, and that even little children evince this faculty in a high degree.‡

These prescriptions are often exceedingly strange, seeming even senseless. If, however, the opinion here maintained, that somnambulism depends on a displacement of the threshold of sensibility, and on partial emergence of the transcendental consciousness,

\* Morin : 'Magnétisme,' 333-336.
† Kieser : 'Tellurismus,' ii. 190.
‡ Ennemoser : 'Der Magnetismus nach der allseitigen Beziehung,' 126.

is right, the singularity of many of the prescriptions is at once explained. For with this displacement the relation of sensibility to chemical substances must be altered; a wholly heterogeneous material of sensibility is brought to the Subject. The prescriptions, therefore, must be frequently as heterogeneous as is this material of sensibility from which they are derived; and the remedies must thus more or less depart from those in use in medicine, which have regard rather to the normal relation of man with Nature. Römer's somnambule said: 'To-morrow morning, punctually at a quarter past nine, I must drink half a glass of shoe-nail water;' adding to the astonished hearers the further direction that fifty shoe-nails should be scalded with boiling water, put upon the fire with a pint and a half of water, and boiled away to half a pint.* That sounds absurd, because for the normal sensibility it is probably quite ineffectual; but we do not at all know what effects there are which remain below the threshold. Indeed, the whole system of homœopathy rests upon such sub-threshold effects.

Many prescriptions recall the sympathetic remedies of the mediæval Paracelcists and the folk-lore of the present day. The efficiency of some of these means is admitted by many unprejudiced physicians, as is the impossibility of a scientific explanation of it.† It seems, however, that somnambulism will explain not only this, but also the origin of folk-lore remedies, by prescriptions given in the ecstatic state. Paracelsus himself, it is related, got up at night and in a half

---

\* Römer: 'Historische Darstellung,' etc., 35.
† Dr. Fr. Most: 'Die sympathetische Mittel und Kurmethoden,' 1842.

ecstatic condition declared the remedies for different diseases. The folk-lore belief in the transference of diseases to plants—*transplantatio morborum*—plays a part in somnambulism also.* A patient of Werner directed that nails cut from her fingers and toes, and mixed with hair of her own and of the magnetiser, and with blood, should be buried under the roots of a tree. When it was all putrified and risen into the tree as sap, her health would improve. This was a genuinely magnetic and likewise sympathetic remedy.

A consequence of the displacement of the threshold of sensibility is that the inclination or repugnance to medicines differs in the waking and in the somnambulic state. Medicaments for which in waking somnambules have the greatest dislike, they often willingly adopt in their magnetic condition, or if the medicaments are made homogeneous to them by magnetic treatment. They like to drink magnetised water, and praise its sanative power. One somnambule required all that she ate or drank to be magnetised, and a cup of coffee, in which her physician's brother-in-law had secretly put his finger, excited in her pains and convulsions.† Another was always made sick by common milk, in whatever composition it entered, though this never occurred when the milk was magnetised.‡ On the other hand, somnambules often know food to be deleterious which in waking they prefer. Selma warned her friends against giving her

* *E.g.*, Werner: 'Schutzgeister,' 289.
† 'Archiv,' v. 3, 83. [For this was what is known as 'cross-magnetism.'—Tr.]
‡ Tardy: 'Essais-Vorrede,' 13.

pears, however much she might beg for them ;* and one of Römer's somnambules prohibited in general everything which she should ask for when not in the magnetic sleep.† They have often no regard whatever to their normal inclinations or the reverse for food and medicines, a somnambule of the physician Heinecken prescribing for herself rhubarb on the following day, to be administered by force, as she had a special abhorrence of it.‡ In other cases this difficulty is got over. Thus, one somnambule prescribed for herself different remedies ; those which she liked to be offered to her when awake, the others she would take in somnambulism, *e.g.* tartar emetic and ipecacuanha. She named the different physics, having read the labels clairvoyantly, now in this, now in that apothecary's shop. Waking, she believed herself incurable; in somnambulism, on the contrary, she was full of hope.§ But though the names of the medicines can be known clairvoyantly, as a rule they are not named, but only described. The faculty is not in the least reflective, but depends on feelings and intuitions which, if symbolised, the somnambules themselves understand only by degrees, or partially, or even not at all. Frau Marnitz could not name euphorbis, buck-bean, or formic spirit, but described the appearance and locality of the former, and of the latter the appearance, taste, and position in the druggist's shop.‖ A somnambule being asked how she knew a herb,

\* Wiener : 'Selma,' 77.
† Römer : 'Histor. Darst.,' 44.
‡ Heinecken : 'Ideen und Beobactungen,' etc., 115.
§ Gauthier : 'Histoire,' etc., ii. 358.
‖ Perty : 'Myst. Ersch.,' i. 264.

whose locality she had given, to be curative, when she yet did not know its name, sensibly replied that herbs have no name in themselves, but only receive them from men.* Yet Puységur's inference that names as abstract and arbitrary denotations can never be known by somnambules seems not in general correct. Some very remarkable experiences of Tardy may be regarded as transitional phenomena to the knowledge of names. From an old work on medicines he had extracted a long list of remedies for tapeworm, the names of which he read to his somnambule, an uneducated girl of the lower orders. She rejected a number of them, but eagerly adopted bitter orange-peel and hemp-seed. She could give no other explanation than that she had heard the names first mentioned with repugnance, but these latter ones with pleasure. Very disagreeable symptoms, from which she had suffered for more than four years, were thus removed.† Another time, for the similar complaint of another patient, he enumerated to his somnambule many remedies; this time she rejected the one used by herself, and recommended one of the others mentioned to her.‡ She once named for a patient a herb not known to Tardy himself, who, however, procured it; in a later sleep he showed it to her, merely asking if she knew it, and she at once replied that it was an advantageous remedy for that patient.§ But the most striking phenomenon of this sort is in the case of the somnambulic boy Görwitz, who, being

---

\* Puységur: 'Recherches,' etc., 148.
† Tardy: 'Essais,' 66; 'Journal de Traitem.,' 94, 95.
‡ Tardy: 'Journal,' etc., 115.
§ Tardy: 'Essai,' etc., 67.

asked by his physician (his brother) about poisons, 'dictated with incomprehensible accuracy the most difficult names of poisons, the enumeration of even a small part of which would fill many quarto pages.'\*

There remains to be noticed a phenomenon which is apparently most difficult to explain by the principle of instinct. Many somnambules prescribe the application of technical apparatus, stating the construction and delineating it themselves. The so-called mineral baquet used in the earlier days of mesmerism was often filled according to the instructions of the somnambules themselves. Römer's somnambule of fifteen years old sketched a machine in sleep, adding explanatory names. This machine had a cylinder, like an electric machine, certain constituent parts of the baquet, but in other respects differed from all known physical appliances; it was of a strictly geometrical construction, and according to the physician was a very interesting contrivance. She devised this machine in a simple form for her own use, in a more complicated one for stronger constitutions; she also made a sketch of this one on a larger scale, cut it out, fastened it on paper, and lastly prepared a model in paste. When a beginning was made with this complicated apparatus, a sketch of which is given in Römer's book, she found fault with departures from her model, and corrected the mistakes. The machine was to be placed by her bed during her sleep to enable her to judge of it.† The seeress of Prevorst also had,

---

\* Görwetz: 'Richards magn. Schlaff,' 55.
† Römer: 'Hist. Darst.,' 11, 12, 24, 26.

early in her disease, a dream, in which there appeared to her a machine, by use of which she hoped to be cured; no attention was paid to her dream, although it was several times repeated. Finally, after an interval of four years, the same dream-image recurred dramatically, her 'guide' holding before her the machine, and reproaching her with her earlier neglect to apply it, as it would have cured her. In the morning she sketched this machine on paper. Every use of it was followed by shocks, as from a galvanic battery, succeeded by spasms, after which she always felt stronger. I have myself seen the sketch\* of this machine in the possession of Kerner's son, the Councillor Theobald Kerner. A similar fact is briefly mentioned by Carré.†

It would be a mistake, however, to ascribe prescriptions, when raised to the point of technical construction, to deliberate reflection. If the wonderful structure of the snow-flakes,‡ or of the protozoa,§ or the mathematical principles followed in the formation of plants, are not allowed to be analogous cases, we may still point to the ingenuity with which spiders spin their webs, and bees construct their cells. To refer such instincts to the understanding would be to ascribe to animals a more than human intelligence. The birch-weevil *(Rhynchites betulæ)* towards the end of May cuts strips off the leaves of the birch, rolling them into funnel-shaped chambers, and marking out suitable cradles for its eggs. A regular

---

\* Kerner: 'Seherin der Prevorst,' 23, 108, 109.
† Carré de Montgéron: 'La verité,' etc., iii. 581.
‡ Semper: 'Der Stil. I Vorrede,' München, 1878.
§. E. Häckel: 'Das Protistenreich,' Leipzig, 1878.

pattern seems to be followed, which, however, can be changed according to the needs of the beetle, if he finds no leaves conformable to it. Debay has copied these leaf-sections with the greatest exactitude, and Heis found, after careful investigation, that for their particular purposes they agree perfectly, even in the smallest technical details, with results of calculations only to be arrived at by help of certain parts of higher mathematics, which had remained unknown up to a recent date in that science.*

It is certainly more permissible to say, with Cuvier, that animals are somnambules, than to attribute to them superhuman intelligence; and so it is also more permissible to ascribe the delineation of technical instruments to instinct than to the conscious deliberation of a girl of fifteen, to whom the very word 'Physics' was perhaps unknown. Readers of the remarkable book already referred to, Ernst Kapp's 'Philosophie der Technik,' will understand this striking phenomenon of somnambulic life without difficulty, and will agree with me that Kapp might have made use of it as a strong confirmation of his theory.

The instinctive character is especially manifest in the prescriptions of somnambules for others, for if these were to be referred to reflection, the understanding of somnambules must be greater than that of men of science. In diagnosis, the method of physicians is to reason reflectively from symptoms to internal causes, while somnambules know the disease in-

* Duttenhofer: 'Die 8 Sinne du Menschen,' 227; Nordlingen, 1858.

tuitively or sensitively. This is also the case when they prescribe for others.

It seems that this can even happen in common sleep. Magnenus, at least, seems to assert it in effect, from his own experience, in his book upon Tobacco. When he went to sleep with his thoughts directed to a sick person, remedies were presented to him in dream which he held to be incomparable when he considered them in the morning, and which he applied with the greatest benefit.* Tertullian also, whose experiences with somnambules made him even a heretic, reports that a person in his 'illuminations'—probably somnambulic—prescribed for other people.†

Deleuze knew a girl of sixteen who dictated medical treatises upon different diseases. She answered his questions clearly and distinctly. But one day she could say nothing whatever about the nature of gout, and the means of curing it. Other diseases, she said, were at least potential in her own constitution, but of gout she had not in herself the slightest germ, and she could therefore only speak of it if placed in rapport with a gouty person.‡ Deleuze, who proceeded very circumspectly and sceptically, had similar experiences with other somnambules, showing that even here, where reflection seems to be implied, the foundation is a pervading feeling of the organism, but perhaps not sufficiently intense to exclude any admixture of mental ingredients; at least in the treatises of the girl above mentioned, Deleuze found that principles of medicine were favoured which were

* Boismont: 'Traktat von Geistern,' 222; Halle, 1721.
† 'Archiv,' ii. 2, 160.
‡ Deleuze: 'Histoire critique,' etc., i. 193.

in vogue then, but which underwent subsequent alterations. As we saw, the health-instinct is much exposed to interference; its ascertainment is therefore very difficult, and blind confidence in the prescriptions is at all events misplaced.

But the directions of the pure instinctive utterance seem to be always attended with success. Medical-Councillor Wezler, of Augsberg, having suffered for years from a nervous complaint, was told by a somnambule to use washings with a soap, the preparation of which she described. He was in a short time relieved from his sufferings, and he considered this cure so extraordinary that he tried the remedy with other patients, and cured the most obstinate cases with it.* I can only refer briefly here to another very remarkable case, the history of the cure of the Countess Maldegem, whose disease, related to insanity, was of years' standing.† With Haddock's somnambule, Emma, also, the curative instinct was so extraordinarily developed that even physicians of high position did not disdain to seek her elucidations upon cases in their practice.

Even prescriptions for others often take on the form of the dramatic self-sundering. In one of such cases a boy was being treated for a disease of the eyes which got continually worse, notwithstanding the physicians. There was a perpetual running from the eyes, and when the lids could be at all raised it was seen that the eyes were wasting. The despairing mother, a Spaniard from the colonies, while sitting at

* Wezler: 'Meine wunderbare Heilung durch eine Somnambule,' 58; Augsberg, 1833.
† Kerner: 'Seherin von Prevorst,' 457.

the sick bed, took refuge in prayer, and in this condition of inward agitation, so favourable to somnambulism, she had a vision in which the Virgin herself appeared. She was heard to exclaim on a sudden, 'Thanks, holy Virgin, I will go seek them!' She thereupon went into the wood, accompanied by two ladies, who could get no reply from her; she there plucked herbs, tearing them out by the roots, and at home made a decoction of them, and of this put cataplasms on the child's eyes. She was much alarmed when in the morning she heard what she had done, and waited anxiously for the physician; but he found the mischief so much abated that he ordered the application to be continued. The mother could not, however, herself recollect what herbs she had picked, but in the evening fell again into somnambulism, returned to the wood, and with a second application of the cataplasm the child was completely cured.\*

According to Dr. Bendsen, prescriptions, both for self and others, not seldom occur in insanity; and he adduces a case in which Frau Petersen in an excess of mania rapidly uttered a very successful prescription. It is true Frau Petersen was a somnambule, but the fact that she herself, in later conditions of somnambulism, remembered nothing whatever of this prescription, is for the expert a sure sign that it did not originate in this state, but in insanity,† for the bridge of memory only connects related states, between heterogeneous ones it breaks down. This is by no means the only characteristic which somnambulism and insanity have in common, again compelling the hypo-

\* Lafontaine: 'Mémoires d'un magnétiseur,' ii. 179; Paris, 1866.
† 'Archiv,' xi. 2, 124, etc.

thesis that in many cases madness may be nothing else than unregulated somnambulism, resting on an oscillation of the threshold of sensibility, with dramatic sundering of the Subject into two persons, and a dramatic explanation of the material of sensibility. In such case the community of characteristics may often lead to the error of putting the insane and somnambules in the same category, whereas regard to the distinctive characteristics requires a separation of these categories. In the Middle Ages, somnambules were confounded with witches, and as long as men of science refuse to study somnambulism there will always be the danger of mistaking it for madness, and of including patients in the same institution who require different treatment.

Now, if health-prescriptions occur in dream, somnambulism, and madness, appearing further in the reports of witch-trials in the Middle Ages, and lastly, as is affirmed by the distinguished witness, Wallace,* among the phenomena observed with modern mediums, that is proof that this exaltation of the health-instinct is common to all conditions which are connected with displacement of the psycho-physical threshold, and which can be so far comprehended under the general conception of ecstasy, that, in them all, the disappearance of self-consciousness proceeds parallel with an inner waking.

(c) *The Health-Prescriptions are not to be explained by rapport with the Magnetiser.*

In the surgical ward at Leipzig, Herr Hansen showed the following experiment in the presence of

* Wallace: 'Defence of Modern Spiritualism.'

different professors. He requested Dr. Hermann to turn his back to him, face to the wall, so that he could not see what Hansen was about. The latter then laid his right hand on Dr. Hermann's head, and with his left hand took a steel pen, dipped it in ink, and drew it through his own mouth. At the same moment Dr. Hermann declared that he had the taste of ink in his mouth, and this lasted an hour, not being even removed by the taste of food taken for the purpose.* I cite this experiment only as an example, which has become very well known, of the rapport existing between magnetiser and magnetised. This rapport can extend itself to all the senses, even to what goes on in the central seat of the senses, the brain, so that even the dispositions and thoughts of the magnetiser are transferred to the somnambule.

It is thus also doubtless possible that even the medical ideas of a magnetising physician rebound, as it were, from the consciousness of the somnambule, especially if the physician, instead of merely exciting the health-instinct, facilitates the interchange by indiscreet interrogation. And so he will be a sort of ventriloquist, hearing his own echo, while he supposes that he is receiving valuable information. Hence it has often been suggested that somnambulic health-prescriptions derive, through rapport, from the mind of the physician. But admitting this possibility, it is still the fact that only a percentage of the prescriptions are to be referred to this source, and the majority of them must be explained by an exalted instinct. That is best proved by the important differences

* Zöllner: 'Wissenschaftliche Abhandlungen,' iii. 529.

existing between medical prescriptions and those of somnambules.

Medical-Councillor Schindler says : ' Finally, we must also regard all *specific* remedies as *magical ;* for our chemical and physical sciences do not suffice to explore the action of remedies, so *it is a relation, unknown to us, of the life of Nature to the individual life which gives natural bodies their healing potency.* The magical healing-instinct, as it expresses itself in sleep and in magnetic conditions, is often far removed from ordinary therapeutics, and somnambules generally prescribe for themselves very simple remedies, often such that we can see in them no relation to the disease, but often also such as seem to be suggested by the mind of the physician. Thus a somnambule patient of mine prescribed for a blindness, following upon an injury to a nerve of the fifth couple in the socket, sponging with *extr. stramonii,* and for another complaint tea of *anagallis arvensis,* a herb which I was not aware had a healing virtue. Another time, I could not make out the remedy desired, and the patient indicated it in the index of a *materia medica* which was brought to her for the purpose, and at the same time improved upon the dose prescribed in the recipe, although she had no knowledge of apothecaries' weights. The magical effects of remedies, by which I mean their specific effects, are very little known to us, and if what the ancients handed down concerning the effects of stones belongs more to the region of fable, the action of metals is yet still obscure to us, and of herbs in this respect we know only a very small part. Very much remains here to be done, and it is a question whether homœopathy in its *similia* *similibus* has already found the key to further investigations.'*

Now, the displacement of the threshold of sensibility affords an excellent opportunity for obtaining new information concerning these still unknown effects of metals and herbs. Those effects do not fall within the sense-consciousness, and are therefore not included in medical science, which might have had a rich field of experience in somnambulism, which, when its prescriptions are based on effects remaining below the threshold, proves that the inner consciousness of somnambules does not draw its material from the mind of the physician.

Were the prescriptions always the result of rapport, somnambules could not, as often happens, energetically oppose the physician's treatment. It is very frequently the case that instinct tends in a direction quite different from that of the physician's deliberate judgment. Usually, indeed, the magnetiser is not a physician, and can form no judgment for himself of the disease and its remedy. But when he is a physician, his methods are often censured, his treatment is corrected, or remedies are prescribed between which and the disease he knows of no connection, because this is only apparent to consciousness below the threshold. The contradiction by the physician often begins at the diagnosis, that of the somnambules being more or less opposed to the professional, in that they treat cases of the same disease individually, as in the regular practice can perhaps only be done by the family physician of many years who knows his patients accurately. Even in the same disease of

* Schindler: 'Magisches Geistesleben,' 268.

the same patient the remedies are often changed according to the season of the year and the weather.* Somnambulists thus do not know the disease as a species, but only in the individual case; every disease is with them a case by itself, the treatment for which is to be changed even according to external circumstances. It is therefore quite possible that the pharmacopœia can be enriched from the prescriptions of somnambulists, though except in the case of very simple remedies, for morbid conditions of little complication, means appropriate to individual cases will not be adapted to all included in the specific concept of the disease, nor can general rules be taken from these prescriptions.

The opposition of somnambulists to the science of the physician also appears in the prescription of remedies, from which, or at least from the doses, he recoils in alarm. This is the more remarkable, as the displacement of the threshold makes the sensibility more acute, influences too weak for external consciousness making themselves known. Therefore when somnambulists, as often happens, double and multiply manifold the usual single doses, when poisons are advantageous to them, of which only a fraction could be taken by the normal man without danger to life, that does not well admit of any other explanation than that not only are new relations between drugs and disease known through somnambulism, but also the old relations are changed or suspended by a change in the whole physiological disposition of the organism. And so somnambulists often prescribe for themselves a very strict diet, even

* Kerner: 'Blätter aus Prevorst,' v. 59.

long abstinence from food and drink, without suffering the emaciation which might have been expected ; a phenomenon forthcoming, moreover, in typhus and febrile diseases. Professor Ennemoser knew a boy who lived for a week on magnetised water only.*

A somnambule prescribed for her child five drops of opium, and on waking was in despair when she heard that they had been given to him. Being again in the somnambulic state, she was easy about it, and the child recovered. For herself she prescribed and actually took 350 drops of opium, all the symptoms of poisoning ensuing, but which again disappeared.† Another replied to the scruple expressed by the magnetiser to the dangerous dose, that in waking she should share this scruple and refuse consent, but in sleep she felt that the dose would do her good, and would restore her in ten days, as was confirmed by the result.‡ Kerner reports of a prescription of poison sufficient to kill twenty men, but the seeress disregarded all representations ; when they offered her half, she pushed it away and demanded the whole, which at last, procured from several shops, was given to her. She drained the glass empty, without the predicted success being accompanied by other evil effects.§

Puységur, to try if a prescription of a somnambule, who had ordered for herself seven grains of tartaremetic, to be taken in an orange, really sprang from her clairvoyant instinct, prepared half a dozen oranges, putting two grains in the first, three in the second,

\* Ennemoser : 'Der Magnetismus nach der allseitigen Beziehung,' etc., 60.
† Archiv, vii. 2, 147, 150.
‡ Puységur : 'Recherches,' etc., 61.
§ Kerner : 'Blätter aus Prevorst,' iii. 181.

and so on up to the last, with seven grains in it. She refused them impatiently one after the other till the last, which she seized gladly.* Nevertheless no case is reported in which a somnambule has killed herself by such prescriptions. A formal change in the disposition of the organism must therefore be supposed, according to which the normal effects of medicaments cease, and abnormal effects take their place. Teste somewhere mentions a somnambule who smoked two large pipes of tobacco without any ill effects.† The physician Despine was treating a girl of eleven for softening of the spinal marrow. In somnambulism she could eat what she liked, in waking she lived only upon milk and eggs ; it was as if she had two different organs of digestion. In waking she was paralysed in the lower extremities ; in somnambulism she could walk, run, swim ; in waking she could only sit between wadding and eider-down, in somnambulism she wallowed in the snow and took ice-cold baths.‡ Only thus is it to be explained that even poisons are taken without injury, as with evident reference to somnambulism it is said in the Gospel : 'And if they drink any deadly thing, it shall not hurt them.'§ It is also reported of the Mohammedan sect of the holy Sheikh Ruffai that the disciples take arsenic and poisonous herbs without harm.‖

* Colquhoun: 'Historische Enthüllungen,' etc., 490. [I have not been able to find any English work by John Campbell Colquhoun (author of several books on these subjects) with a title corresponding to the above.—Tr.]
† [It should be added, presuming this to be implied, that she had never smoked before.—Tr.]
‡ Pigeaire: 'Electricité animale,' 272, 277, 278.
§ Mark xvi. 18.
‖ Görres: 'Christl. Mystik,' iii. 548.

Now if chemicals act otherwise on somnambulists than on persons in the waking state, the opposition of the former to the medicaments offered to them, and their choice of those which seem unadapted to our system, are intelligible, as also the fact that the treatment of such patients according to the principles of science is for the most part unsuccessful. Koreff, who found, not without a feeling of humiliation, that his patients rejected his remedies and chose others from which he could anticipate no effect, draws the right inference—that the physician who has satisfied himself of the somnambulists' clairvoyance should trust entirely their prescriptions, for which he has no scientific gauge; that he can only choose between two methods, not combine them.*

Somnambulists often depart from the practice of physicians in the opposite direction also, for heroic remedies substituting others apparently quite inadequate, or reducing the customary doses. The Seeress of Prevorst, by means of an infusion of lime blossoms, pear juice, and castoreum, put into a long sleep a sufferer from delirium tremens, on whom the strongest doses of opium were no longer of any avail.†

Independence of the physician is further shown in the insistence upon the exact time to a minute for the administration of nourishment and medicine, for which particularity the rational system has no data. Julie, who was very exact in this respect, referred an indisposition to the fact that coffee had been brought to her three minutes too late. Once she received

* Deleuze: 'Instruction,' etc., 455, 460, 461.
† Kerner: 'Scherin v. Prevorst,' 102.

it thirty seconds too soon, and declined it with a 'not yet,' but that time having elapsed, she got up of herself to take it. It is the 'watch in the head' by which they estimate the time, like the ordinary sleeper when he wakes exactly at a predetermined hour. It is also often an impulse from the transcendental will giving effect to itself. So Julie felt impelled to take a walk; in half an hour she bounded back as if pushed, and said it was as though her feet were urged.*

The critique of somnambulists extends not merely to the physician's medicines, but also to the magnetic treatment applied by their magnetisers. Somnambulism awakens not only instinctive knowledge of the mode of magnetising advantageous for each particular case, but it imparts to somnambulists, or exalts in them, the power to magnetise themselves or others. A dropsical patient stretched out her hand towards the physician, as if to charge it fully with magnetism, and then magnetised herself over the whole body.† Already in the Report of the Paris Academy (1784), it is said that the patients sought for and magnetised each other. A young man who was frequently in the crisis then went quietly and silently through the hall and put others in the same state by magnetic passes. On awaking he remembered nothing of it, and could no longer magnetise.‡ Puységur had a servant who, being asked what was the best way to magnetise a deaf person, gave the directions: 'With the thumb of one hand in one ear, and

---

\* Strombeck: 'Geschichte,' etc., 32, 36, 115.
† Deleuze: 'Hist. crit.,' etc., i. 240.
‡ Gauthier: 'Hist. du Somnambulisme,' ii. 244.

the little finger of the other hand in the other ear.' This somnambulic servant was largely interrogated by Puységur without coming to be the mere echo of his magnetiser. The physician is thus not the source of this critique of the magnetic passes, but it is the sanative power of nature reaching up into the sphere of ideation, the best proof of which is the fact that somnambulists in sleep magnetise much more effectively than in waking. To this magnetism is even the greatest curative action ascribed. Koreff knew two somnambulists who could put anyone into the sleep, even if he had shown himself hitherto quite unsensitive; they produced very beneficent crises, stopped the most violent pains, and in obstinate diseases often suddenly introduced such revolutions that effects were accelerated which otherwise would be slowly attained. The most remarkable scene, says Koreff, is when two somnambulists of different degrees of lucidity magnetise each other; the more elevated subjects the other to his will, evokes in him unexpected crises, rules his feelings, and compels his limbs to movements recalling the most expert jugglers.*

Rapport, then, will by no means explain all the prescriptions. When that is the source, it may be known by the excogitative mode of speech, agreeing with the reasoning judgment of the physician upon the case. In very many cases rapport cannot even possibly be the source—those, namely, in which somnambulism is not induced by a magnetiser, but by nature herself for beneficent ends. Moreover, even in artificially-induced somnambulism the instinctive

* Deleuze: 'Instruction,' etc., 407, 408.

source could be brought to a test by a decisive experiment. It would only be necessary to magnetise the physician himself, after he had deliberately concluded his scientific diagnosis and therapeutic, and to see if his somnambulic deliverance agreed with it. I find only one notice of such a case, which is in the letter of a lady to Deleuze. She was magnetised for months without success. One day the magnetiser, not feeling well himself, intermitted the operation, on which she offered to exchange parts, and the physician having become the somnambulist, she interrogated him concerning her disorder, and got rid of it by means of his prescriptions.* Such an experiment would be very instructive for the physician, who could thus compare the conceptions of his intellect, the inferences from external symptoms to internal causes, with his instinct, which proceeds reversely. I am convinced that this experiment would very seldom result in the agreement of the two diagnoses, but that the dualism of the two persons of the *one* Subject would be reflected in that of the diagnoses and prescriptions.

When in the year 1831 the professional Commission, which had been engaged in its investigation since its appointment several years before, caused its Report, confirming all the substantial phenomena attributed to somnambulism, to be read in the Medical Academy of Paris, the deep silence of the assembly betrayed the disturbance of their minds. Then, when as usual it was proposed that this report should be printed, an Academician, Castel, rose and protested against the printing of it, *because*

* Archiv, iv. 1, 127.

*if the facts reported were true, half of our physiological science would be destroyed.* So: down with truth! live the system!—that has ever been the principle of all the prejudiced.

But it has been shown by the foregoing dissertation that what somnambulism threatens is our supposed, not our true, physiological science. With regard to health-prescriptions especially, their exact analysis has exhibited them as the combination of two parts, each of which is quite familiar to physiology, so that henceforward the union of these parts can only be objected to by that scepticism which cannot do an addition sum. These two parts are: 1. The reciprocity of Will and Idea;* 2. The displacement of the psycho-physical threshold.

The will excites the idea, and the idea the will. If the intuitive representation of a thing homogeneous to my present condition occurs to me, that excites the want; as, for instance, the sign of an inn with its suggestion of foaming beer glasses may excite thirst. If, conversely, the want of the thing is already in the will, it excites in waking the thought, in sleep the representation of the thing. So, for example, in erotic dreams. Thus the Neoplatonist, Plotinus, says: 'When desire arises, then comes imagination and presents the object.'† That will can excite thoughts is everyday experience, and the great

---

* ['Will' here stands for the teleological activity of the organic forces, and is distinguished from Idea, the representation of that activity, or of its end, in consciousness. It is not necessary to refer these expressions here to the philosophy of Schopenhauer in the full significance there attached to them.—Tr.]

† Plotinus: 'Enneads,' iv. 4, 17.

majority of men have no capacity for objective*
thoughts, but only for such as are evoked by the
egoistic will, interest, or want ; and even the great
majority of scientific books are open to Bacon's
censure, that 'human understanding is not a pure
light, but suffers influences from will and feeling.'†

Now, were we not so unphilosophical as to lose
surprise in regard to daily experience, retaining it
only for what is rare, this surprise would be regulated
solely by the objective content of a phenomenon; and
then we must unavoidably confess that it is far more
wonderful that will can excite thoughts in waking
than that it should excite representation in sleep.
For all thinking by concepts and all language are
rooted (as Lazarus Geiger has convincingly proved‡)
in intuition ; representation (Vorstellung) is the
radical, the primary in our thinking, and all
concepts, all words, are only condensed representations. In sleep, therefore, the action of will remains
*stationary*, in the sphere of representation, whereas
in waking it *protrudes* into the sphere of abstract
thinking—into thoughts of what is willed. The

* [*I.e.*, non-egoistic; egoism here, of course, including all that is related to the self by the affections. But the proposition is surely too broadly stated, since all the intellectual work of life requires objective thinking in some degree. Intellectual capacity is in fact measurable by the degree of objectivity attained by thought. This is its abstraction from all egoistic intrusion, as from prejudice, preconceptions, and prepossessions, not less than from the importunities of sense or personal concerns which dis-tract us, and prevent the object of thought from developing its pure reality in our intelligence.—Tr.]

† Bacon: 'Novum Organum,' 1, § 49. And Schopenhauer: 'Welt als Wille und Vorstellung,' ii. Kap. 19.

‡ Geiger: 'Ursprung der Sprache,' Stuttgart, 1869. And 'Ursprung und Entwicklung der menschlichen Sprache und Ver-nunft,' Stuttgart, 1868.

latter case is thus, notwithstanding its familiarity, far more mysterious than the other. The sceptic who disputes the possibility of vision of remedies in dream is therefore to be referred to this fact of waking life.

The other factor of the somnambulic health-prescriptions is the displacement of the psycho-physical threshold. The threshold divides those influences from the outer world which are conscious from others which remain unconscious, but yet go on of themselves, only are not felt. The displacement of the threshold thus makes the unconscious conscious: it must increase the material of sensibility. Thousands of experiments with somnambulists have proved that they receive from substances influences of which in waking only sensitives are susceptible, or which show themselves in idiosyncrasies. Our waking capacity to react upon all things with inclination or disinclination is exalted in sleep, so that somnambulists even feel the chemical constituents of compounds. It is therefore natural that they are also informed upon the beneficial or hurtful tendencies of the same; for in sleep, as in waking, pain is the accompanying sign of what is injurious, pleasure of what is advantageous to the organism. Had we not this impulse to seek the suitable and to flee from the unsuitable, we should be incapable of life.

As well, then, as the faculty of sensibility in waking can produce in a thirsty man the thought of water, can this greatly exalted faculty in sleep produce in the diseased organism the representation of chemical substances advantageous to it.

Thus the so-called miracle of health-prescriptions is in both its parts quite conceivable, and, in view of the great quantity of evidence, must be recognised as an intelligible fact by everyone who can add the two parts together.

There are sceptics who do not indeed deny the facts of somnambulism, but disparage their value because they are of a morbid nature. They are that, certainly—every displacement of the psycho-physical threshold is at the same time a displacement of the normal sound condition; but they are only morbid in regard to the exciting cause and for the Person of the external consciousness, not at all in regard to their transcendental content; and this scruple cannot better be removed than by the proof that dream is a physician, that the transcendental Person is the physician of the empirical Person.

This language will no doubt sound strange to many; but, since the faculties of somnambulists cannot be explained from the external consciousness, we must even have the courage just to say that somnambulists are inspired. But by whom inspired? It is not necessary to accept their 'guardian spirits' and their 'guides' as realities and as the inspirers, because the phenomena are as well explained by the simple hypothesis that the somnambulists are inspired *by themselves*. These inspirations originate, however, from the region of the unconscious; it is the Ego below the threshold that lets itself be known when external consciousness disappears. A psychical relation of some kind must be at the foundation of the appearance that these inspirations come from without, and no other explanation is to be found than that the inspiration originates from the same Subject, indeed, but yet from another Person than that of the external consciousness. This second Person, however, can then be only relatively unconscious for the Person of external consciousness, but not in itself. To sum up the result in a few words, that is to say: Our normal self-consciousness does not exhaust its object, our Self—it comprehends only one of the two Persons of our Subject. Man is a monistic double-being—monistic as Subject, dualistic as Person. The contention of monists and dualists is thus resolved by comprisal of alternatives.

www.ingramcontent.com/pod-product-compliance
Lightning Source LLC
Chambersburg PA
CBHW032047220426
43664CB00008B/893